ly told us the production line in Kerry was finished

RÓISÍN SCACKS CRAT
Trevor
Siún

2006 2007 2009 2014

KIERAN

DONAGHY

What Do You Think Of That?

KIERAN
DONAGHY
What Do You Think Of That?

MY AUTOBIOGRAPHY

With Kieran Shannon

Sport Media

I dedicate this book to four very special ladies:
Mom, Nan, Hilary and Lola Rose.

Mom, I grew up wanting to be a good son for you
because I knew how hard you worked to give us a
chance to succeed in life.

Nan, to all those nights hatching by the fire at 1am in
the morning, I miss them. I also miss the laughs, the
prayers, the kisses and the constant candle lighting
through the years.

Hilary, you are a great wife and a fantastic mother.
You have always had my back and your constant
support helped me live out my dreams.

Lola Rose, you have brought so much joy to our lives
and we can't wait to see you grow up, make mistakes,
learn from them and drive on again.

Sport Media

Kieran Donaghy:
What Do You Think Of That?

© Kieran Donaghy

Written with Kieran Shannon

First Edition
Published in 2016.

Published and produced by: Trinity Mirror Sport Media,
PO Box 48, Old Hall Street, Liverpool, L69 3EB.

Managing Director: Steve Hanrahan
Commercial Director: Will Beedles
Executive Editor: Paul Dove
Executive Art Editor: Rick Cooke
Marketing and Communications Manager: Claire Brown
Editing & Production: Roy Gilfoyle
Editing: Chris Brereton

ISBN: 978-1-910335-51-2

With thanks to Eddie O'Donnell and Gill Hess Ltd.

Photographic acknowledgements:
Kieran Donaghy personal collection, Tony Woolliscroft,
Sportsfile, Inpho, Eamonn Keogh (MacMonagle.com),
Irish Examiner Archive, Domnick Walsh Photography.

Cover design: Rick Cooke.
Cover photo: Tony Woolliscroft.

Printed and bound by CPI Group (UK) Ltd, Croydon, CR0 4YY.

Contents

CHAPTER 1

KINGS OF FLAMINGO PARK

'Everything makes sense in hindsight, but when Kieran Donaghy came in there was a totally new dynamic to the Kerry attack. He created panic in the Dublin defence for the first time in the match, and had that been there from the start it might well have resulted in more scores for Kerry. It begs the question: should he have started?'

John O'Keeffe, Irish Times, September 21, 2015

JANUARY, 2016, MIAMI

I'M BOUNCING A BASKETBALL ALONG THE STREET, just like I used to going to the shop for a Mr Freeze as a kid in Tralee. Only I've just bought this ball, this street has palm trees and I'm not on my own.

I'm here going along Washington Avenue with a group of teammates and some of their partners, breaking in this ball I just got for $30 in a sports shop. And as the ball bounces, making that loud thump followed by that high-pitched, hollow ring, we take in the other sounds and smells of South Beach. The salsa and the hip-hop coming from the open-door bars and restaurants. The cigar smoke from the old boys playing dominoes. The revving engines of the lunatics on their motorbikes roaring past without any helmets.

And most of all, there's the baking heat. Instead of having to contend with the cold, rain and wind of home, we're going about in our T-shirts, shorts and shades.

We're here on the Kerry team holiday. Part reward for reaching an All Ireland final, and part rehab to help with getting over losing it.

It still pisses me off, last September. The six weeks before Christmas back home, I was training at least twice a day, up by six every morning to be in the gym for seven. The day of the All Ireland final I weighed 16 stone 6, just as I did for the final the year before when we won and everyone was delighted with me. In the middle of November, I went to Portugal for a blowout and some golf with a few friends, and tipping seventeen stone. This morning on the scales I was 15 stone 9. Everybody's been saying it to me over here: Jesus, man, you've lost some weight!

A few years ago we were playing Dublin in the league and some of the Hill on tour, being the witty boys they are, were roaring down, calling me Duckarse Donaghy. But as Barry John Keane said to me there earlier this week, the duckarse is gone now!

I just want to have no excuses in 2016. The past few seasons I've allowed myself to become too one-dimensional. Pigeon-holed. Staying between the two big posts that support the nets behind the goals and not going beyond the 45m line. Some of my best football over the years has been when I've come out a bit more and won ball out in front, or roamed out to around the middle of the field, like the 2007 All Ireland semi-final when we were the ones beating Dublin in the big, close games. By losing the bit of weight I'm letting our manager Éamonn Fitzmaurice and his selectors know I'm ready to play more like that again.

Éamonn's not out here with us, he's at home making preparations for the McGrath Cup and the season ahead, but I've to sit down with him early next week once we get back. Because right now I don't know if I'm going back playing in 2016. I need Éamonn to be able to look me in the eye and say that he really wants me back. I can't go through a year feeling like I'm a spare part, a luxury item, something to be broken out only in the case of an emergency. I've done and been through too much in the game for that.

I've had a great run, more than I could have imagined. As a young fella I couldn't make the school team. I was the last player called onto the Kerry minor panel in my last year at that grade. Even after I was called into the Kerry seniors, it took me the third season to get on the team. What followed after that – all the big games and All Irelands, the joy and honour of playing alongside some of the best to ever play the game, the craic and the friendships I've had and made – was a dream; I got to live out my dreams. But the last five seasons there's been a lot of tough days and I just don't want or need any more.

In 2011 we threw away an All Ireland. In 2013 I was dropped for the All Ireland semi-final. In 2014 I was gone, and Kerry were too until with five minutes to go against Mayo up in Croke Park I was thrown in at full forward and caught two balls. Those balls could have gone in another ten times and I wouldn't have won any of them: Mayo would have gone on to play Donegal in the All Ireland final and my retirement would have been a small column along the side of the paper, squeezed in beside the reams of stuff on how the winners won their All Ireland. But I did win those two balls and we went on to win one of the sweetest All Irelands Kerry ever have. Yet a year later I found myself back on the bench for the All Ireland, even though I was team captain.

To be honest, 2015 was one of the toughest years of my life.

My nan passed away; she was more like a second mother than a grandmother after she took us all into her house when Dad left.

I left my job in the bank, for numerous reasons, the main one being there was only so far I could advance with my dyslexia.

There was a terrible rumour about my private life that was rampant throughout the county and spread around the country, even though it was complete and utter bullshit.

And then there was the All Ireland. A nightmare I'm still trying to wake from…

In it Éamonn calls me to the side the Tuesday before the match to tell me what I've already suspected from the teams being picked in training – I'm dropped from the starting fifteen.

I take it the only way I know how. "Alright, man, I'll be ready for you when you need me."

So on the Sunday I'm looking out from our bench in the Hogan Stand and all I can see through the driving rain are Dublin backs bullying my boys. Philly McMahon bumping and pulling and dragging Colm 'Gooch' Cooper. Johnny Cooper mauling James O'Donoghue. Rory O'Carroll welded to Paul Geaney. *Jesus, let me out there.*

Six months earlier we played Dublin in the league down in Killarney. My first game as Kerry captain. Early on O'Carroll was pinching me, turning the skin, so I just grabbed him by the throat, walked him twenty yards into the goalmouth, threw him into the goal, then ran back out to win a ball and lay it off for a point. When he came back over I told him that if he didn't stop the bullshit, I'd bring him to the ground. Then we'd both get yellow cards which, me being the forward, would suit me fine. Was that fine with him?

I've had loads of exchanges like that with full backs over the years. Eoin Cadogan and Michael Shields from Cork. Stephen Lucey of Limerick. The McGee brothers from Donegal. "Look, man, I'm here to play football. But if you want …"

Between the white lines for those seventy minutes, I'm ready to kill you to win. It's the only way I know how. It's the way I've always done it. Can I change? Can I stop giving out to the refs? I fuckin' can't. It's just the way I am.

Away from football, I'll be all on for having the craic with you. I'd say there were plenty of lads who went to Australia with me on the Irish International Rules team who might have initially thought I was an absolute bollix from what they'd seen of me on the field; then once they got to know me on the trip and saw me being the ringleader of the jokes and the banter, they probably thought, "Your man Donaghy's sound, in fairness." But on the field, when we're competing against each other, again, I'll do whatever it takes. I know my limitations. I know I'm not a Colm Cooper. I can't feint or solo or shoot like James O'Donoghue either. But what I will do is stand up to anyone so the likes of James and Gooch can play. I'll do what it takes for the team to win.

So I'm itching for Éamonn to let me out there. Eventually, with just over twenty minutes to go, I get the nod. I run over to him, he puts the arm around the shoulder. I'm in for Paul Geaney.

"We need you here. Do what you do best. Lead from the front."

As I run on, I'm thinking: *Any bullying from now on, we'll be the ones doing it.*

I'm barely in when Darran O'Sullivan plays a little dink ball in. I fist it off to Donncha Walsh who pops it back to Darran and he puts it over the bar. It's back down to two points.

A few minutes later, they win a free about fifty yards out from our goal. They call Stephen Cluxton up to take it and of course he starts walking up like he has all day, time wasting. I run over and start pushing him up the field.

He breaks into a small jog but he's still taking the piss. I give him another little push, and he slides along the ground on his knees, trying to make a big scene of it and have the ball moved forward, but David Coldrick doesn't fall for it.

Finally Cluxton arrives up. I point to where I think the ball should be, a bit further back, and after his shot trails wide I jog back alongside him. You're getting nothing easy now, buddy.

But still they're in control. The game's stop-start which favours the side that's in the lead, and when Paul Flynn kicks another score, the gap goes out to three. There's little ball coming my way until with five minutes to go, Paul Galvin, who has just been brought on, gathers a ball around midfield and floats it in towards the right edge of the big square.

Rory O'Carroll is in front of me. In many ways it's a ball I have no right to win. But I'm able to jump over O'Carroll and get my hands on it. I haven't quite secured it though and I fumble it but I fight on my back for it and manage to grab it again. I'm trying to get up but I'm surrounded by Dubs. One of them is nicking the side of me. Next thing there's a finger pulling at my eye.

I'm just getting to my feet with the ball intact when David Coldrick blows his whistle. Good. Free in.

But no. It's a hop ball. Why's it a hop ball?! Some fella's nearly taken the eye out of my fuckin' head!

I run a few steps towards the ref, ball under my arm. I don't roar, I don't show any anger. I just inform him. "He gouged my eye on the ground, Dave."

"Ah, I didn't see that now, Kieran," he says.

Philly McMahon sticks his head in. "It's two boys competing, that's all!"

I just look at him, bemused. At this stage I've no issue with him; I think it's someone else who did it. I'm not wanting anyone sent off, I just wanted a free we should have had, and now that we didn't get it, I just want to win this hop ball. The clock is ticking; there's no time for any big remonstrations. We have to win this hop ball. Focus.

Coldrick throws it up between myself and Michael Darragh

Macauley. I hold Macauley off, grab it, spin, and lay it off across goal to Killian Young. He's clean through. He has Paul Galvin backdoor with no-one on him straight in front of the goal…

But the conditions are the worst I've ever known for a final and the ball slips from Killian's hands. James McCarthy takes the ball and passes it out to Alan Brogan who has just come on.

As Brogan carries the ball upfield, I have words with O'Carroll. "That was a fuckin' low blow, man! You nearly pulled the eye out of my head!"

But he insists. "Honestly, man, I didn't touch you."

Twenty-four hours later I'll realise he's right. When our train stops off in Rathmore, a couple of our county board officers come up to me all flustered, saying RTE News want my reaction to 'the Philly McMahon incident'; supposedly it has been highlighted on The Sunday Game. I'll tell our officers not to worry, I'll handle it, and when I'm asked by the reporter about it, I just give the old line about what happens on the field staying on the field. But it's only there in Rathmore that it clicks: *So that's why McMahon was so eager to talk to me that time…*

As O'Carroll is telling me it wasn't him, up at the other end of the field Alan Brogan kicks a point to extend their lead to four.

We need a goal now. I collect a ball out by the corner, pop it off to Gooch and as it's recycled I run across into the big square, looking for a high ball. Paul Murphy kicks it in. I've good position. I'm backing into O'Carroll and he's panicking. I raise my arm about to punch it into the net when O'Carroll puts his arm over my shoulder and pulls me to the ground.

It's a foul. It's a penalty. But again it's not given.

And that's the game. A few minutes later, Dave Coldrick blows it up. Dublin 0-12, Kerry 0-9.

I turn looking to shake hands with O'Carroll, but he's run over to embrace McMahon. The nearest man is Stephen Cluxton. Their captain. As our captain, I put out my hand.

"Well done, man."

"Hard luck."

"No bother."

A little later John Costello, the Dublin county secretary, comes over. We've got on brilliantly ever since the 2008 league final when myself and Micheál Quirke were left stranded in Parnell Park after we'd been drug-tested. John's own son Cormac has just won an All Ireland as a sub but John bends down to me on my honkers and gives me a hug.

I rise to my feet and stand there in the rain, hands on the hips, watching the Dubs laughing, going up the steps to lift the cup.

I can't take this. I head towards the tunnel and as I do I'm thinking this is goodbye to Croke Park. I'm gone.

The worst part about it is that we didn't do ourselves justice. Other times when we've lost here, at least we've made the opposition play out of their skins. This time Dublin didn't have to.

The only thing that saves me is seeing my four-month-old daughter Lola Rose underneath the stand with my wife Hilary. I kiss Hilary and pick up Lola Rose. And as long as she's in front of me it's like the game's been wiped from my mind. On the bus back to the hotel I still have her in my arms. For that hour she is my saviour. She's saving me from this.

We get to the hotel, the D4. I come down late to the function. I've already done fuckin' three of these – 2005, 2008, 2011 – and know what it's going to be like, the old rigmarole and rhetoric that's going to be thrown out.

"Kerry will be back!" "Hold your heads up proud!"

I can't be listening to it. So I start with the white wine. I don't even like white wine but tonight keep it coming to me. The waitress to our table cops this early and leaves another bottle in the ice-bucket stand for me. That's lovely, thanks.

I don't want to deal with we should have done this, you should have done that, I should have done this. Woulda, coulda, shoulda is after an All Ireland loss. That's all that happens. With teammates, with everybody. You sit down and at first you skirt around it but eventually it comes up and you try to figure it out, but who cares? You're wasting your time! You'd be better off just getting pissed, going up to bed and forgetting about it until you wake up the next morning.

After the function we move out from the main hall and a few of us take up a spot by the bar in the lobby. Tommy Walsh and his father Seán; David Moran and his dad Ógie. The Tralee gang.

"Go on, Kieran," says Seán, "give us that song."

Hilary hands me a pint of water – the first sign I'm in trouble – and I go into my party piece, a song Christy Moore's covered.

My little Honda 50, she's rapid, and she's nifty...

I've my eyes closed, making a balls of the lyrics, slurring some of them. "Time for bed, Keek," says Hilary.

I wake up the next morning. *Fuckit, we lost.* Now you have to deal with what you didn't want to deal with last night – another All Ireland lost.

Again, drink is the first port of call to numb the pain. I go downstairs and start on some brandies and Bailey's with Charlie, my dad's brother. On the train down with the lads I drink some more until just before we come to Rathmore; at that point it's time to sober up because as captain I'm going to be called upon to say a few words.

In Kerry we make it as hard as possible on ourselves after losing an All Ireland. We always have to get off in Rathmore because Aidan O'Mahony's from there and either Tom O'Sullivan or now Paul Murphy is from there too. So we get up on the tractor stage and all the players are introduced and we hear the local mayor give his mandatory few words.

Then the chairman has to come on and say something.

Then Éamonn has to come on and say something.

And we're still only in Rathmore.

Next is Tralee. We've to get up on a double-decker bus for a lap of the town, then get up on the stage on Denny Street, and more talking.

Then, back onto the team bus, and off to Killarney. Another lap of the town, another stage, more speeches. By now it's half-eleven, seven hours after we stopped off in Rathmore. There's barely a dozen players onstage. Fellas have scattered. "I'm not going up on the stage in Killarney – I'm going into Jimmy O'Brien's in Killarney." If I wasn't the captain, I'd have been in there with them or else I'd have just got off in Tralee. We appreciate the support but lads are just wrecked, mentally and physically; if we lose we should just go to Austin Stack Park in Tralee or Fitzgerald Stadium in Killarney, thank the supporters and then go to a hotel for a bit of peace and quiet.

The rest of the week is tough, but at least we're together and it's the one town for the night. The Tuesday's always the captain's hometown. And as that's me, our spot is my old stomping ground, The Greyhound Bar, where my uncle Aidan keeps the food and drink coming down to the lads all night.

By now there's no more hiding from the game. You're talking about it in corners and corridors with a couple of your closest buddies on the team. For me that's Paul Galvin, who has just played his last game for Kerry.

"They outfought us, Paul. They wanted it more."

"I know, man."

And for a while we just stand there, sipping our beers, saying nothing. We just gaze blankly at the floor and the wall, knowing that as long as the last few days have been, the winter is going to be even longer…

But now it feels like summer. It's sunny. It's 2016. It's Miami. We're moving along Washington Avenue, past the Playwright Bar where we've had a few great nights, on our way to the outdoor courts of Flamingo Park.

For the last few months I've been back playing basketball for the first time in five years. The team I play for in Tralee have gone on a bit of a run in the intermediate National Cup and we've the semi-final the day after we fly back. To keep my eye in, I've already been down to the park here a couple of times, playing pickup with some of the locals like I have the three previous times I've been in Miami. Now I've some of my Kerry boys with me.

We rock up to the gate. It's a fine facility: beside us are six tennis courts, a soccer pitch, chin-up bars, weights. If I lived in Miami I wouldn't bother paying for a gym; I'd just come here, shoot some hoops and have my little workout, under the sun with the light beach breeze to cool me off.

The basketball courts are immaculate. There's no bend or give in the rings. The surface is smooth and clean. And soon it's squeaking like tens of thousands of other playgrounds around

America right now, though this is probably the only one completely taken over by a bunch of Kerrymen.

Some of the lads can play. Tommy Walsh played a season in the Superleague alongside me with the Tralee Tigers. Barry John Keane is a handy point guard having played in school; Jack Sherwood, whose sister was an underage international, the same. A lot of the other lads then just want to go up and down to sweat out the previous night's beer: David Moran, Shane Enright, Stephen O'Brien, Pa Kilkenny, Brian Kelly, Alan Fitzgerald, Donncha Walsh.

After a while I sit out a game and notice a couple of guys shooting down by the bottom rings. One of them in particular looks a player. He's lean, long arms, like a panther with his shaven black head and his serious skills and moves. I ask a couple of guys doing weights nearby. "Hey, guys, know who your man is?"

And they tell me: Oh, that's Curtis Joseph, man. CJ. He's like the King of Flamingo Park; that is, until he hands over the mantle to his younger, slightly taller sidekick there, The Bird.

Sure enough I look up a bit about him on my phone. Curtis Joseph. The original IRobot, streetball legend. There's a clip of him dunking over seven girls in a huddle from a few years back. I look back over at him. He's mid-thirties now, I'd say, and lost some of his hops with those bandaged knees, but I can see by the way he moves he still has game.

I fall back in with the lads. It's getting darker now. More players have congregated by the side of the court, in their Jordans and LeBrons and long shorts. CJ and The Bird begin stretching. I know what's coming. They're going to pick their best five, ask us for a game and basically try to take over the court for the night.

Sure enough CJ approaches me. "Hey, want to pick your best five out of those guys and play us?"

I tell him we're up for that and ask how the scoring works here. It's standard playground rules. One point for a basket, two for anything outside the three-point line. First up to fifteen, winners stay on.

I go back over to our boys and go straight into coaching mode. Barry John, you and me will take the ball up. Jack, you stay on the wing, go to the basket. Tommy and Dave – horse all round you on the boards. The rest of ye, stick around and support us. We're going to need it because these guys look shit hot.

And they are. First time down the court CJ pulls up a few feet outside the three-point line and drains it in my face. The Bird backs David down low, spins, shoots and scores. We make a bit of rally, but we're tired from our own runaround earlier and they finish us off, 15-7.

CJ comes over. Hey, man, thanks for the game; want to play the one after this next one? There's still not another five guys.

I tell him thanks, man, but no thanks; it's 7.15 now and we've a dinner reservation for 9.00.

"Alright, man," he says. "Well, nice to meet you."

So I'm heading away with the lads, fairly thick having to leave on a downer like that, when I notice Barry John Keane and his girlfriend Aoife are sitting down on the steel bleachers. He says they're going to stick around for another bit, savour some more of the playground experience, watch these other fellas go against each other. So we tell him, sound, we'll catch them later in the restaurant, and we start walking when I pause at the gate.

"Fuckit, lads, will we give them one more rattle?!"

The lads: We will so!

So we turn around and join Barry John and Aoife on the bleachers. About quarter-of-an-hour later CJ sinks a nice floater in the lane. Game. He asks if we mind if they take a five-minute break? No bother, I tell him, go ahead. But then I spot another five have gathered at the bottom basket. One of them was there when we were playing CJ's crew and now he's bouncing his ball out around midcourt, as if to mark out his territory.

"Sorry there, bud," I says, "but we're next."

"No man, I got my five!"

"Yeah, but you'd only two when we called Next."

"No! You had your go! Our turn!"

He's trying to intimidate me. He thinks these boys in their sorry shorts and low-cut runners will back down. But I just explain: Look, man, we're a football team from Ireland. We're heading home first thing in the morning. Win or lose, this is the last time we'll play in Flamingo Park.

He starts laughing to himself. Like y'all might win?! Okay, go ahead then and get your sorry white asses kicked.

CJ and his boys return. The floodlights are on now. On the sidelines, more and more onlookers and ballplayers have gathered.

I'm all over CJ like a rash, bumping him with my forearm. In the first game he was making fadeaway threes. Now he's clanking them off the rim.

Tommy Walsh sinks a lovely fadeaway shot. Jack Sherwood makes a drive to the basket. Barry John knocks down a three-pointer. David Moran is playing ferocious defence on The Bird. When one of their lads finally gets a rebound off him, Dave just rips it out of his hands. Someone hollers from the sidelines, "Goddamn, these white boys are strong!" And when I pull off a behind-the-back move before finger-rolling it into the hoop, there's more whooping from the sidelines.

But CJ's the King of Flamingo Park for a reason. He whizzes a brilliant pass right by my ear to The Bird inside who dunks. Then he puts a Jordan crossover on me, pulls up and knocks it down which brings them back to 13-11.

It stays that score for ages. An old unwritten law of the playground is in full effect now: no blood, no foul, so with no-one giving an inch, no-one's getting a shot.

The ballers on the touchline are getting so restless, they're standing on it, glaring at us.

Tommy drives to the basket but he's hacked. Even they have to put the hand up on that one: foul. As Tommy takes the ball back up top to be checked in, someone calls, "C'mon! Put a clock on this! Three minutes!"

CJ tells them to chill: that ain't happenin'. This is going to fifteen, however long it takes.

I'm over on the wing and smile to a few of the bystanders: "Don't worry, boys, I've got it!"

One of them is there with his headband and braids, holding a ball against his belly-button, a big old frown on him. "Yeah, c'mon! Finish this, already, damn!"

So Barry John checks it in. I've my mind made up before he even snaps it to me: I'm taking a three. CJ's guarding me. I give him a bit of a shake down low, step back, and cock my wrist. The ball arches towards the rim, spinning, and spinning...

Swish! Nothing but net! Game!

The place goes wild. They can't believe these sorry white boys have beaten CJ and The Bird! I sprint along the sideline, high-fiving all the outstretched hands, including the guy with braids whose frown has been turned upside down. Tommy's jumping around and the two of us do the NFL chest-bump. Again, the locals love it.

CJ comes over and clasps my hand. He invites us to this top nightclub he's deejaying in later on – tickets, drinks, he'll take care of us. I tell him thanks a million but we're off in the morning early; it's a pity we didn't meet a few days ago. He extends the offer to the next time we're over and we exchange numbers. Then he and his boys have their photos taken with us, all of us kings of Flamingo Park, at least for that night.

Heading back to the hotel, I'm raving to the lads how this is like something straight out of White Men Can't Jump. Wesley Snipes and Woody Harrelson at the end beat two LA playground legends, The King and The Duck; now in Miami we've taken down The King and The Bird! We're floating, as if we're just after winning an All Ireland.

And in the restaurant afterwards I say it to the lads. "Boys, in thirty years' time you'll have forgotten about the theme parks and where we stayed and where we ate and drank. But we'll be old fellas, sitting down having a pint together, and one of us will say, 'Do you remember that time in Flamingo Park?!'"

JANUARY 2016, TRALEE

IT'S a cold, blustery Monday afternoon, the rain hopping off the car windscreen. And already it seems a while ago since we were kicking it by the pool of the Nautilus Hotel, and myself and Mikey Sheehy were rubbing our hands, taking money off

Johnny Buckley and our kitman Niall 'Botty' O'Callaghan on the eighteenth of the Blue Monster at Doral.

I'm on my way over to Éamonn Fitzmaurice's house that's at the back of the local cemetery and I'm just hoping that when I'm leaving it's not the passing of an inter-county career that we'll be looking at.

I've known him all my senior inter-county career. He was first a teammate and a friend, a leader and an inspiration; then a selector with Jack; and now, the last three years, our manager.

One of Éamonn's greatest qualities is that he's straight and honest and he wants you to be straight and honest with him. I remember my first year starting on the team, 2006. One night myself and Gooch were trying to work a goal in training. We were throwing it around like a basketball. He was open to shoot it, then slipped it back over to me. But I was on my left leg so I popped it back over to Gooch. He fired off a rasper of a shot which hit off the post and came back out the field. The ball broke to Eoin Brosnan who burned Éamonn and banged it over the bar.

Next thing, Éamonn came pacing up the field, his arms pinned behind his back. For the most part, he's a very measured, soft-spoken man. He also has the loudest voice of anyone I've ever played with. And now he let me and Gooch have it. "WILL YE KILL THE BALL AND STOP FUCKIN' AROUND?!"

And he was right. We overdid it. Just get it and kill it.

I met Éamonn in his house back in November, a couple of days before I went for that blowout in Portugal. As always he was very honest, very humble. "I've learned an awful lot about myself over the last eight weeks," he said.

He went on to say the first mistake he made was not bringing me on at half-time. That he probably should even have started me. That he possibly put too much store on form and not enough on matchups and experience. That he could have factored in more the league game in Killarney back in February when I got the better of O'Carroll and the 2011 final too. "You've never let Kerry down on the big day," he said.

I'm not going over to him tonight though to rehash 2015. This is about 2016.

I knock on the door. Éamonn answers and brings me into the sitting room. His wife Tina pops her head in, smiles hi and then waves bye, knowing there's a serious chat on the way.

The two of us start off making small talk about the holiday before he remarks on what great shape I'm looking in, that he'd heard good reports from Miami.

"Yeah, man," I say, "I've worked my arse off since I was last here. I told you I was going to train hard to see if the appetite was still there for 2016 and it is.

"But Éamonn, what do you see for me this year? I'm after getting lighter and quicker for you now, but I need to know where I am in your plans."

And straight away he says, "Full forward. When you're on that's the way I want to go." Yes, he likes playing the small-ball game, but he likes the long-ball game as well; he reminds me that when he was player-manager with Finuge he'd played himself at full forward and instructed the lads to beat everything in on top of him.

It's huge to hear that so I have just one more thing to run by him. He'd hinted over the last few weeks that he was looking for me to go back training tomorrow night and be available for the opening league game against Dublin in Croker.

I tell him straight. "Éamonn, I've been going two and a half years non-stop. Declan O'Sullivan told me to take a break last year after the club All Ireland semi-final and I didn't listen to him; I wanted back in right away with Kerry, probably because I was captain, and maybe in the long term it hurt me. 2015 only finished up for me Christmas week when I walked off a pitch above in John Mitchels with the hailstones hitting me on the side of the face and all I could say was 'Thanks be to Christ this is our last game of the year.' I can't look at a field for another six weeks."

And again, he's great about it. He understands. I'll come back in the Tuesday after the team's second league game, against Roscommon, which will give us a three-week run-in to our third game.

We start rising to our feet. "Look, Kieran," he says, "after the year you've had and for you to go away and do what you've done the last eight weeks, I've no worries about you now."

So driving back, I'm buzzing. I start my new job in a couple of days, for PST Sports, installers of artificial grass for clubs and schools. I have a national basketball cup final at the end of the month. And then, ten days after that, I'll return to Kerry training for one last crack at it.

It's weird. Walking down the tunnel in Croke Park last September after watching the Dubs lift the cup, I was sure that was the last time I'd seen the place as a player.

But obviously I haven't been able to leave it at that.

Those November and December mornings when the human alarm clock that's Lola Rose would go off at about 6.00, I'd get up, give her the bottle, and when she'd drift back off to sleep, bring her back up to Hilary to snuggle up beside her. By 7.00

I'd be in the gym in John Mitchels where my trainer Damien Ryall would put me through real balls-to-the-floor stuff. I'd be boxing, swinging left and right at his pads, my eyes closed, feeling the sweat fly off my head each time I threw a punch. And he'd be roaring, "C'MON! YOU'RE NOT HITTING HARD ENOUGH!"

At the end of the six weeks and I'd lost nearly a stone and a half he put what I lost into a bag. "Lift that." I put it over my shoulder. It felt heavy. "You've been running around with that on you."

Why did I lose all that weight? Why did I do all that work, with Damien, and with Joe O'Connor? When I'd be coming to the end of a rep and wincing, struggling to complete it, Damien would shout to me, "Push through it! Think of some image, something, why you're doing all this!"

And all I could think of was Croke Park. And me being up there on those steps, Sam above my head, again.

Back in my mid-teens, I'd pal around with the Smith brothers, Brendan and Finbarr. I wasn't lucky enough to have PlaySta-tion at home but the boys were. So I'd be over in their place, along with a couple of other buddies, playing this game called Pro Evolution Soccer. A lot of the time I'd be Holland. Edgar Davids, Patrick Kluivert and the boys. Brendan and Finbarr's mum, Joan, would come in to us: Would ye not go outside and play football instead of that bloody game?! But we'd stay there for hours, having our own competitions. We'd have a league, which was important, but a bit like the GAA league, it wasn't the be-all and end-all. The Cup was the big one. Do-or-die. Only, if I lost, I'd beg for a Go Home game. Brendan or Finbarr might have won the Cup and been tired and wanted to go to bed but I couldn't leave it at that. I'd plague them. "Tell you what, if I lose this, I'm going home!" Or "Win or lose, I'm going home!" So they'd give in. Alright so, one more game!

So I'd cycle back in the dark, either pissed off that I'd lost again, or, more often than not, buzzing because I'd won.

I don't know what it is, whether it's being a winner or being a stubborn bastard or what, but I've always been like that.

I was like that with Pro Evolution Soccer.

It was the same in Flamingo Park. We lost that first game but I had to turn back for a Go Home game.

And now it's the same with Croke Park. *Fuckit, will we give it one more rattle?!*

CHAPTER 2

DAD

"This all goes back to Oliver.
I think Kieran has adopted the
best parts of him – the charm, the
charisma. As for the other side of
Oliver, well a part of that we see when
he's playing: the hyper-aggression, the
ferocious energy. It all goes back to
the father"

Kieran's former Superleague coach Rus Bradburd

FOR A GOOD WHILE GROWING UP I THOUGHT my childhood was a happy-go-lucky one – normal even. And that my father wasn't just normal, he was great. We'd kick football in the Caherslee pitches behind my nan's place, watch cowboys on TV together, ride horses with my brother and sister. And at Christmas he was the star of the show in my eyes, greater and bigger than even Santa, because he'd make Santa and Christmas so special.

Then some things made you realise that maybe your dad and your situation weren't so normal.

Like the time we came back from school to find my mother's clothes all over the front garden after he'd fired them out of their bedroom window.

Or, a little while after Mom eventually threw Dad out, he came round to the house and started thumping on the door, pleading to be allowed in, swearing that he'd changed, that he'd stopped the gambling and drinking.

And then there was the time he came over and Mom wasn't there; she was working the nightshift in the local hospital as a nurse. So when our poor young babysitter Stephanie innocently opened the door, he just barrelled straight past her and stormed up the stairs. "Where's my son?!"

I was asleep, in my pyjamas, like Sarah and Conor in their rooms. But maybe because I was the oldest and he could only carry one of us, it was me he lifted. Before myself and Stephanie knew it, he was carrying me down the stairs and into his car and driving off to the other end of Ireland, to his native Tyrone.

For hours we drove through the dark, me up at the front with him, in my pyjamas and now a tracksuit top and runners he must have grabbed in the house.

The closer we got to the border, the more I'd point out to him the red needle and flashing petrol light. But he'd dismiss it. "Naw, we'll be fine!"

Sure enough, we ran out of petrol. Chug, chug, splat! On a pitch black country road.

And so even though I was only about eleven, I'd to get into the driver seat as he shifted the gear into neutral and pushed that old blue Ford Orion off the road and onto a small farmer's lane, calling out instructions to me.

"Keep it either side of the grass, Kieran!… Don't drive it into the ditch… Now, when we get up here, I want you to push the brake, the middle one… Brake, brake, brake!"

After we'd pulled the car over by a ditch, he started ripping down branches from an overhanging tree. I was still in the car and could hear the sound of the breaking bark. What was he doing? Then I watched him place the branches over the car until it was completely camouflaged. He obviously didn't want anyone passing by the main road being able to see his car, especially with its southern registration plate. Things were still tense in the North. And this was a tense enough situation he was in as it was.

So picture it. We're stranded off some country road somewhere around the border, the fugitive father and his abducted son, hundreds of miles from my distraught mother.

What did we do then? I'll come to that later.

What was I thinking, feeling? The one thing I can tell you is that I wasn't scared. Even though I could smell he had some drink on him, I had no fear whatsoever. If anything I was excited. I was with my dad, on my way, as he'd explained, to visit my uncles and aunts and cousins. And though I knew this wasn't exactly normal and maybe wasn't the right thing he was doing, he was my dad. As long as I was with him, I was happy out.

MY first conscious memory is of another trip up North. Again, there was me and Dad in that same metallic Ford Orion, but this time we'd Sarah alongside me in the back and Dad's co-pilot was my mother, Deirdre, pregnant with Conor. I was four years old and everything I knew was packed into that car. At the time I was under the impression that we were just going visiting our relatives, but in actual fact we were leaving my mother's hometown of Tralee and moving to Omagh.

I can still recall that journey. Sarah in her babyseat, battling like Harry Houdini suspended over a water trap, trying to rid herself of her straps. Me recognising the arched bridge on the slip road outside Abbeyfeale, and naively thinking if we'd travelled that far, we must have been nearly at our destination. Snaking through all those small midlands towns and up and down all the humps and bumps on the roads – no motorways back then, the fuckin' torture. And I'll never forget when we came to the border: the checkpoints, the flashing lights, the soldiers, the guns. At first I thought it was cool, but Dad turned and fixed me with a look that told me to stay quiet.

Next thing, a soldier was butting his gun off the car window and barking at my father. "OUT! OUT!"

It was the winter of 1987, around the time of the Enniskillen IRA bombing in which twelve people were killed and more than sixty others were injured. In that climate a southern car was going to arouse some suspicion. First they searched the car, upturning everything we'd packed, even tossing my toys and Sarah's dolls about. Then they aggressively frisked Dad. After he produced his documents, we were let pass, but I'll always remember suddenly realising that there was a big bad world out there and the anger on my father's face.

In no way was he a 'Fuck The Brits, Up The 'RA' man. He'd even worked for one form of the British security services when he lived in London in the 1970s, somehow talking his way into the Queen's Guard – you know those guys with the bright red blazers and bear-skinned tall black caps that stand motionless outside Buckingham Palace. (It was hardly going to be a job for life, that. Oliver Donaghy couldn't stand still long enough.) I can't remember Dad ever being remotely political. But the vibe the security forces gave him at that checkpoint was *What are you doing, coming into our country?* and that had him fuming, *No, what the fuck are you doing in my country?*

He was from Beragh, a small village about eight miles outside of Omagh, one of seven boys and five girls. Granddad John was a stalwart with the local GAA club, the Beragh Red Knights, and all his sons would play for them, including my dad. Oliver Donaghy wasn't known for his skill or talent or for being particularly strong or tall but he had a reputation for being ferocious once he crossed the white lines. He was a wiry buck who'd fight on his back for the cause; he wouldn't back down from anyone. I suppose I must have got that streak from him.

Anyone who worked with him would talk about how he could be this whirlwind of manic energy, an absolute powerhouse. In London he worked some time on the building sites, like so many other Irishmen of his generation. In Kerry he'd work for the county council. An old colleague of his there would tell me about the time they'd to erect these railway sleepers down by Banna Strand to keep the access road free from the blowing sands coming in from the dunes. It took two men to lift those giant sleepers but my father was having none of it. He would horse one of those sleepers up on his shoulder and power on by himself. "Your father was an animal of a man for physical work, Kieran," he'd say.

Our first Christmas in Tyrone was my first time seeing snow, but what I remember most about it is Dad. The night Santa was to visit us, Sarah and myself couldn't get to sleep with the excitement, constantly peeping out the window in the hope of catching a glimpse of the great man and Rudolph and all the boys. I tiptoed into our parents' room, taking little Sarah by the hand, only to be ordered back to our own room fairly rapid. But on the third time of entering, Dad hopped out of bed. "Okay, follow me."

He crept to the top of the stairs, like a special forces marine officer leading out an ambush. "Quiet now!" he whispered, putting his finger to his mouth. Mom, who was next in line, repeated the same gesture back to me, and I turned and made the same sign to Sarah.

We advanced down, one step at a time. Then he got to the bottom and approached the door when he suddenly stopped. We all froze. Had Santa come yet? Had he seen us? Was he still in there munching on the goodies we left him?

"Go back!" Dad hissed.

We flew up the stairs and shot into our beds and under the blankets.

We'd reassemble on the stairs a few minutes later, make our

way down undetected, and storm the sitting room where we'd make quick work of the wrapping paper. To our delight, the big man in red had delivered. I'd written to Santa asking for an electric racing car track. Dad had put the letter up our chimney and let the wind suck it up and fly, all the way to the North Pole. It had obviously arrived there, because on Christmas morning that racing track had arrived in our house.

I can still see my dad, putting that track together in its fig-ure-of-eight shape with the loops and Daytona-style curbs and barriers on the bends, showing us how the cars worked; then kicking back on the couch, drinking his cup of tea, looking content. All through the years I'd rarely see him so at ease. He'd either be bounding about the place at 100 miles an hour, or else he'd be down in the dumps. That Christmas morning when I flung one of my electric cars off the track, crashing into one of Sarah's dolls, I looked over my shoulder, wondering if Dad had seen it and would disapprove. But he just grinned and nodded and hoisted his cup to me as a sort of salute.

I've only good memories of our eighteen months living in Tyrone. We'd go over to my Nana Rosie and Granddad John's where there was always a big fire and an even bigger welcome. Nana Rosie would pour me an ice cold glass of Maine, a fruity fizzy drink made locally that on a roasting hot summer's day was simply to die for. Granddad John had a bird aviary out the back which was a place of wonder for my little eyes and ears, with all the budgies and finches chirping, the eggs hatching and the chicks popping out, these alien-like creatures that Grandda would carefully place into my hand. I'd freewheel around our estate in my cousin Stephen's go-kart. We'd play matches between Tyrone and Kerry, with myself and Kerry always seeming to get stuck with the smaller, weaker kids. To this day I'm close with a lot of my cousins and uncles and aunts.

But Mom never really settled up there. When a good job offer came her way back home, the decision was made we'd all return to Tralee.

I ALWAYS knew Dad liked a drink but at first I didn't see it as a problem. I'd often fix him a hot whiskey, especially on Monday nights. That was boys' night: me and Dad. While Mom would be off working the graveyard shift in the hospital and Sarah and Conor were asleep in bed, the two of us would settle onto the couch and put the feet up in front of the fire and TV.

First we'd watch Italian football, a highlights show with the goals flying in left, right and centre – *Go-laçoooo!* AC Milan were my team and Ruud Gullit my main man; that's how I'd come to support Chelsea, when he joined them. Then during the nine o'clock news, I'd get the prompt which I was more than happy to oblige: "Get me a hot whiskey there, Kieran, like a good boy."

I'd it down to a tee: boil the kettle, reach for the bottle of Powers, one sugar, a slice of lemon, four cloves. I'd bring it in and he'd be delighted: a hot whiskey in his hand, his son by his side and a good ole Western on the box.

Dad loved Westerns. A lot of his favourite films were in black and white and a bit dated for a nine-year-old but there was a show at that time called The Young Riders, starring Josh Brolin and one of the Baldwin brothers, Stephen. Riding for the Pony Express, showdowns at noon, bar fights at night: it was all in a day's work for those cowboys. And for a couple of other cowboys in Tralee, watching them and Italian football on a Monday night was the high point of our week.

There was definitely something of a cowboy in my dad. He even bought us a horse, a palomino breed, duly named Palo. It had a cream coat, four snow-white socks, white mane, white tail: beautiful. Dad would keep the horse in a friend's field a bit outside Tralee. On weekends then he'd take us there: me, Conor and Sarah.

Sarah was the best of us on a horse. Fearless. She'd go on to win rosettes at county fairs in showjumping and all. I used to love those days out too – when Dad's mood was good. We'd feed our horse sugar and carrots and then Dad would put us up on the saddle, tighten the girth, and give the command: "Right – flat out to the top of the field!" And away we'd gallop, feeling we were going faster than the wind.

But a darker mood could emerge out there as well. He'd build these massive jumps, which to us seemed bigger than you'd find in the Grand National, and tie a lunge rope onto Palo's bridle. Then he'd have the horse going around in circles while he'd be in the centre, roaring like a lunatic.

As we'd get close to the jump he'd show the horse this large whip. More often than not the horse would still refuse.

"Dad! The fence is too high for Palo!"

"Fuck's sake, Kieran! You're not driving him into it hard enough!"

So he'd bring me around again on the lunge rope, this time using his whip on Palo, "UP! UP! UP!"

Out of pure fear, Palo would try to clear the fence, with me holding on for dear life. And sometimes we would miraculously make it over, and for a moment, you'd be thinking: Yes, we did it – we're over! But that would only mean Dad would make the fence even bigger. You'd nearly have to crash off the horse for him to call it a day out there.

One time I saw him get kicked by one of the horses out there, hard in the ribs. He just grimaced and punched the horse right back in the face. The horse wobbled and nearly keeled over before gathering itself and tearing off up the field.

Dad loved horses though. The problem was he loved betting on them too. Them and the dogs. It'd be pure drink betting. Lose and he'd come home and you didn't dare say boo to him or he could take his belt off to you.

It was the ruin of him, the gambling and the drink. Later in life if my father came up in conversation with someone, for every person who'd rave about what a great workhorse he was, there'd be someone else a lot cooler about him. "Oh, I knew your dad alright." And I'd know by the way they said it, they meant, "He feckin' caught me for a few bob."

When he won, he would be as good as gold; he'd have run around town giving money back to people. In that game though, you always lose more than you win, and Oliver Donaghy was no different. From time to time he'd go to Gamblers Anonymous but he'd just keep falling off the wagon.

We tried to get him off the drink as well. When I was about ten, he was in Talbot Grove in Castleisland for a couple of weeks to try and dry out. One day the kids could go and visit. I couldn't get over how subdued he was. They probably had him up at seven in the morning planting spuds or something to try to keep his brain occupied but after a week of it he just seemed worn out. Bate. Defeated.

He'd never defeat the drink. It was a fuckin' demon and with it he could be a demon as well. Poor Mom could only take so much. Looking back, she was a saint to put up with him for as long as she did. So when I was about eleven, Dad had to leave the house.

He'd try to get back in. One evening he came round and started thumping the front door. "Deirdre! Kids! It's me! Let me in!"

"Go away, Oliver, or I'll call the Guards!"

He dashed around to the back trying to enter through there. Mom had to scurry back to make sure the back door was locked. He banged on the window. "Open up! Listen! I'm not drinking! Give me another chance!"

So I'd try to open that window before Mom would frantically dash over to close it again. By that point, I was crying and shouting at her. "But Mom! Let him in! It's Dad! Why can't ye get back together?"

I just didn't understand.

Mom would eventually chase him, but I'd learn that not long after that she seriously thought about letting him back.

This was Ireland, 1994. There was still no divorce. Separation was a big thing. There was almost a stigma to it, with the shame beginning in your own mind. 'In sickness and in health, until death do us part.'

Mom's brother Brian, the rock of our family, came down from Dublin where he worked for An Garda Síochána and pleaded with her to stay strong; that she'd be throwing away her life and damaging the future of her children if she let Oliver back into the house. He followed it up with a heartfelt ten-page letter. That swayed it for her.

Looking at it now, it's hard to believe how the two of them ever got together. And yet I still can see how someone as beautiful as my mom fell for Oliver Donaghy in London in the Seventies. He could be extremely charming, bursting with personality and life. He loved his Elvis and Joe Dolan and giving it loads on the dance floor.

> *Me oh my! You make me sigh!*
> *You're such a good-looking woman!*

I remember one night in my twenties being up in Beragh at some GAA function and watching him: dancing with everyone, shaking his long arms and legs all over, everyone smiling and laughing back. And I could picture the young Oliver in London, the one who'd have swept Mom off her feet. I'd say he would have been great fun up until the point he'd have had too much to drink.

Sadly, that point would almost always arrive.

One night he landed on the house when only the babysitter was there with us and he took me over to his apartment. I hadn't a problem with that but Mom did and later that night gardaí had to break down the door of Dad's flat to get me back to my mother.

Then, a few weeks later, he again ambushed the babysitter. That was the time he lifted me out of the bed and started driving up North until we ran out of petrol.

SO he's pushed the car off the main road and covered it in branches and leaves. What to do, what to do, what do we do now? He's out of breath, exhausted. He gets back into the car and says we should have a quick nap.

About an hour later, he stirs me, fresh as a daisy. The sun's coming up so it's time we got up as well.

We start walking. And walking. I don't know where we're going but he does: he knows these roads like the back of his hand. We arrive on the outskirts of some small town. There's a factory. So he strolls in with his son in pyjama bottoms, and he charms some of the staff into letting us into their canteen and offering us some tea, buns and scones. Later a man takes us in his car, stops off to get a can of petrol and drops us off to where Dad's hidden the Ford Orion. The man waits for Dad to pour in the petrol and see if his car starts, and when it does, Dad heartily thanks the man, and heads off towards Omagh, delighted with himself.

The smile wasn't long disappearing from his face when we landed back at his parents' house. I ran over to give Nana Rosie and Granddad John a big hug and a kiss, delighted to see them, but I could sense a tension in the air. Dad was quickly called to the kitchen, and as I stayed sitting in the living room, I could hear hushed tones and the odd raised voice from the conference inside. More of his brothers and sisters arrived. They must have got word from my mom. Eventually I overheard: "Oliver, would you get that boy back down to his mother!"

I cringe trying to imagine the anguish my mother must have gone through that night. No mobile phones, no way of knowing where I was or whether I was dead or alive…

And yet I still loved him. I'd constantly tell him in those years: "I love you, Dad."

It probably helped that Mom was gracious enough never to

badmouth him. And he always had access to us on Saturdays from twelve to six. I'd still look forward to those Saturdays with him – Conor and Sarah too. We would have some great days out with him. We might go to the beach or the park or out to the horses. He'd sold Palo, probably from a gambling debt, but he'd promise us that within a few weeks he'd be buying an even better horse, and to be fair to him, he'd be as good as his word – whenever we'd go out there, there'd be a new horse waiting for us.

But then there'd be Saturdays where we'd be at home in the garden and by one o'clock there'd still be no sign of Dad collecting us. *Where is he?*

Mom would see me and softly say, "Look, he's not coming, I'm sure he'll be here next week." We'd be devastated, especially Sarah: no horses for her that day. It would fall on Mom as usual to try to lift our mood.

There'd be other Saturdays when Dad would come round but I could tell by his mood from the moment we got into the car that there'd be no beach or horses. Instead he'd just bring us back to his apartment and he'd mope about there, leaving three children stuck in a dark room staring at the TV for the day. You could tell from the ashtray full of butts that he'd been gattin' the night before. It would depress me going round there. I hated that fuckin' dive of a place. I'd say the drinking he must have done there was cruel.

The first year or two after Mom and Dad broke up, I'd plague her: Bring back Dad, Mom; I miss my dad. I was nearly blaming her that we were no longer all one big happy family. But by the time I was fourteen or so, I'd come to realise she was the rock. I'd more empathy for her and less sympathy for him. He might wait outside mass on a Sunday for me or at the Stacks or after school, just to talk to me and ask about how Mom, Sarah and Conor were. I'd fob him off.

"Dad, I'm not sure I'm supposed to be talking to you now. I'll see you on Saturday, sure."

He'd get upset. "You don't have to tell your mom! Fuck's sake, you're my son, Kieran! I can see you whenever I like!"

After a while it sank in with him: Mom wasn't going to take him back. And if he only had access to us for a few hours every week, what was the point in staying in Tralee?

When I was about sixteen he flew off the handle and told us that he'd sold all the horses and he was finished with "this fuckin' town"; he was heading back up to Omagh to live. And at the time I thought: Fine. You can head up there for all we care.

But, of course, after a while you cool down, you mature, you forgive. And with every birthday and Christmas card he'd send – with maybe £10 sterling thrown in as well – you wanted to give him another chance, you still wanted to have some relationship with your father. So a week or so after I'd played minor for Kerry in Croke Park, I took him up on his invite to stay with him in Omagh for a week.

I was with him on 9/11. He'd his own mobile shop, driving around Tyrone in a red van with everything from teabags to toilet paper that he'd have bought in a cash and carry. He'd just gone into a house in Fintona when I heard something on the radio about a couple of planes crashing into the World Trade Center. At first I thought it was a trailer ad for some new movie but then Dad came out and told me to come in with him and see what was going on in New York.

We'd call into lots of houses that week. Just random houses. And a lot of the time it wasn't so Dad could try and sell some of the goods from his shop. He just wanted to introduce people to his son who had played minor for Kerry in Croke Park.

It would go to a ridiculous level altogether when I went up there again a couple of years later with Conor. That's when I got a notion that maybe the old man had issues more than just gambling and drinking. We'd call over to one of my uncles and aunts and we'd be sitting down having the craic with them and our cousins, when Dad would suddenly declare, "Right, boys! C'mon, we must go see John Moriarty now!"

Now, the pair of us didn't know John Moriarty, and we were comfortable where we were, but Dad would insist. So we'd head over to John Moriarty's. He'd be up at six in the morning trying to get us out of bed to go around to some fella's house so he could introduce us to him. At that age we liked our lie-in, especially when we were meant to be on holidays. But Dad would be knocking on the door. "Breakfast's on the table! C'mon, you can sleep when you die! You can sleep when you die!"

So after breakfast we were knocking on some poor fella's door. The man answered in his nightgown, rubbing his eyes. "Oliver, it's seven in the morning."

But Dad just talked over him and around him. "Oh, but my sons are up from Kerry! This here's Conor! This is Kieran – he plays Under-21 for Kerry! Put on the kettle there, sure, and we'll have a quick cup of tea!" And in he went, bustling past your man, with the rest of us having to follow him in.

It drove Conor mad; I don't think he ever visited Tyrone again after that. But it was one of those nights up there that I said it to him: Conor, that's not normal behaviour.

I'm not a doctor but I think that Dad was undiagnosed bipolar. I've read up on it a good bit the last while and regret I didn't do so much earlier. If he'd been diagnosed, it could have helped him so much. I'm sure there were strategies and medication that would have moderated his mood instead of him being so high or so low so much of the time.

Of course, it would have been some job trying to convince him he was bipolar, to take the medication, to explain to him that at least one in every forty people have it, including a lot of famous people that have been able to manage their lives with the right support. He'd have viewed any admission like that as a sign of weakness, any diagnosis as an attack on his manhood.

I remember going to see him in rehab and how resistant he was to saying the words: "I'm Oliver Donaghy and I'm an alcoholic." He said it through gritted teeth. So I can just hear him: "I'm not taking any tablets! I'm not fuckin' bipolar! Bipolar, my arse!"

But he was bipolar. Or at least, I'm almost certain he was. If you look at all the classic symptoms of the condition, he ticked nearly all of them. Those states of hypomania like when he could lift those sleepers on Banna Strand by himself. The constant irritability and fidgeting and inability to sit still. The pressured speech in which he'd be talking over you and talking so fast, he'd find it as hard to get all the words out in time as you would find it hard to interrupt him. In a manic state, he'd sleep very little yet never feel tired; then in a depressed state, he could sleep all day and still feel flat.

And he definitely experienced what the experts call a sense of grandiosity, when he'd feel the whole world knew and loved him and that he could do anything, like bet and drink without any consequences. As I understand it, one in two people with bipolar are estimated to have a drink and drug problem. In a manic state, they'll drink to slow themselves down; then when they're depressed, they'll drink to try to lift their mood.

There we were, thinking the gambling and gattin' were the problems, when maybe they were just the symptoms. Underlying them both was a bigger problem.

These days there's a greater appreciation of mental health and the idea of it being okay to not feel okay. But when Dad was still with us, there wasn't that same awareness. So he had to struggle on as he was. We had to struggle on as he was.

AUGUST, 2004, and I'm playing a Munster Under-21 final midweek against Cork at home in Tralee. It's one of the biggest football games of my life up to this point, so Dad wants to come down and share in it.

The day before the match, he lands down in a new Merc and looking a million dollars. He probably spent every last cent that he had on that car but he's giving off the impression that he's doing well for himself up North, that he's changed.

So on the Tuesday I tag along with him as he struts and bounds down Main Street like John Travolta in his pomp. He's this fine leather jacket on, smart jeans, big boots, and he's stopping and talking to anyone who'll open their ears to him.

"Here's my son, Kieran Donaghy!" he announces, slapping my shoulder. "He's playing midfield for Kerry tomorrow! Are you heading up to it?!"

All this time I'm tagging along. I'm twenty-one now. Not as

well-known as I'll be, but fairly well recognised around the town as a sportsman, and can tell people need the cringing introduction and sports bulletin just about as much as I do.

And before they can answer him, he might spot someone else vaguely familiar on the other side of the road, leave the people he was talking to – "Right, see you later!" – and bounce over to this other fella, dragging me along. "Timmy! How's it goin'?!"

We head into John Dowling's sports shop, then up to Hennebery's Sports. He gives the same spiel. I want to say to him, "Dad, will you fuckin' relax?!" But I can't. He's already moved on to someone else.

Anyway, any form of resistance is pointless. He's learned that I'm working in Supermac's. The franchise in town is owned by Mick O'Dwyer. So he wants to meet Micko! Shake his hand and tell the great man who's playing midfield for Kerry in the Under-21 game tomorrow. I try to explain to him: Dad, Micko owns the franchise, his son John is the one who manages it. The only time we've seen Micko was at the launch. He won't be there. He's never there.

But Dad's not having it. Oliver Donaghy is in town with his son who is playing midfield with Kerry tomorrow, and so he has decreed that Mick O'Dwyer must be in town as well and Supermac's while he's at it.

So Dad blazes in, me trudging along behind. Up to the counter. He doesn't want a Mighty Mac. He wants the mighty Micko. Is he here? But of course he's not. Dad has to settle for a free meal instead.

The rest of the day is like that: Dad in his Merc driving up unannounced in the driveways of people he hasn't seen in donkey's years.

The day of the game, we have lunch in The Greyhound before I head off to do my own thing and leave him off to do his. We lose by a point in a fuckin' game we had won, throwing away a four-point lead with ten minutes to go.

I don't put the loss down to the appearance and distraction of my dad, I played reasonably well, but after the game I don't want to see him.

I'm out with the rest of the team and steer them away from haunts like The Greyhound or anywhere else I think he might be. Instead we go to younger spots, like Ruairí's.

Every time I come out of one of them I'm looking around. Is he about? No. Good. Then we cross the road over to another bar and again I'm cagily scanning around. Because if he's here I know he's going to be devastated that we lost and he's going to want to talk about it and then I'm going to be stuck with him for the night, just as I was the day before. But again, thankfully, there's no sign of him here.

Three days later and there's still no word from him. By now I'm worried: where the fuck's the old man? We all have mobiles now; it's strange he hasn't called. So I ring him. The phone's dead. I presume he's headed back up North but then we hear from my uncles up there that they thought he was still down in Tralee. My cousin Aidan from my mother's side summons a search party. On the Sunday morning we get word that he's in this fella's house that he used to gat with back when he lived down here. We call Dad's brother, Anthony, to come down and bring him home.

Later that evening Aidan and Anthony knock on a door a stone's throw from Austin Stack Park. I stay in Aidan's car, anxiously biting the zip ring of my tracksuit. Will he go with them quietly? Will he cause uproar? Dad could do anything here. Then I see him emerge from the house, his forearm trying to block the daylight, wearing the same clothes that he had on when I'd seen him last.

Aidan and Anthony usher him across the road before bundling him into Anthony's car. Aidan tells him to stay away from Tralee until he's sorted himself out once and for all.

All the while I remain in Aidan's car and just watch Anthony drive off, his brother a shell of the man that blazed into town days earlier, slumped in the back, a beaten docket.

I DON'T think we spoke for more than eighteen months after that. We certainly didn't see each other. But of course I often thought of him and would ask the cousins in Tyrone how he was. And around the time Kerry won the 2006 league and I'd broken onto the team in midfield, I picked up the phone. He was thrilled to hear from me. He said he was keeping well. Hadn't taken a drink in four months and had a few ponies he looked after. I was glad to hear that.

He came down for the drawn Munster final and behaved himself. Then when we were drawn against Armagh in the All Ireland quarter-final, I knew how high he'd be with how well I'd played at full forward in the qualifier against Longford, and, as a Tyrone man, how much he'd love to share in the craic and the banter of us playing their fiercest rivals.

"Hey, Dad, do you want a ticket for the game in Croker?"

"Oh, I'd love that, son! And c'mere, would you have another one for a friend of mine?"

That was the famous game I grabbed the ball over Francie Bellew and blasted it past Paul Hearty. After the final whistle went and I'd embraced a few team-mates, I ran off to a corner of the Hogan Stand, section 335, and took off my jersey. There was a certain man I wanted to have it. And sure enough, along came Dad, breaking through security to get to the railing where we hugged and I handed him the jersey and we hugged again.

Over the next couple of years he got to share in the adventure. He'd go to all the big games in Croker. We'd talk on the phone. He'd visit Tralee a few times and there were a couple of occasions I was up in Tyrone to visit him and all the relations.

He'd ask how it was going with Hilary. And how Conor and Sarah were. Whenever he passed away, he said, he'd be leaving the worth of his little house to us. And he'd enquire and rave about Mom. "A gem of a woman, son," he'd tell me one night with a few pints in him. "I fucked it up. How did I fuck that up? What a woman. What a woman." I knew by the way he said it too that it wasn't just the drink talking.

And, of course, most of the time we talked football. That was our glue, and it was never lost on me that football was a big reason we were still in touch.

One night I was up in the clubhouse in Beragh where there was a John Donaghy Memorial trophy in honour of Granddad John being presented to the local Player of the Year. And naturally that night my dad was again going around the place like a blue-arse fly, introducing me to every Tom, Pascal and Larry…

But unlike that time of the Munster Under-21 final, I was fine with it and fine with him. At least he knew these people.

THE day after we beat Cork in the 2008 All Ireland semi-final replay and Tyrone beat Wexford on the same bill, I rang Dad. For the final there'd be reporters onto him, wanting to take the angle of me having a parent in both counties. "When they call, Dad, don't bother opening your mouth." I was everywhere in the papers throughout 2006 and 2007 but in 2008 was keeping the head down. "Could you do that, please, Dad? For me?"

"No problem, son," he promised.

The day before the final, the team was on the way up on the train when one of the lads opened one of the tabloids. There, splashed over a two-page spread, was the old man. Wearing a Kerry hat and Kerry jersey and waving his Kerry flag with some Tyrone colours flying in the background. And shooting his mouth off all over the rest of it.

Some of it was harmless if stupid stuff. How he had me out soloing a ball from when I was three years of age and how at five I could shoot into the goals from all angles. But then he went on to say that if I was living in Tyrone it would be Mickey Harte's team going for three All Irelands in a row. And worse, that he expected me to score something like 2-3 against them in this final. As if anyone would get 2-3 off a defence like theirs in an All Ireland final.

Sure enough, some of the lippy Tyrone backs would bring it up the next day. "Your old man…"

I was raging with him. Hadn't I pleaded with him to stay out of the papers?

I was a lot less trustful of him after that, and a lot less in contact. I wasn't going to cut him off completely, though. I suppose he'd always get the benefit of the doubt in my eyes, a fellow member of the old Monday Night Cowboys Club.

But then he went and fuckin' did it again. One day I got a call from O'Neill's sportswear. A few weeks earlier a man had walked into their factory in Strabane, Co. Tyrone, claiming his son was Kieran Donaghy who played for Kerry and could he take away some Kerry jerseys and a tracksuit. He hadn't paid for them, so would I settle it up?

I tried to laugh them off. Stop the lights, lads, are ye having me on or what? I'm afraid that's your own baby, you'll just have to write that one off and have a word with whoever was stupid enough to give free gear to a man coming in off the street. But when I put the phone down I wasn't laughing. I was livid. That was definitely, finally, the last straw. At least for a while until I'd thaw out and no doubt give him another chance.

MARCH 16, 2012, Gold Cup Friday, and after gathering up everyone's tenner at work in the bank for the rollover for the big race, I'm alone in the office kitchen having my lunch when a Northern number comes up on my phone. Straightaway I sense the news is not good.

"Hello?"

"Och, hello, Kieran, it's Gloria here." Gloria, my dad's sister, the family's matriarch. And before she goes any further, I know. Dad's dead. At fifty-nine. Passed away in his little house in Omagh, all alone, with just his scrawny dog for company.

I'm sitting there by myself and I start crying. My manager knocks on the door. Everything okay, Kieran? I tell her no: my father is dead. And in fairness, she's great, very supportive. Everyone is. Jack O'Connor calls and tells me not to worry about this league game down in Cork on Sunday, go be with my family. But I tell him I want to play. For one, it's Cork. And Dad's not being buried until the Tuesday. I'll go up early on the Monday. I want to play on the Sunday. Dad would have wanted me to play.

So I do. Before the game there's a minute's silence for the late Oliver Donaghy. Either side of me, linking arms, squeezing me, are my boys – Paul Galvin, Aidan O'Mahony. They have me.

I can barely remember anything else about that game. I couldn't even recall who won until I looked it up recently and saw that we did, by two points in a goalless game, and that apparently I played my part.

On the Monday I headed up North with Mom; being the lady that she is, she wanted to be there for me.

The wake was in the same house where Dad died, but as is usually the way at these things in this country, there was a good bit of laughter and black humour. The uncles and cousins laughed about the game the previous day and how Oliver would have loved the minute's silence for him. Páirc Uí Chaoimh coming to a standstill over him? The recognition, the respect – Oliver would have been in his element looking down on that!

And I was struck by the amount of people who came over to tell us about all the good turns Dad did for them.

A pensioner told the story about how, when his boiler was broken and the house was freezing, Dad went over and fixed it for him. Another old lady talked about how he'd change her light bulbs for her.

The Tuesday morning, just before they put the lid on his coffin and took him to the church, I was left alone with him in the room.

I bit my lip as I looked at him there in the coffin, his face all beaten and worn down by life and drink.

Jesus Christ, Dad. You had it all, man.

A saint of a woman in Mom. A gem of a daughter in Sarah; as tough as nails yet a pure dote. A son, Conor, thriving as a stone mason in Australia, with the same work ethic you had on your best days.

And me, man. Even me. How did it end like this, the two of us not having talked in two years and now never will again?

And at that, I broke down, uncontrollably, until my mother came in to escort me out of the room as they put the lid on the coffin.

Part of it stemmed from guilt. Me and my pride and getting so thick about some poxy article; the fact he'd the nerve and, fuckit, the charm, to walk into O'Neill's and get some free gear off them.

Really, Kieran, really? That's why you stopped talking to your old man? Why couldn't you just get over yourself?

I'd been planning to give him a call, even to meet up with him. A few months earlier I'd got engaged to Hilary. Of course I was going to tell him. Of course I was going to invite him. But I wanted to sit him down and clearly explain that I didn't want him coming down and upsetting my mother or sister or brother on the big day. "Listen, Dad, this is what I want from you around the time of the wedding…"

But I never got that chance. I never gave him the chance.

Maybe, I began thinking to myself, that's what triggered his last drinking spree. Maybe he'd heard that I was getting married so he went on an unmerciful bender, the man who was so worthless that his own son wouldn't even tell him he'd got engaged.

That thought haunted me for a while after. It was the drink that did it for him in the end and maybe he wouldn't have been on that last bender if it weren't for me. Maybe he'd still be alive if it weren't for me.

In time I'd come to forgive myself. I'd come to forgive him. I now try to recall the good times we had – those early Christmases; the Monday Night Cowboys Club; when he'd make sure I'd practised my spellings and then his delight when I'd get them all right; the trips out to the horses; and later, seeing him after the big games in Croker, bursting with pride.

And I try to have a greater understanding of why there were all those hard, testing times. Some family members are less sympathetic, saying my bipolar theory is only excusing inexcusable behaviour. But in my eyes he wasn't a bad person, he was just a troubled person who made some terrible decisions under the influence of drink and the pressures of gambling and an illness we didn't even recognise or know. In many ways they combined to rob me of a dad. But to me he was, and always will be, my dad.

A LITTLE over a year after he passed away, Kerry had a league game against Tyrone in Omagh. I said to Éamonn Fitzmaurice that I'd like to travel up ahead of the rest of the team, that I had some flowers for my dad. So, that Saturday evening, I stood and bowed my head in a graveyard in Beragh.

He's buried alongside his mother and father, resting in peace, as they say, though I wonder if even now Oliver Donaghy is still.

The day after we laid him down in that grave, myself and Hilary called over to his brother Benny's house just before heading back to Kerry. Benny was keeping Dad's dog, the one that had found him dead. The poor thing was probably going to be put in a home, but as a couple of dog lovers with a few terriers already at home, we said we'd like to have a look at him first.

He was skinny and smelly, probably because of the rough last few weeks my father would have had. But there was something very distinctive and classy about him with his silvery wavy-curly coat and long head and black overgrown facial hair. Hilary and myself looked at each other. "We've got to take him," she said.

It was a Kerry Blue terrier, a breed no doubt Dad went for because of the name. He'd even called it Star, just like the little Jack Russell he'd had when I'd last visited him. We hadn't spoken in two years and still the old man had called his dog after me. The least I could do for him was to take care of his dog.

For the first while down the road, the dog was scampering from side to side across the back seat, whining and whimpering, still probably wondering where his owner was. Then, just as we got to the Ballygawley roundabout, he suddenly settled down, and with his paws on the edge of the back of my seat, eased the point of his chin up against my shoulder. And that's where it stayed for the rest of the journey – his head tilted next to mine while I steered the wheel. The dog had only met me, just as it had only met Hilary, yet it was my shoulder he had leaned on. Was it that he recognised something about Dad in me?

We weren't long back in Kerry when we certainly recognised something of Dad in the dog. First time I brought him down to the beach, he started off being so lovely and playful, but once my friend from basketball, Vinnie Murphy, came along with his dog, our fella was straight in its face and hair was flying. I'd say the old man would have loved that, walking about with the toughest dog in town.

We renamed him Buddy – I wasn't going to have anyone say, "Yer man's so full of himself, he even calls his own dog Star!" – and that's exactly what he came to be to us: our Buddy. Dad would be true to his word and leave the worth of his little house to us, but the greatest inheritance of all was that dog.

So, when Hilary came back from work one day and found him virtually paralysed, we were in an awful state. The first couple of vets were sure he'd had a stroke. He seemed on death's door.

We couldn't leave it at that. We went to a third vet, Thomas Brosnan in Killarney. He said there was an outside chance it might be a spinal injury and put us in touch with a college friend of his with the only canine scanning equipment in the country. So, that same day, we headed up to Dublin, forking out the €1500 for the appointment without hesitation. It turned out there'd been no damage to the brain. Instead, Buddy was suffering from something called FCE, a blockage in the blood vessels of his spinal cord, probably from jumping and landing on his neck.

The vet warned us that it was still a pretty bad case. Buddy had ninety per cent paralysis. The rehabilitation could be too much for him.

Every day for the following six months I'd do exercises with him, moving his shoulder and paws. We'd bring him up to a swimming pool in Naas where the top racehorses go and the specialists would bring him around on this rope, getting him to swim and move his limbs. I'd hook him up to these electric pads I bought to help stimulate and build his muscles back up. We'd even have him undergo acupuncture from a fella that had returned from China.

His front right paw would return to its full capability, his back right to about seventy per cent and his back left to about fifty. His front left is basically redundant, but still he struts about the place as if he owns it, and if there's a sniff of a fight, he's up for it.

Still proud, still moody, still headstrong, still feisty out.

As long as Buddy is close to me, it's as if something of Oliver Donaghy is as well.

SLEEPING WITH THE BALL

"Donaghy's very evasive for a big man. In basketball you have to have your head up all the time so you see the hits coming earlier. You're drilled to use both hands. Donaghy's assists are very noticeable. The timing and weighting of his handpasses are brilliant. That's definitely from playing basketball"

Liam McHale, 2006

NOT LONG AFTER DAD LIFTED ME FROM bed that night and drove up to Tyrone, Mom was hauling me in her banger of a car down to Cork. When I asked why, stewing in the passenger seat alongside her, she wouldn't let on, but the two trips were not unrelated.

I had been in a massive fight in school with a good friend, Stephen Enright. I can't remember what started it, probably some comment he made that was harmless enough, but it was enough for me to snap. Before we knew it, the two of us were crashing from one classroom table into another. When we were pulled apart, we were sent straight into the principal's office, our school-uniform cream shirts splashed with each other's blood.

As the pair of us sat across from one another, waiting for our parents to come in, we knew we were in trouble. What I didn't bargain for was that it would trigger Mom to drag me down to Cork for a meeting with some psychiatrist or psychologist. I realise now why she did, that my fight with Stephen wasn't the kind someone in primary school should be having. By nature I was a cheerful, friendly kid; the situation at home was obviously affecting me. But back then I was in denial. I resented the notion. I resented her. Why had she driven Dad away and why now was she driving me here to see some stranger?

There was a sand dial in the psychiatrist's office, and for as long as we were in there, I just gazed at it, turning it over, watching the grains of sand stream down. I didn't engage at all. It was a complete waste of everyone's time, something I'd make very clear to poor Mom on the way back. "That was a bloody joke, Mom! Don't ever take me down there again! I'm fine!"

It's the front I'd try to give to everyone: I'm fine. And for the most part I was. But my uncle Brian recalls coming down to us from Dublin one evening and popping up to my room and on the landing being able to hear me sobbing behind the door. When he knocked, I hopped up, flicking a tear away. "Hey, B, how are you?!" He asked if I'd been crying. I'd say no but the red rings around my eyes gave me away. So he lay down there on the bed with me, and I'd open up to him, about Mom and Dad and how I felt, in a way I never could to some shrink.

And that's how we'd get by. I had my uncles, I had my nan whom we lived with and adored, and I'd Mom – always. I didn't need anyone else. I had more than enough love there in that house on the Caherslee Road.

Still, in my head, everybody else in school had a dad at home, and whenever friends would call around, I'd be wondering what they'd be thinking of our situation. I remember when I was about thirteen, a friend's parents had a bust-up and were living separately and I finally felt I had someone I could relate to on that count. Then his mom and dad got back together and with it our special bond was lost.

At school you'd see the other kids being dropped off and collected by their dads and it would sometimes hit you: *Jesus, it's always my mom collecting me.*

And as for the car she'd be in… Money was tight back in those days in our house, so when Uncle Brian said he'd a new Japanese sports car for us, we were delighted. That's how he'd pitched it to us: a Japanese sports car! It sounded so cool, so exotic! Then it arrived: the ugliest heap of shit you've ever seen. Brian and his Garda colleagues in Dublin had found it abandoned in the mountains, the front window completely smashed. When they returned it to the owner, she said she was done with it. So off it went down to his sister in Kerry, this white car now almost orange from the rust. There was even a small hole in the flooring through which we could see the road. We were like the flippin' Flintstones.

Whenever I'd have basketball training, I'd ask Mom to drop me about half a mile from the gym. I couldn't be seen in that yoke.

SCHOOL was something of a love-hate affair. I loved the craic there but hated the books.

Some teachers I was fierce fond of. Our principal at Holy Family primary was a pure gentleman called Michael Hayes who would still provide me with grinds in Irish and Maths up to my Leaving Cert and remains a friend to this day. In second class we had a Sister De Lourdes who'd show us National Geographic videos and run quizzes in which the grand prize could be vanilla buns. But in secondary school in Tralee CBS, The Green, I must have been a nightmare for the teachers.

We'd an Irish teacher who hated noise, so of course we'd make plenty of it. My buddy Andrew Dineen used to sit in front of me, over by the window. On the other side of the room then there'd be a couple of other friends, Martin Courtney and David Conway, that we'd try to get in trouble. Dineen and myself would hop our pens off the window, then flash a look over towards the two boys.

"For God's sake, Courtney, stop it, will ya?!"

The trick to it was for the two of us to look over simultaneously; then we'd have the teacher fooled and the boys busted. Years later I'd serve that teacher in The Greyhound Bar and we'd laugh about it, but back in the day we were probably the bane of his life.

I suppose I was disruptive because most of the time I didn't know what the fuck the teachers were on about. Maths with its algebra and theorems was a complete write-off, even though my teacher Des Healy tried so hard with me. I'd fierce difficulty with reading in general though I didn't know why at the time – I just thought I was thick. Mom and Nan would make me go upstairs to do my study but after two pages I'd get dizzy from it all and just close the book; instead I'd switch on Atlantic 252, my fingers hovering over the play and record buttons, ready to tape a favourite song. The next morning then I'd copy homework off the smart guys, but be smart enough to get a few answers wrong so no-one could be accused of any cogging.

The one subject I was good at was geography – and that was as much out of spite as a genuine interest in it.

One afternoon myself and Brendan Smith skipped the first class after lunch to stay on playing soccer in the town park, right behind the school. We breezed in for our next class but our geography teacher, Dan Nolan, could tell from the green patches on the knees of our pants what we'd been at. We'd get suspended for three days which we'd spend up in Smithy's playing ISS Pro Evolution Soccer. I'd it in for Dan after that, and all the more when he'd tell me not to take honours in the Leaving because I'd fail. Not only did I take honours, I'd get a C+. I did next to no study in school but fuck me did I study for geography.

That suspension had been coming though. One Wednesday myself and Martin Courtney went on the hop down to Cork for a big FAI Cup game Cork City were playing that afternoon. We made our way out to Turner's Cross and into The Shed, joining in the taunts of the Shamrock Rovers fans.

Oh they're all a bunch of wankers over there!

Of course the Rovers fans gave back as good as they got.

Oh they're all a bunch of sheepshaggers over there!

Over and back it went. Juvenile stuff, maybe, but for a few juveniles from Tralee on the doss for the day, gas craic altogether. Even when we'd get reported by the school and killed by our moms the next day, we were still laughing about it.

Later, I'd discover a more respectable way of getting out of class – playing and coaching basketball.

WE were all visiting my Aunt Gloria's in Tyrone when I noticed an orange metal hoop with a tattered net hanging from the red-bricked gable wall.

"Oh, that's a basketball ring," Dad said. "It's more of a girl's game."

Years later he'd learn how wrong he was about that, but it was a game alright that my cousin Nicola was familiar with, and she'd produce a ball from the garage. From the moment my hands felt the pimpled grain of that ball, I was fascinated by it, and when I finally got a ball to drop through that rim, I didn't want to leave.

Up to the age of ten or so, football would have been the game I played most; Dad was around back then and there was no mistaking what his favourite game was. But basketball was the game my mom had played, winning a schools All Ireland. So when Dad left and we moved over to Nan's, she got my uncle Ciarán to put up a red-rimmed hoop out the back. She probably thought I could do with a distraction from all the upheaval, and over the years, that ring and backyard would be my refuge.

I started out there wanting to be a Tralee Tiger. I remember the opening night of the 1993-94 season, going to the Sports Complex in town to see them and their new American, Ricardo Leonard, and just being in awe of the man.

He was about 6'7", just a year out of Old Dominion College whom he'd helped get to the famous March Madness NCAA tournament. He ended up scoring fifty-two points. There was one play where one of the local stars, John Teahan, threw an inbound ball from the sideline and Ricardo just spun off his man, jumped, caught Teahan's alley-oop and slammed it into the ring before he returned to earth. I had never seen anything like it before. I had never seen anything like him before. All of them: their size and speed and the sweat coming off them as I watched on from the first row of the bleachers; I was transfixed. I went straight home and out the back, shooting in my finger-less gloves, until Nan called me in, saying one of the neighbours had phoned, complaining of the racket.

The next week I'd signed up with the Tigers Under-12s. On Saturday mornings Ric would pop his head in. Of course we'd all start showing off at the sight of him, putting it through the legs and stuff. He was like something from another world. The only other black men in town back then worked in the hospital and they were hardly as tall or as cool as Ricardo Leonard.

That first year with the Under-12s, I'd have been one of our weakest players, but when that season ended I didn't stop. Every day and into the night I'd be out shooting into that cheap, price-less ring Mom got Ciarán to put up.

It was so much easier to play around with a basketball than a football. You didn't have to run forty yards to retrieve it and then jog back to kick another point. You could just shoot, get it, shoot again.

I'd also learned to shoot properly. A great Tralee basket-ball man called Seánie Burrows was watching me over at the side baskets while the Tigers Superleague team were training. He spotted my elbow was way out to the side, an awful habit probably rooted in me being so small and trying to generate enough power to reach the ten-foot basket.

He called me aside. "Right, I'm going to put my hand here so you keep your elbow in. Now, push it straight up and follow through."

I wanted to go back to my old way – "I can't do it, Seánie" – but he'd tell me if I wanted to be a good basketball player, it was the way to go.

Seánie would keep looking out for me. He'd give me one of those old video tapes. "There's three NBA games on that, now. Take it away with you." I'd sprint home then insert the latest tape into the VCR. And there'd be six hours of basketball to marvel at, though I couldn't watch it for that long – I'd have to go out the back and try some move of Larry Bird's or Magic Johnson's.

The main man though was Michael Jordan. I'd a video of his all to myself which I'd watch every day. I'm not joking. The gravity-defying dunks, the game-winning buzzer beaters; to this day I can quote about every line that's in Come Fly With Me.

One morning in third year, one of our classmates got word

that Michael Jordan was playing golf out in Tralee Golf Club. Straight away, myself and David Conway dropped our school-bags and were out the gap. It was hardly as if we were members there, so we sneaked down along the beach and onto the course to find the Jordan party on the eleventh.

The thing that struck me most following him was his sheer size: he was an absolute monster. I also couldn't believe how far he could hit the ball; with the downwind that was blowing that day, he must have hit it well over three hundred yards off the eighteenth. And, of course, with his Nike hat and puffing his cigar, he just oozed cool. Afterwards, when he and his entourage were getting back onto his bus, I worked my way into position to reach and grab his hand. Just to touch the hem of that god's garment.

I still had local heroes. Every night the Tigers trained or played, I'd be there. I'd shoot on the side rings. Every now and then the ball would bounce off the ring and onto the main court and the coach would roar, "SIT DOWN, KIERAN!" But then after a while I'd rise from the bench and shoot again, making sure to scurry in for every rebound before it hit the ground.

As much as I'd shoot though, I spent more time watching and learning from the Tigers. I'd notice how John Teahan hustled on defence. The hours Ricardo would put into his shooting. And then there was Vinnie Murphy at point guard.

I loved his attitude. He was a rebel. He'd have these mad haircuts, anything from a bleached, semi-Mohican to my personal favourite, the tiger-stripes look, when he'd dye his hair black and orange. And he was a big, big talker, bossing teammates and games like a fellow Corkman of the time, Roy Keane, though he probably looked more like Vinnie Jones.

I became so much part of the furniture with the Tigers, I got to sit on their most precious piece of furniture – the team bench. I'd walk into the hall with all the other kids, then strut over to the boys. "Hey, Vinnie! Hey, Ric!" And of course they all knew me. "Hey, Kieran." All this in front of my friends. So I'm cool, like; I'm the coolest twelve-year-old in Tralee. I'd get to say to my buddies, "Sure, I'll catch ye after the game, boys," and then just hang there, while they'd to head over to the bleachers where they and the rest of the town could get a fine view of that lucky bollix Donaghy sitting over with the team.

The Tigers would win the Superleague in 1995-96. There's a photograph that was in all the papers from the night they were presented with the trophy, and popping up on the right shoulder of their inspirational coach Timmy McCarthy – the same Tim now famous for his orgasmic 'DOWNTOWN!' 'BOOMSHAKALAKA!' television Olympics commentary – is a beaming, big red-lipped kid who'd just turned thirteen.

To this day that memory is as clear in my head as any All Ireland final I've won. Before the game they switched off all the lights. *What the hell's going on here?* Suddenly, a spotlight beams to the mid-court. "Ladies and gentlemen, please welcome the Superleague champions, YOUR TRALEE TIGERS!" Next thing, the intro to Eye of the Tiger. 'DUN! DUN, DUN, DUN!' And the team runs out, all in their cool new shooting tops, and I'm like: *Wow!*

By this stage I was the best player on our Under-13 team. I remember that season's Castleisland Christmas Blitz. For a lot of kids in Kerry, the Blitz was as big as Christmas Day itself. The crowd crammed around the court, your game being played either side of maybe a Superleague team; everyone, from eight-year-old girls to forty-something beer-bellies, looked forward to and took part in the Blitz. But when the morning arrived, the day after Stephen's Day, I was gawking inside the toilet bowl on my knees with the team bus waiting outside and Mom standing at the bathroom door, telling me I couldn't go. "Mom," I said, "out of the way."

I'd all my gear from Christmas; my new Nike Air Huaraches, my new tracksuit, and my earphones and walkman that I wanted to rock up to the gym wearing. Mom wouldn't budge. But I wouldn't either and when I turned on the waterworks, she eventually let me go.

We got down there and I nearly passed out from the heat of the radiators and the intensity of the game. But I refused to quit. I refused to lose. I wanted to win. Looking back, I think that's where a lot of it started. That 'YEAAHH!' thrill of winning and of turning over an arch rival or a more fancied team, or both, as was the case with the Castleisland Under-13s.

And deep down there probably was a certain rage there, a rage from all that went with Dad leaving the house. I suppose I needed an outlet for my anger, and sport, winning, provided it.

The only thing I loved as much as winning was the game itself. The summer of '97 I plagued my mother to let me go to the well-known residential camp in Dungarvan, County Waterford. One of the American coaches they brought over recommended that we sleep with the ball. That we become that familiar with it. So when I got back after one of the greatest weeks of my life, that's what I'd do; every night I'd cuddle up to that ball, watched over by all the posters and photos on the wall of Jordan, Pippen and Rodman that I'd cut out of Slam Magazine.

The following season I was one of forty kids to try out for

the Under-16 Irish squad. I was one of the smallest there but I didn't give a shit. I was making that team.

I made the provisional sixteen-man squad, and every weekend for a couple of months I'd head up to Dublin with another lad from Tralee, Daniel Boylan. Our mothers would put us on the train, waving us off with the sandwiches they'd packed and £2 for our tea and bar of chocolate from the aisle trolley.

It would be by post that we'd find out if we'd made the final twelve or not, so when the letter dropped through the box, I was never as nervous in my life. I wanted to be by myself opening it in case it was bad news. I slipped in to Nan's room and braced myself. And there it was: 'You have been selected…'

I was ecstatic – and relieved. By then I'd come to fully appreciate how much Mom was doing for us, especially for me with the basketball. You'd hardly ever see her head out for a night. She was either working or she was at home looking after us. Putting that hoop up out the back in the first place; then after me plaguing her about the loose chippings out there, somehow forking up enough for us to get it tarmacadamed; all the spins to and from Tigers training; buying and washing and ironing all my gear; finding the money to send us to Dungarvan; then all she'd have paid out for me to go up to Dublin: when I made the cut, it was like repaying and justifying all she'd invested in me.

Even after I'd made the team, I'd to raise £500 to fund the trip to Sweden for our European Championships qualification tournament. Mom would take the sponsored cards into work or over to anyone she knew to get a line signed. All to help me with my dreams, never to live her own through me.

With Dad it was different. In that sense I think it suited me that he went away. It allowed me to go about my sport without any pressure. I didn't have to put up with any "You should have done this, you should have done that." I'd come home and Mom would just ask, "How did ye get on?" If we won or I'd played well, she'd say, "Brilliant. Well done." And if I didn't, she'd say, "Hard luck. Next time."

When I was older alright, playing for Kerry, she'd give out to me for giving out to the refs. "You're always sticking your neck out! It looks terrible on television!" But as a kid, there was no judgement, no interference.

Daniel made that Irish Under-16 squad as well, so on Tuesdays and Thursdays he'd cycle over to our backyard. We'd been given these shooting programmes and we'd to chart them, how many free-throws and outside shots we'd make out of a hundred. Then on the Saturday we'd go up with those sheets and our sandwiches, and train with the squad for the weekend.

The pair of us would stay with the team coach, Joey Boylan. With his wild, overgrown beard, Joey looked like the Tom Hanks character in Castaway, while his thick Dublin accent lay somewhere between Ronnie Drew and Christy Brown; for the first couple of sessions I couldn't understand him at all. His flat wasn't always the tidiest either from all the cigarette butts, but we were mad about him. We'd eat pizza and listen and laugh to all his great stories about old ball-players and watch videos of him and his beloved St Vincent's winning Cups.

His assistant, Dave Fitzsimmons, was a real polished, technical coach; he'd take us through our offences and how we were going to run Play X, Y and Z. Then Joey would step in and roar, "DE-FENCE!" And you'd have to roar it as well, slapping your hands on the floor, or else you'd be running sprints for an hour. I loved it.

Joey was my kind of coach and I was his kind of player. I might have been the smallest player on the squad – I'd be the smallest player among the five teams at our European Championship qualifying tournament – but I was all about hustle and all about the team. If I found our big man hadn't got a few touches the previous few possessions and was getting antsy, I'd feed him the ball next time up, then give him a pat on the back coming back the court after he'd made the shot.

And I brought a bite to it, just like Vinnie did to the Tigers. I was like a Jack Russell on the court. I'd be the one yapping on defence. "Ball, ball, ball!" "Help, help, help!". If a teammate was slacking off, I'd let him know. I'd be barking at our big fellas. "Box out! Get rebounds! Get back the floor! C'mon!"

One day Joey and Dave called me aside. They were making me captain. I was astonished. Ger Quinlan from Neptune in Cork was our best player; why wasn't he the captain? But, no, Joey felt I was the leader. He noticed I got on well with everyone. If during lunch I'd a spare orange, I'd open it and half it with a teammate, maybe one I'd been snapping at earlier. I wanted to be cool with everyone.

Our first night in Sweden, there was a reception for all the teams. Right away I said to myself: *We're in trouble.* All the other teams had boys 6'8", 6'9". Our tallest fella was 6'2". We were well beaten in our first three games – by the hosts and then two powerhouses of the European game, Lithuania and Spain. The one winnable game was England.

We came into the locker room at half-time, ten points down. The floor was still wet from the game before ours. Dave started off making a few technical points, in that calm, measured way of his. Then Joey took the floor.

He nodded to one of our players: "That water bottle over there, pick it up."

So your man rises from his seat, rather baffled, picks up the water bottle, and casually hands it to Joey.

Joey goes spare. "SEE! That's exactly our problem! We're too casual going for the ball!" He plonks the bottle on the floor, takes three steps back, then dives full length across the floor, splitting the water like an Olympic swimmer. He jumps up, slams the bottle down in front of your man so hard, water shoots out. "*THAT'S* HOW YOU GO AFTER THE BALL!"

In the second half, fellas were diving all over the place for balls they had no right to win. But in the last quarter as we tired, England stretched out their lead some more, and when I drove down the lane, this big black fella, about 6'7", swiped away my shot and turned round to me. "Get out, you little Paddy!"

I was fuming. *You're a great man now with the game in the bag to start talking.* Running back the court, I snapped and kick-tripped his back leg, sending him splashing to the floor. For a moment everyone just stopped where they were: is that little kid after kicking that big fella? Just as it dawned with the English lads and they started making a beeline to strangle me, one of the refs marched me to the opposite side of the court and the-atrically pointed to the changing rooms. All he was missing was the red card.

It was a lonely walk of shame to the dressing room, and when I got there, I hung my head, absolutely disgusted. We'd lost again, we hadn't brought the fight from the start, I'd let down the team with my temper.

When the rest of the team trooped in, I didn't know how to look at them, especially Joey as he came over and sat down beside me. I was just about to mumble sorry when he slapped me on the knee, and, speaking out of the side of his mouth, said, "Fair feckin' play to ya. At least you took nothing lying down!"

If I'd been in the stand that day, watching my own son do what I did, I'd probably have cringed. But it was the last game of the tournament, I was team captain, and I think Joey appreciated how much it had meant to me and that I shouldn't let that moment overshadow the whole experience. In giving me that pick-up, he had me for life, if he hadn't already.

A few months later we'd win the Four Countries, beating England on their own patch along the way. Again I was the captain and again that big 6'7" fella was playing for them. There was no "Get Out, You Little Paddy" that day.

BEING an Irish international gave me huge confidence and a certain status and leeway around school and town. Two of the teachers, Liz Doyle and Geraldine O'Dwyer, were brilliant to me, organising all the basketball in a football-dominated school and giving me the responsibility of coaching the first and second years. I was all on for it, not least because I'd a pass from class for the day anytime we had a blitz or some big game around the country.

At lunchtimes in the school hall I could either practise myself or coach the second-years. John O'Keeffe, the Kerry football legend and our PE teacher would section off at least half the gym so we could get in our work.

Often he would help me physically train the teams. I'd use

drills I'd seen Joey and Dave do. Between us we'd help the team make it all the way to the All Ireland final, only to lose by a basket.

By this stage I was too cool to sit on the bench of the Tigers. I'd outgrown that. I was regularly falling in at training with the likes of Vinnie and Teahan, not stargazing at them. On game night I'd be more in to eating Stinger bars and commenting on the female talent in the Complex with my buddies.

The gear and look was all part of it. I'd do all kinds of things for show and a laugh. One time my buddy Andrew Dineen came back from LA with two pairs of the new Kobe Bryant Crazy 8s. So before a Kerry county final against Castleisland we came up with the idea of mixing up our shoes; he'd wear the right black one and left white one and I'd wear the opposite.

We won the game and afterwards the pair of us came out of the hall, buzzing, to find five or six of the Castleisland boys leaning against the wall.

One of the ringleaders, smoking a fag, piped up, "Ha, the two faggots leaving together, look!"

Dineen turned but I grabbed him. "C'mon, forget them."

Dineen walked up to your man.

"Sorry, what did you say?"

Your man was there, flanked by his boys. "Yer two faggots, wearing the same shoes."

With that, Dineen dropped his can of Lucozade and swung, sending your man's head against the wall; down he went, in a heap.

"Well," asked Andrew, "has anyone else anything to say?"

The silence was only broken when Dineen picked up his can again and complained to me that there was a dent in it. And off we continued then along our way, in our one black and one white Crazy 8s, the crazy pair of us.

I'D ALWAYS had big feet and big hands, just short legs and short arms; Vinnie has told me I was the goofiest kid he'd ever seen. Then in the space of a year I went from about 5'6" to 6'4"; I grew into my hands and into my feet. It's why I'll often say to a kid that might look awkward, "What size shoes are you, man?" They might say size 11 and I'll go, "God, you're going to be tall, boy!" No-one ever said that to me; not to worry about being a bit uncoordinated now, you'll grow into yourself.

It worked out great for me, though. I'd good ball-handling skills from being a point guard. Then when I grew, I could attack the basket way more, and eventually could dunk it.

It was around then that I had some falling out with the Tigers while they had fallen out of the Superleague for a couple of years. So Vinnie dropped down to intermediate national league and the pair of us teamed up with St Brendan's, another club in the town.

Not everyone could handle playing with Vinnie. I'd see him bark at other players and they'd go into their shell. He was definitely old school, but the way I looked at it when he'd shout at me was, *Right, I messed up there, I can't do that again.* Vinnie says that's why he knew I'd make it in sport – anything a veteran like him would say to me, they only had to say it once.

One time we were playing in the Neptune Stadium. One of our players, Joe Quirke, was trapped in the corner and I just stood in the opposite corner, waving for the ball. In the end Joe got called for travelling. Coming back down the court, Vinnie roared at me. "Fuck's sake, you're our main man! If you see a fella in trouble, don't just stand there! Go get the ball!" I nodded: Okay. And I went on to have a massive game. It's something that's stayed with me, football or basketball. Stand up and show for the ball. Never hide from it.

SATURDAY, JANUARY 30, 2016

OVER four months on from the All Ireland and I finally bring myself back up to Dublin. I've avoided the place over the winter. This weekend is National Cup weekend, the biggest in the Irish basketball calendar when the sport's community comes together out in the National Basketball Arena in Tallaght.

At midday I'm playing for St Brendan's in the intermediate final. It seems as if all of Tralee is up here to support us. And probably the best part of it all is that my brother Conor is here rooming and playing with me.

The day after I got back from the Kerry team holiday in Miami, we beat Cork Celts in Portlaoise in a dogfight of a semi-final. Afterwards I hugged Conor and I said, "We'll make up for that Under-19 Cup final in the Arena."

That 2002 All Ireland A Schools League final was a moment that was stolen from us, or more like I stole from us.

Conor was only fourteen back then but still on our starting five, he was such a big strong young fella. We were playing for Tralee Community College where I was doing a Post Leaving Cert course, against Coláiste Éanna, a Dublin school.

We were up seven points at half-time but something that was pissing me off was that the referees – from Dublin – were calling the Éanna players by their nicknames. Midway through the third quarter I made a great block on one of their star players. Next thing, I hear the whistle. Foul on Number 10, black. That's me. And that's my fourth foul.

No fuckin' way, I'm thinking, and then without thinking, I kick the padding under the basket. The whistle goes again. Technical foul. And your fifth.

Ah, Jesus Christ, ref! You're not serious?!

Okay, that's it. You're out of here, Number 10!

I went over and got a drum from one of our supporters, marched up to the top of the bleachers and started banging the shit out of the thing. "DE-FENCE! DE-FENCE!" I was like a psycho up and down the aisle, and following my lead, our crowd deafened the place.

The lads on the floor dug deep. Conor. Daniel Boylan, my old Under-16 international team-mate; Wayne Riordan, an international swimmer; Aidan O'Shea; Martin Ferris, son of the politician. Our coach, Paul Coffey. To a man they were heroic.

They'd lose – by a single point. No defeat up to then had devastated me more. Even now it would still be in my top five. Never have I let my team down more than I did in that one.

So that's one of the great things about this Cup run with St Brendan's. All these years later I've got to play again with Conor, and now we get to play again in the Arena.

It's just fallen this way. Some time between last year's All Ireland quarter-final and semi-final, Pa Carey, the chairman of St Brendan's, rang to tell me that Basketball Ireland was starting a National Cup for intermediate clubs like them; Brendan's were entering it and he was thinking of registering me. I told him not to bother but Pa said he'd put my name down anyway and we'd talk again in October. Sure enough, when I came back from a little holiday in Portugal to try to beat the All Ireland blues, Pa called again and before I knew it, I was togging out for a county league game against Gneeveguilla in the Moyderwell gym in town. It was my first competitive game of basketball in seven years. I hadn't even trained with the team. But that night it seemed like I had never been away.

In basketball I always know I can influence the thing. I nearly always feel like I'm the best player. I don't feel that confidence or control in football. I've never been the best player, not at inter-county level anyway. I've had to rely on the ball coming to me. In basketball if I want the ball, I can go demand it.

The whole town seems to have fallen back in love with the sport. Tralee hasn't had a Superleague team since 2009 but now a few of us are looking at bringing it back. I'd say Irish basketball needs it as much as Tralee basketball does. There's a great tradition in the town of the sport and the past few months has shown there's still a huge passion for it.

That's why we need Superleague back in Tralee. That the talent we have in the town, like Ryan Leonard, Ricardo's seventeen-year-old son, can play at a level that will push them. With Brendan's, we've a lad called Paul McMahon; good shooter, tall, athletic, who could do with bulking up. But at the moment what's he going to do weights for? County league next year?

In a way though that's part of the charm of this weekend, how casual the lads are about preparation; I used to be like that myself before entering the Kerry setup. We're staying here in a hotel near Newland's Cross. With Kerry you come down for breakfast and it's all yoghurts and poached eggs and porridge laid on; no sausages, no rashers, no black or white puddings. This morning Jason Quirke ate a full Irish and a bowl of Coco Pops. All the lads tucked in to their fry, delighted with the free breakfast. I'm going, "Lads, we're playing a National Cup final at twelve o'clock! And where the fuck can I get some poached eggs around here?" I didn't want any fried eggs while the scrambled eggs looked a bit dodgy. The lads thought it was hilarious; Star getting so worked up about what kind of egg to eat!

We head over to the Arena and about ten minutes before the game, the lights go down. The players are waiting in the tunnel, to be called onto the floor, and I find myself welling up.

In front of me is Conor. For six years he was away in Australia. He came back because he missed everyone, especially Nan, knowing she wouldn't be around forever. For the last six months of her life he minded her, with the rest of us, lifting her to bed every night. This month was her first anniversary. God, I'd love it if she was here to see the two of us.

Now the third special lady in my life is Lola Rose and she's sitting in the stand on Hilary's lap, right beside Mom.

Coming into the Arena, Conor and myself met Daniel Boylan and Paul Coffey walking in. The last time the four of us were in the same hall was that Under-19 Schools League final here in 2002. The two of them changed their ticket back to Canada to take in this game. Seánie Burrows, who showed me how to shoot all those years ago, is here; I only wish his brother Bruddy, a former Irish captain who passed away last year, was as well. Everyone from Tralee that's alive and well seems to be here. I spot Andrew 'Crazy 8s' Dineen in the stand. Ger Power and Seánie Walsh too. We must have over four hundred people up

here. God, imagine if we got a team back in the Superleague…
But we've got to win this to make our case to Basketball Ireland.
We've got to win…

It takes us a while to settle. Our opponents, BC Leixlip
Nemunas, jump into a 17-7 lead. Their entire team are from
Lithuania where basketball is the national sport and a few of
them played for Dublin Inter in the Superleague Cup final only
two years ago. I've got to step up, demand it, no hiding. I get
the ball in the corner, throw a fake, drive to the basket, draw the
foul and still make the shot and the free-throw. After that, I'm
off. We're away. By half-time I'm on sixteen points and we're
up 40-32.

In the second half the rest of the lads take it away. The Lithuanians are double-teaming me and it's leaving other lads wide
open. Even when the Lithuanians make a bit of a run to bring
it back to a couple of baskets, Darren O'Sullivan hits three
three-pointers in a row. And looking at him, punching the air
repeatedly running back the court, I'm skipping back myself.
There's a guy that has lived this Cup run; for me it's been just
a bit of fun. Our player-coach Fergal O'Sullivan also lights it
up to finish on fourteen points. I'm delighted it's them boys that
win the game for us. I'll end up with the MVP because the stat
line of a triple double is supposedly a first for an Irish player in
a men's National Cup final – 18 (points), 26 (rebounds) and 12
(assists) – but only two of my points came after half-time. When
it had to be won it was the boys who made the big shots.

After the buzzer goes I dash over to Conor and we embrace;
finally the ghost of that Under-19 Schools final has been
banished. Hilary brings over Lola Rose and I have her in my
arms collecting the medal and the MVP golden ball. Mom,

Sarah, Hilary and of course Conor join us for a lovely family picture out on the floor.

I meet everyone out there. Joey Boylan, who gives me a big grin and hug. Daniel Boylan. Paul Coffey. Andrew Dineen. Seànie Burrows. Ric Leonard. It feels like it's all come full circle, like it's all connected. That's a good word for how I feel right now. Connected.

The only thing that brings my mood down a bit is watching the football on the TV in the Boar's Head later on. The national league opened with Dublin and Kerry again in Croke Park, this time under the lights. Dublin again won comfortably enough.

But tonight is all about the Brendan's boys. I call on a few contacts and in we all go into Dicey Riley's and later Everleigh Gardens nightclub, four tables sectioned off with the sign: Reserved: St Brendan's Basketball Club. The boys are loving it, laughing and clinking their glasses.

VIPs, the lot of them, or at least for tonight.

CHAPTER 4

STAR AND THE HOUND

"The biggest thing about being a barman is personality. Anyone can fill a pint. People don't just come for the pint. They come for interaction. When you strike up that connection with the person on the other side of the counter, there's a magic to that. Star could make that connection"

Aidan 'The Hound' O'Connor

WHEN I TELL PEOPLE ABOUT HOW AVERAGE an underage footballer I was, I tell them about the Under-16 county final against Beaufort.

It was out in Spa, a few miles from Killarney, on a lovely summer's evening, so it wasn't like I could blame the conditions for what happened out there.

I was in at full forward, not because I was tall; I'd still to have my growth spurt. It wasn't like I was some great finisher; our coach Frank Courtney would always be telling me not to kick the ball because I was no good at it. My job was to lay it off to those who could kick it, like Kevin Walsh, David Conway and Frank's own son, Martin. I had good movement and quick hands from the basketball and as long as I stuck to winning the ball and getting rid of it, I could do a job for the team.

With a few minutes to go there was only a point or so in it when I won a ball out in front of my man. But everyone else had been dragged out the field; I'd no-one to pop it off to. I was running and looking around, panicking, until eventually, the whistle went. Free out – over-carrying.

I turned around to find my marker was still on the ground, clutching his ankle. I had been straight through on goal, about ten yards out from the posts. It had never occurred to me to face the goal and go for a score myself.

We'd end up losing, and walking off the field I was sick; if I'd scored that time we'd likely have gone on and won it. That evening I went up with Martin to Timmy Lynch's house where the three of us slumped into the sofa and played Pro Evolution on his PlayStation, typical teenagers with our hoodies up.

Timmy's dad, Pa the Jap, came in the door from the match.

"Jesus! Fuckin' disaster, wasn't it?"

We all mumbled, barely looking away from the screen. "Yeah."

"I mean, Jesus Christ almighty, your man inside at full forward! The biggest waste of space of all time! Who's that fella anyway?"

I could see the two boys wincing beside me, so instead of making it awkward for the three of us, especially Timmy, I rose up and put up the hand. "Oh yeah, Mister Lynch, that was me. Sorry about that, I was brutal, I know!"

Well, I've never seen a man turn red so fast.

"Well, em, I suppose you gave it your best," he spluttered, his eyes never leaving the ground until he'd whisked himself away.

To this day whenever I meet Pa, he always has a slight cringe, a wink and a smile for me. It's like our own little private, unspoken joke.

I'll always have a big welcome for him. "Well, Pa!"

"Well, Kieran, how's it going?"

He's never actually come out and said, Jesus, was I wrong about you!

There's no need. Sure what he said was dead right. Back then I was a complete waste of space when it came to football.

JAP was in good company with his assessment. I couldn't make the school team either, not until the year I repeated my Leaving.

In sixth year alright I felt I was good enough to make the panel though maybe not the team, but that year they won their third Munster title in a row, so obviously they were fine without 'the basketballer', and the basketballer wasn't too upset about it either. I was happy enough to line up like the rest of the school and pay my fiver to go on one of the fifty-seater buses they'd roll out for their big games.

I'd close friends and Stacks teammates who would have played three years senior on those successful Corn Uí Mhuirí teams, the likes of Brian Dennehy, TJ Hogan and Mikey Collins linking up with the gifted Declan Quill from Kerins O'Rahilly's. If you were to ask back then who'd be the kid from Tralee that would go on and win All Irelands and All Stars with Kerry, any of those four lads would have been championed. My name wouldn't have been mentioned. It would have been laughed at, probably most loudly by me.

It wasn't that I was indifferent to football. Like the rest of Kerry, I grew up on The Golden Years video. I'd watch the tape of the 1986 All Ireland final with Dad and hear him harp on about how Tyrone should have beaten Kerry that day. On Sunday mornings I'd go down to the Austin Stacks club in Connelly Park where I'd learn the basic skills of the game from the master coach, James Hobbart, just as he used to take the likes of Mikey Sheehy and Ger Power long before me.

He'd line us up and throw the ball up in the air and encourage us to catch it at the peak of our jump. "Out of the clouds, Kieran boy! Out of the clouds!" he'd shout as I'd leap, mindful of his other instruction to have my two thumbs behind the ball. When I think back now on why I'd develop into a good high fielder, I put a lot of it down to James. Whenever I'm coaching young kids now to catch the ball overhead, I find myself echoing James. "That's it, thumbs behind the ball. Out of the clouds, boy! Out of the clouds!"

Sadly, James would die prematurely, suffering a massive heart attack on the sideline. Not long afterwards, I was lying on a field myself with my life in possible danger. I got knocked out playing an Under-14 match with the Stacks and my tongue got lodged in my throat. My body went into a half-fit and all, but then Frank Courtney came dashing onto the field and had the presence to turn me on my side, stick his finger in my mouth and free up the airway.

That would be typical Frank: he'd never quit on me, though he'd no hesitation being on my case if he felt I needed it.

That same year we went down to Cork to play a tournament in Na Piarsaigh. We'd reach the final but while we were waiting around before the game, I came up with the bright idea of running up the massive hill that was beside the pitch and then rolling down it, just for the craic, like. Soon I'd the whole team at it, under the blazing sun.

By half-time in the final, we were shattered with Setanta Ó hAilpín and John Gardiner leaving me for dead in midfield. Frank was livid. "You were full of running and laughing before the game, Donaghy! I don't see you running or laughing now!"

Poor Frank, I'd constantly give him reason to be on my case, even when he wasn't coaching me.

A few years later I'd be playing soccer for St Brendan's Park along with his son, Martin. We were playing Ferrybank from Waterford in a big cup game and in the eighty-eighth minute I scored with a bullet of a header in off the crossbar. A few of us at training had been messing around about what goal celebrations we might do. The film Any Given Sunday was out that year and we loved the bit where the guy who scored the touchdown pretended to use the ball as a gun and shoot his teammates. So after I scored, I ran to the corner flag, picked it up, pointed it at the lads running towards me, and one by one I'd shoot and reload and they'd collapse on the ground. Everyone else was falling around the place laughing at it as well, except the Ferrybank lads, and one familiar, screaming voice.

"Donaghy, put down that flag, you fuckin' eejit! It's not over!"

And, of course, Frank Courtney was bang on. If we'd conceded an equaliser, I'd have looked an awful eejit is right.

Frank would always be looking out for me. If I missed a training session with the Stacks, he'd phone the house and Mom would tell me Frank Courtney had been on; there'd be training again on Thursday at five o'clock. When I wouldn't be getting a game in my bad year, say when I was fifteen playing Under-16, he'd still have Martin on to me, telling me to stick at it. And then when I was in my good year, he put me in at full forward where I played in the county final against Beaufort.

Only I made a balls of it, like I had a habit of when it came to football. *Fuck that for a game of soldiers*, I remember thinking that summer. *I'm an international at the basketball and I'm shit at the football so I'll leave it.*

I'd better things to be doing and other things I was better at.

AROUND the time I was retiring from Gaelic football at the age of sixteen, I started my first job. My mom's cousin Aidan O'Connor owned a bar in town called The Greyhound, and with the Rose of Tralee festival in full swing, he said to her for me to come down one night and make a bit of money of my own, glass picking.

So I saunter in through the door a little after nine o'clock to find the place is chockablock, clouded with cigarette smoke. I'm getting bounced around by drunks dancing to the live band but make a drive to the counter and eventually get there.

A member of the bar staff glowers at me. "Are you a glass picker?"

"Yeah."

"You're five minutes late!"

"Oh, yeah, sorry. Is Aidan here?"

"No! You're working for me tonight! I need you to fill a bin of Budweiser out the back."

"Right, yeah. Where's the bin?"

"Bin's outside! Budweiser's in the storeroom!"

"Sorry, I haven't been here before. I don't know where the storeroom is."

So he starts cursing under his breath, takes me out the back, heads off, then returns with this big green wheelie bin. "Fill this! Then bring it up to me in the bar."

And before I can nod okay, he's gone back in to the madness.

So, I'm there opening up these crates of Budweiser and trying to reach down to the bottom of the bin, gently placing each bottle in so none of them break. Next thing, I hear your man's footsteps. "What the fuck's going on?! Jesus Christ!" And he starts just turning the crates of Bud upside down and into the bin. All I can hear is the sound of breaking glass but he doesn't give a shit. They need Budweiser back inside right away and he doesn't care if he loses ten bottles; he just fires them in before chucking some ice in on top.

That was my introduction to The Greyhound and the real world, but like everything else that would happen there, that baptism of fire would serve me well. The Greyhound is where I grew up, in so many ways.

That first night manager might have been a sergeant major but for the most part I was dealing with Aidan. From him I'd learn how to work with and treat people.

He'd a great way of making someone feel welcome. It didn't matter if you were a big brass around town or if you hadn't washed in four days; Aidan would have a big handshake and hug for you. He'd kiss old women on the cheek. A fella who might be getting too rowdy, he'd just place his hand on his shoulder and softly usher him out. He'd drive home a loyal customer who might have had one too many.

One of our regulars was a fella called John The Mop. John supposedly had curly hair until he stopped washing it and it turned into a ball of hair just matted together, like a mop, hence John The Mop. He was a droll, witty kind of character. He'd blame Aidan for cutting short his football career. He'd tell us about when he was man of the match in a minor game out in Dingle, then came in afterwards to The Greyhound to meet his uncle Charlie. Aidan gave him a pint bottle to salute his performance and sure that was that then, according to John.

At weekends The Greyhound would be jammers but during the week on dark winter nights you might only have two or three people in the bar and John would be one of them. Sometimes it would be just the two of us, him up on his stool and me behind the counter, serving. I might join him then on the other side to throw darts and we'd play away for two euro, which John would almost always win.

Often on those cold nights when he would be getting ready to leave, I'd want him to stay. I might have given him back £2.10 change from his fiver and I could tell from how slow he was drinking that his budget for the night wouldn't allow for another.

So I'd say, "Is there a bit left in that, John?"

Then I'd wink. "How about an old Castleisland Medium?"

That was our term for a glass of Guinness but for John I'd make it a pint. Of course, he'd have his pint glass over as quick as a flash.

"Yeah, Star, I'll have a Castleisland Medium."

"There you go, John. I'm always looking after you!"

Now you could say I lost money, charging John only a half-pint when I basically served him a full one. But I had John in there every night. It went back to what I learned from Aidan: treat them well and they'll keep coming back.

I'd learn all kinds of tricks of the trade from the staff. We'd a great barman called Donie Houlihan, the Silver Fox. He was as cute as one too.

Donie caddied out on the Barrow golf course and one day he rang the landline, telling me he'd caddied for six well-off Yanks and they were on their way into us.

"Go out the back," he says, "and cut up some blocks of cheese, slices of tomato and red onion. Then pour loads of salt on the lot of it so they're gasping. You'll get two or three rounds out of them that way."

True to his word, they land in about half an hour later.

"Hey, eh, are you Star?"

"Yeah, how's it going, lads? Come in!"

"Donie sent us down from the golf club?"

"Oh, no problem, sit down! What do ye want?"

So I usher them to their seats, go fill the pints of porter, then bring them out with these two massive plates I'd all ready inside.

"What's that, Star?"

"Oh, that's an Irish speciality, boys. You'll love it. I'll show you now. Grab a bit of red onion like this here, look, a bit of tomato, a bit of this cheese here…"

The cheese is fuckin' raked with salt now.

So the boys try it anyway. Five minutes later they're looking back up at me behind the bar. "Hey, this is lovely, man! Can we get some more?"

Donie came in three hours later. "They're still here?!"

They must have stayed for eight rounds before leaving, absolutely pissed, raving about the great Irish hospitality they'd been treated to. And they'd leave a £50 tip, which the bould Donie insisted I split with him.

The Greyhound used to do a roaring trade in those days. It was the time of the Celtic Tiger so you'd have people in construction clocking off at Friday lunchtime to come into our place; they'd more than enough money made for the week.

We'd have to be in at 9.30 on a Sunday morning to get ready for them again and prepare the sandwiches, chips and drisheen they'd hoover up. By lunchtime the place would be packed. You'd have old men waltzing with each other around the floor to Neil Diamond.

Hands, touchin' hands
Reachin' out, touchin' me, touchin' you…

They were the old stock of the town. Labourers and builders, and if they had money in their pocket, they were spending it and enjoying it, and no better place than The Greyhound.

It was in the bar where I'd get notions for girls for the first time. Before that I'd no time for them or the drink; I was just too busy and interested in sport, especially the basketball. Then I started that job picking glasses. You'd see what the fuss was about then: the makeup, the hair all done up, the short skirts. I'd be walking around with maybe ten glasses in my raised hands trying to limbo weave through the gaps in the crowd, but if I just happened to rub against some young wan in the process, well, Way-hay!

Some nights then I might get my bum pinched and the guilty party and the sixteen-year-old glassboy would laugh at the frivolity of it all.

It was just pure craic, harmless fun, great times.

THOUGH he's technically a second cousin, I always call Aidan my uncle, and during those Greyhound years he was more like a father. He was always looking out for me as if I was his own, and it's him that I have to credit for roping me back into the football.

Aidan had long been a passionate Stacks man. He would have been a fringe player on the powerful team of the late 1970s and early 1980s when the likes of Mikey Sheehy, Ger Power, John O'Keeffe and Ger O'Keeffe were playing. He was that fella who'd be there for every league game and then when all the county lads came back he'd be dropped every time.

There was this big championship game though that Ger O'Keeffe did his hamstring in the warm-up and Aidan was told he was in at corner back. So John O'Keeffe is the team captain and he's striding around the dressing room with his magnificent chest out, telling his teammates in his cool, commanding way how exactly they're going to play and win. He starts then talking about the referee, how they'll have to keep their composure, that he's a terrible whistler, that they'll have to watch out for him.

All the while Aidan's completely wired, his knees shaking, his steel studs clanking against the concrete, his head racing. He catches Johnno mentioning something about some fella being a terrible so and so that they'll need to watch out for. So Aidan jumps up off the bench. "I'll fuckin' mark him, Johnno! What number is he?!"

That was pure Aidan, hugely excitable when it came to his football and the Stacks, whether it meant being ready to mark a whistle-happy ref or years later taking the C team in the club.

I suppose the C team was something of a pub team. It was for lads who just wanted to play a bit of football for the craic. The older lads with their potbellies didn't want to put in the commitment the senior and intermediate team were, and the younger fellas weren't quite ready for the physical demands of senior football either. So they'd train on the Monday and Wednesday and then on the Friday they'd have their game before heading to the 'Hound where Aidan would tell me to bring a round or two down to their table.

One night Aidan sort of twisted my arm that I should play for them. I hadn't kicked an O'Neill's in about nine months, ever since that night I made a fool of myself in the Under-16 final, but after seeing the craic the Cs were having and figuring I'd at least make that team, I went along one night to training and found that I enjoyed it.

My first game was down in Lispole. Aidan wasn't there and five minutes before it was even half-time the other selectors took me off. I was shocking. They had me in at corner forward and I got cleaned out by some fella twice my age. Walking past the

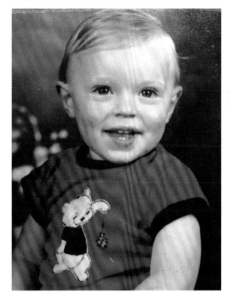

House angel, street devil: I had no problem with photos as a baby but when I was three I was having none of it

In the midst of greatness: There's three All Ireland winners inside the wire at this 1987 Cork-Kerry game: a grimacing Pat Spillane, a concerned Jack O'Shea and a four-year-old Kieran Donaghy at his first Munster final

The rock: My mother Deirdre was always there for me (right), Conor (second right) and Sarah

Oliver: My father (middle) looked a lot like me when he was a young man. He is here with my uncle Anthony and my granddad John

Home and away: Wearing the Kerry jersey on Tyrone soil for the first time, aged five

Time with Dad: With Dad, Sarah and Conor on a holiday in Omagh

Pet loves: Teaching Conor to ride our horse Palo, with Sarah following behind, while I've always been a dog lover; this was my first dog, Bran

The shadow don't lie!: Countless hours were spent shooting out the backyard; neighbours complained I was keeping them awake at 1am

International captain: I was the smallest player on the Irish Under-16 team – and I would have been the smallest player for Spain as well!

Busting moves and breaking ankles: Driving past Killarney's top American Kenny Gamble in a local derby

Number one: The first of the four major trophies we'd win with the Tigers. In 2003-4 we went from last to first place under our coach Rus Bradburd (bottom right)

Tiger teeth: Mom always gave me grief about giving out to refs; here I take her advice while still showing them I'm not happy

Better times: Slapping five with Chris Craig after winning the 2005 Cup. We had no idea of the troubles poor Chris would have later on

The three amigos: Myself, Micheál Quirke and John Teahan enjoying a few gats after that 2005 Cup win

BOOMSHAKALAKA!: White men *can* jump – or at least some can

On the up: Getting down and dirty as a 17-year-old playing for the Stacks; then as a Kerry minor in Croke Park; then making my league debut for the seniors in 2005, also against Dublin

Out of the clouds, boy!: Following my late great mentor James Hobbart's advice in my first start in a Munster final, the drawn 2006 game against Cork

Destiny is calling me: The day I knew I could make it at full forward, when I rounded Armagh legend Francie Bellew and blasted it past Paul Hearty

Goal for Nan: When I scored a goal in the 2006 All Ireland final, I ran straight over and pointed to a special, wheelchair-bound woman above in the upper Hogan Stand: my grandmother, Mary Fitzgerald nee Moriarty (pictured above left with me after the 2007 Munster final)

sideline I threw my gloves on the ground and headed to the back of the dugout, trying to hold off the tears.

Never fuckin' again. What did I come back to this poxy game for?

Then one of our subs, a DJ around town called Francie Breen, got up from the front row of the dugout, picked up my gloves, and came over to me.

"Head up, Kieran, we're on again next week."

No way, I said to him. This was like the Under-16 final all over again. I wasn't cut out for the football. I was sticking to just the basketball.

But Francie kept at me. You have talent. Stick with it. Aidan will be disgusted if you don't. "I better see you at training on Monday," he said in the dressing room afterwards. But he didn't; I was a no-show. Himself and Aidan had to call up to the house to persuade me to go back down on the Wednesday. Thank God they did.

It was real 1975-style training; kick around at the posts for ten minutes, a warmup, a few hard runs and then a game of backs and forwards, but Aidan's enthusiasm was infectious. Any time I did anything right, I could hear his voice. "Brilliant!"

After that I wouldn't miss a night of training and Aidan wouldn't miss a game. And sure the craic after matches in The Greyhound would be mighty.

A constant source of the craic would have been Aidan's right-hand man, Charlie Healy, or Chazzy Boy as we called him. He'd start out the game as cool as a breeze on the line, looking out for the more animated Aidan, pulling back his jumper, making sure he wasn't giving out to the refs. Then at half-time Charlie would produce some poitín and rub it into the legs of the older fellas to get them going, or if you were a young fella that wasn't motoring so well, you'd be summoned for some special treatment as well while Aidan stomped around, barking instructions. If the game was tight, Charlie could be prone to taking a few sips of the poitín himself. In the second half so you'd have a role reversal: Charlie himself would be flying onto the field, roaring at the ref, with Aidan the one trying to hold him back.

They were some double act, not just for the comedy but for the football. Over seven years they would help the club to four county junior championships on the trot and a couple of leagues and bring through many players who would play senior for the club and beyond.

There were a lot of lads my own age on that C team. Charlie's Angels, we were known as. There was Martin Courtney; Billy Sheehan, who would later play for Laois; Daniel Bohane, who would play with Kerry. We'd some other great players to go along with them then. Anthony Moriarty who'd won an All Ireland vocational medal. Gareth Clifford, a star Kerry minor. And Aidan's own son, Tommy 'Stones'.

Tommy was our leader. He once broke his collarbone with five minutes to go in a big championship match against Lispole. He was on his knees, wincing on the ground, unable to move his hand, yet he insisted on staying on. Sure enough, with just the one arm, he'd manage to win a ball and a free which Courtney would stick over to force a replay which we'd win.

Tommy went straight from the game to the hospital and then from there straight to – where else? – The Greyhound where he'd be charioted into the bar to a rousing cheer from all of Charlie's Angels.

There were at least five forwards better than me, possibly six, on that C team, but Aidan gave me every benefit of the doubt to squeeze me in at corner forward.

He'd also give me my nickname around that time. Well, him and a certain Monday night regular. I'd just got back from captaining the Irish Under-17 basketball team to that Four Nations tournament win. The C team had a junior league final replay on the bank holiday Monday and we'd won, so afterwards when I was working in The Greyhound, Aidan saluted me before a few punters. "Beat England on the Sunday! Then Annascaul the Monday! What a star!"

John The Mop was perched by the counter. "I'll have a pint of porter there so, *STARRRRRRR!*"

Soon it had caught on with everyone in there. Donie would spot me daydreaming or yapping with someone. "Come on to fuck out of your spaceship, Star!"

To this day when I pop the head in to see Aidan and the gang down there, they'll all greet me the same: "Hey, Star!"

So that's how it started, before I ever slipped on a Kerry jersey, or even an Orlando Magic jacket with its signature blue star. With a typically affectionate line from Aidan and a typically droll quip from John The Mop.

BECAUSE I was enjoying my football with the Cs, I was all on for playing with the club minors that summer of 2000. I was in the middle of my growth spurt and my confidence was rising from being able to take and ride tackles from men.

We'd reach the county minor semi-final where we ended up facing South Kerry. It was my first time playing in Fitzgerald

Stadium and I lined out at left wing back, marking Declan O'Sullivan. Even then he had a reputation for being an exceptional talent, but although we lost, I did well on him. After that I started to see myself as one of the main men on the team rather than just someone there to make up the numbers like I would have before.

I was even practising, out kicking points and frees with Brian Dennehy. Coming up through the ranks, practice was something I only did with the basketball. In football because I'd often be on the sideline when I was a year underage, I'd lose interest, which meant I wouldn't practise, which, looking back, only increased my chances of remaining on the sideline. Now that vicious circle had been broken.

I still wasn't thinking in terms of Kerry heading into 2001. Myself and Daniel Bohane were called in for a couple of trial games during the spring and early summer but nothing came of them. Then that July I went down to Cork for the Munster final and saw Donncha Walsh and Paddy Kelly play midfield in the minor game. By then I was 6'3" and playing midfield myself for the Stacks minors and cleaning up around there. Standing in the City End terrace in Pairc Uí Chaoimh, I was thinking: *I could do a job for them, easily. Donncha has a bit more football than me alright but in the air I'm better than him and Paddy. Yeah, they're able to go box to box, but so am I. Fuckit, I should be on the panel anyway.*

Years later over a few pints, Mikey Sheehy, who was a county minor selector to Charlie Nelligan at the time, would tell me that they didn't think I was serious enough about football. And I can just imagine them alright, looking at the townie strolling into Austin Stack Park with his baggy basketball tracksuit on and lounging around the dressing room, laughing and joking with all the boys he knew.

But what they failed to see was that on the pitch I was serious; there was no laughing or joking out there. So the week after watching that Munster final from the terraces, I went out with a bit of a temper for the Stacks in a minor county quarter-final in Connolly Park against East Kerry and dominated the game.

I got called in for a few more trial games after that but even though I did well in them, I still didn't gain full panel status. So when they asked me to come in again the Tuesday before their All Ireland semi-final along with Bohane, it wasn't like I thought, *This is my big chance to impress.* I went in, played well again, and thought little more about it. The Rose of Tralee was on with a big disco in The Dome so all I wanted to do was get home, showered and go on the piss. I was sick of doing well in trial games and hearing no more.

It must have been about five in the morning by the time I fell into bed. It seemed like I had just fallen asleep when my mom was rapping the door; Mikey Sheehy was on the phone downstairs. So there I was with my hangover, listening to this Kerry legend telling me I was on the panel for the game in Croke Park on Sunday and I'd probably be getting a game at some stage.

It turned out Bohane got a similar call, and the following Sunday against Dublin we were both on before half-time. I was more than holding my own around the middle of the field, only my feet were killing me. To mark the occasion, Mom had gone and bought me these classy new boots, Predator Precisions. Of course, greenhorn here never broke them in, so by half-time my feet were raw and I'd to change back into my old moldies.

Dublin would go on to beat us, reeling off the last four points of the game, but by the time we'd arrived back to Killarney you'd never have known. I was in my element. On the train down I had got talking to Séamus Moynihan. The man must have been low in the cage, only hours after one of the most humiliating defeats of his career, a fifteen-point hammering to Meath. The last thing he must have wanted was to have this minor, half-pissed already, blabbering away to him. And yet he couldn't have been nicer or more tolerant. He never looked away from me, he retained eye contact all through. I'd always admired him but from that day on I loved Séamus Moynihan, for how he handled himself and that situation.

That night then out with the minors, it was like I had been on the team all year. Colm Cooper, Declan O'Sullivan, Donncha Walsh, Bryan Sheehan in goal: I was best friends with them all, the life of the party. To make a great night even better, I kissed a girl from Tralee I had been mad about for ages, Hilary Stephenson. A huge gang of us ended up crashing back in Gooch's house, which Ronán Ó Flaitheartaigh nearly burned down trying to fry sausages at about 4am.

The following morning Gooch's mother got up and showed Ronán how it should be done, cooking a massive breakfast for all of us. Then Daniel and myself said our goodbyes and thanks. We stepped out into the light, walked into town and waited for my mom to collect us. Not having a clue what else lay ahead for us, only knowing we loved where we'd just been.

CHAPTER 5

THE AGGRESSORS

'What we had to endure in the first half was nothing less than disgraceful. Hard to know why there was such naked venom from the moment the game started but it seems each team wanted to set a marker that they would not be surrendering by hook or by crook'

Eugene McGee, Irish Independent, March 7, 2016

THURSDAY, MARCH 3, 2016

I'M BACK WITH KERRY A MONTH NOW BUT IT'S hard to know where either of us is at. Last Sunday up in Newry we beat Down easily to give us our first win of the season at the third attempt. They were as poor as I've come across in eleven years playing Division One football. Any other northern team I've met, even if they were average enough, they still brought it to you physically. These boys just rolled over.

It'll be a different story next Sunday. Donegal are coming down here to Tralee and along with Dublin are the in-form team in the country having won their first three games. You can be sure they won't keel over, that they'll bring that physicality. We'll know a lot more about ourselves after that.

I'm feeling more confident after tonight though with some of the stats Éamonn had back from last Sunday's game. It was my first match of the year and I've played very little football at midfield for Kerry the last ten years, yet the GPS readings showed that only Donncha Walsh covered more ground.

I'd felt alright that I was moving well in training. A fortnight ago we trained on the beach and I finished in the top eight in the four-mile run. For a tall old slow fella, I took encouragement from that, and I'll take more now from last Sunday.

It was a bit by chance that I played midfield in Newry – or that I even played at all.

My first few weeks back, I was in at full forward any time we'd a game in training, but sure we'd hardly any ballwork done and the conditions didn't help at all. We'd a game among ourselves in Ballybunion, the worst afternoon I can ever remember training with Kerry. The pitch was basically quicksand; during the week they literally dumped a lorry load of sand in the field. I've always played better in the summer when the ground is hard and I can get my feet under me to jump. Then the lashing rain and hurricane howling in from the sea made whatever ball coming in my way a complete lottery. I actually thought I did quite well in the circumstances. I worked hard, forced a couple of turnovers, set up a few scores, and my team won. In my head I was going: *I did okay, Éamonn will be happy enough.*

The next day though, he told me he thought I looked a bit rusty. We even talked about whether I should play with the club against Nemo Rangers instead of heading up to Newry, that the guaranteed sixty minutes might bring me on more. But I told him I didn't want to be playing some challenge game with the club and finding out on Twitter that Kerry had lost. I'd prefer to be a sub and be able to come on and help some way, even at midfield if the team needed, with David Moran an injury doubt.

As it worked out, I was given the nod to partner Bryan Sheehan in midfield. And this time I couldn't complain about the conditions; they were lovely and dry. I said it to Liam Hassett, who is a selector with us this year. "If I can't play well in this, I'll pack it up now."

I played well enough there. I enjoyed it. I'm not the fastest but I can read a game, I can take up the right positions. I'm good at distributing the ball. I can link up well with someone like Bryan playing alongside me. And I'm feeling really sharp and agile from the winter playing basketball.

But again, I can't take last Sunday on its own merits because Down were so bad. I'm a bit worried whether I can stay with Donegal's high-powered running game. Can I track all the runners, tackle hard and still boss the midfield area? A part of me is afraid of falling between two stools and that come the summer I won't be playing either midfield or full forward when we have all our big guns back: the likes of David, Anthony Maher, James O'Donoghue, Paul Geaney.

But that's out of my hands for now. All I can do is put the head down and make it as hard as possible for Éamonn to leave me off.

THE weekend after the lads lost at home to Roscommon in the second round of the league, Éamonn took us all down to the beach: first to Banna on the Saturday, then Ballyheigue on the Sunday.

Both days it was wild out. The wind was blowing strong while what Eamonn put us through was raw enough as well. He split us into teams named after leaders of the 1916 Rising – Éamonn is passionate about history and the Irish language – and had us run up the sand dunes twenty-five times and then do a set of jumping-jacks and sit-ups at the bottom every time. He had us wrestling in a circle; I won my first one fairly handy but then got drawn against Tommy Walsh and sure with his superior strength he pinned me down – fight over. On the Sunday we'd tug o' war. Luckily enough, our Thomas Ashe team had Shane Enright in our ranks. Shane is from Tarbert where it's a Christmas Day tradition to pull rope, so he'd the technique and strategy to a tee. I was our anchor at the back, and following his every call as to when to hold and conserve our energy and when to really heave, we'd win it out.

Sometimes when a team is after a loss, an exercise like that can almost be a form of punishment. That wasn't how we looked at it. Win or lose Éamonn always planned to bring us to the beach, especially with the pitches around the county being in the state they are. On top of that, a lot of the weekend was fun. More than anything I wanted to strip everything back to basics.

Maybe he felt we'd be getting a bit soft, that we'd be getting things a little too handy. Yeah, you can train hard in Killarney, but then you go down to the hotel and have some chicken handed to you on a plate and fellas are giving out that there's not enough salad or sauce to go with it.

Out on the beach, he was taking us away from all the frills and fancy stuff. No GPS. No pasta and chicken. No showers. Instead we could wash ourselves in the sea and drink our milk and have our sandwiches there on the beach, out in the nipping cold.

BACK when I was playing Under-16 for the Stacks, we had this game against Tarbert. Even at that age they're hardy bucks out there; it's pure North Kerry, Shane Enright country where they have their young out doing tug o'war on Christmas mornings. I was fifteen, at full forward, and I'd this big fucker marking me.

He started digging me in the back. I was nearly afraid of him, he was so big, so I didn't do anything at first; I just took it.

Then he began kicking my ankles. This time I turned around to him. "Hey, knock it off, man, will ya?" But he just clipped me with his forearm into the back of my head.

I turned around to the umpires and could see one of them

was our club sponsor, Denis O'Regan, a butcher in town known to everyone as Dee Butcher. I'd learn soon enough the other umpire was from Tarbert. When I brought it to their attention that my marker was digging me, Butcher shouted in, "Stop that, Number Three!" The other fella just grumbled, "Play away!"

So Number Three keeps thumping me, catching me in the ribs. The ball is down at the other side of the field when I go into Butcher. "Will you call the referee over and tell him about this fella?"

Butcher tells me he has an even better idea: Stand up for myself. Then he looks around and nods discreetly over at his colleague by the opposite post. "I'm going over to distract this fella," he whispers. "You know what to do."

So I go back out to the edge of the square. Your man rattles into me again. I look around and see Butcher has his arm around the other umpire's shoulder, pointing his finger at something over by the sideline. I'm gazing at my man, like Michael Corleone in The Godfather looking at Sollozzo and the crooked cop after coming back from the jacks with the gun in his hand. This is it! It's now or never!

Next thing – BANG! I swing back the elbow and suddenly your man's laid out on the ground, his nose pumping blood! There's absolute uproar! But since the umpires saw nothing, no-one is put off and we go on to win the game.

I'm walking off the field afterwards when Butcher comes up behind me and grabs the back of my head.

"Hey, next time, don't wait for me to tell you to sort it out! Sort it out yourself!"

That was the day I suppose I lost my football innocence but learned a valuable lesson: don't let it get to that point. Don't be a reactor. Be the aggressor. If you think your man is the type who'll start something off, start it before he starts it.

It's a line I've been using the last three or four years with the Stacks and with Kerry – are we going to be the reactors or are we going to be the aggressors?

The thing about when you're aggressive, you're actually the one more in control: of yourself, of the situation. Sometimes fellas in the Stacks will be looking at me and shout, "Calm down, Star!" They think I'm after going haywire. But I'm in complete control. I'm on the verge of going out of control but I'm not going to do anything stupid that's going to jeopardise the team.

This season just past, the club almost lost our senior status even though we won the county championship in 2014. We played a relegation semi-final against Milltown Castlemaine and they beat us. Why? Because they were the aggressors and we were the reactors.

I'd warned our lads at our last team meeting: These lads are coming for us; be ready to fight fire with fire. And I knew there were lads looking at me, thinking, "Ah Star is always on like this. Milltown, who do they have? We'll beat them over the phone."

Milltown have a lad called Marcus Mangan who has been in and out of the Kerry panel the last few years; actually he was there on Banna Beach, helping my Thomas Ashe team plough through those sand dunes. He'd cut you in half for a ball. And sure enough, Milltown were six points up on us with about five minutes to go when Marcus got a big hit in on one of our lads, forcing the ball to spill. Then he pounced on the loose ball and won a free, bounced up and raised his fist to the Milltown supporters, as if to tell everyone: We have them!

One of our lads tried to get in his face and goad him. "Who the fuck are you? You're shit, boy!" I cringed when I saw that. I was thinking: Marcus Mangan is in training with Kerry, man. And he's just after leading his small club to a huge win over us. That's who Marcus Mangan is.

With Kerry it's a bit different. There's no complacency, no undeserved arrogance. But sometimes not enough of us are suitably aggressive.

I've been guilty of it myself. At the start of 2007 I had gone soft mentally. We played Fermanagh in a league game and early on a couple of their backs had a few pops at me. Then their number six shouldered me in the back running out for a kickout. I reacted and tried to trip him. It was straight in front of the referee and sure the man couldn't get the card out quick enough. Most red cards handed out in the GAA are shown to the reactors, not the aggressors. In that dressing room afterwards, I vowed never to let that happen again. I've never been shown a straight red card since.

The Tyrone team of the noughties were full of aggressors. If one of them turned you over, he'd have four other teammates roaring at him, "Well fuckin' done! Drive it into him!" That image of Joe McMahon roaring in Tommy Walsh's face in the 2008 final rankled with Kerry people and it stuck in my craw too. Then during the International Rules series a few months later, I saw him doing the same to some huge Aussie and I got pumped. I realised then that Tyrone were just smart in that 2008 final. Pound for pound we had the better players but they were ready to do anything to win.

In Kerry we don't tend to go to those lengths because we're seen as pure footballers first and foremost and whenever we go over the edge there's outrage – 'Ah, Jesus, if Kerry are at the dark arts, the game's fucked.' Even the time I stuck my head in Paul Hearty's face in the 2006 quarter-final, my Uncle Brian said: "It didn't look good, Kieran. You should probably apologise." The next day out against Cork when I was interviewed after the game, I duly apologised. I should never have apologised. I played with an edge and on the edge that day against Armagh because that's where Kerry needed me to be.

That summer when I went to full forward, Jack O'Connor told me to have Gooch's back. In the 2005 All Ireland final Gooch got a bad slap early on and no-one jumped in to back him up. If someone had flattened Peter Canavan, there would have been murder with the Tyrone boys barging in. Sometimes in Kerry we can be too timid, too quiet, even at training. I remember being up in Limerick and watching the Munster rugby boys training – O'Connell, O'Callaghan, O'Gara, the lot. The level of talk and encouragement was through the roof. We don't have that which is pissing me off so the other week in a huddle I had to address it.

"Boys, we're like a bunch of mice around the place. I can hear myself all the time and that's not good. I'm sick of listening to myself and I'm sure ye are too. Can we all get talking and encouraging each other more?"

You need that: when a fella does something well, especially when it's something he's not known for doing, let him know. Urging fellas on through the hard runs on the winter nights. "Dig in, boys! That's the stuff!"

And having an aggressive mindset isn't all about belting people or roaring at them. I remember Declan O'Sullivan saying to us before the 2006 final against Mayo, "First chance I get, I'm gone. I'm getting the ball and going straight at James Nallen and I'm sticking it over the bar." He ended up sticking it in the net. That's what he was about. Winner. Warrior. Aggressor.

That's what we need more of this year. Starting this Sunday against Donegal.

SUNDAY, MARCH 6, TRALEE

THE calm before the storm.

I get up at about eight, make my porridge and throw a few blueberries into it, then put on the Conor McGregor fight from Vegas I Sky Plussed last night. I'm sitting on the carpet, with little Lola Rose crawling between my outstretched legs, and I'm munching my breakfast, when after a round I say to Hilary on the couch behind me, "God, he looks in a bit of trouble." Turns out he lost! The Notorious is no longer the undefeated. Going up a weight division and carrying the extra couple of stone, he gassed out.

After another quick bite to eat at 11.30, I drive in to town. I've a friend, Padraig Locke, AKA Flourisher, whose family have a shop premises a stone's throw from Austin Stack Park. He has a 'No Parking' sign out which to me basically means 'Reserved'. I leave the car there, lob my gearbag on my shoulder and put my hat and earphones on, only to take them off when at the roundabout I meet a special supporter of ours with a collection bucket.

Mary McCarthy is collecting for the local Down Syndrome support unit as it's a condition she herself has, but even if she wasn't out with the bucket today, she'd be at the game. After almost every match we have in Tralee or Killarney she'll be outside the dressing rooms with her mom, and win or lose, the two of us will always have a big hug for each other. The day of her twenty-first birthday we had an All Ireland quarter-final in Croke Park but David Moran, Anthony Maher and myself made sure we got back down to Killarney with a signed jersey for the real star of that night.

It's heart-lifting to run in to her today, though I'm mortified; I haven't a cent on me.

"Not to worry, Kieran," she laughs giving me another big hug and a kiss on the cheek, "just get us the win today."

For you, Mary, anything.

It's a big day for the town, not just the team, today. It's the opening of the new pitch they've put down in Austin Stack Park. On Friday night we trained here, to get familiar with the changes. Just before the warmdown we formed a players' circle and both Bryan Sheehan as captain and myself made it clear the mentality needed for this one.

There's bound to be needle today. There's a bit of history between the teams. They ended our championship in 2012. We ended their All Ireland dream in 2014. So Éamonn doesn't have to say much to us before we head out; he just repeats some of the bullet points from what we spoke about on Friday. Move the ball fast. If we're playing with the breeze, don't let them slow us down. Northern teams are masters at it, Donegal especially. When they have the wind, they're happy to play full throttle. If they're playing against it, they slow everything down. If we win a free, get it out quickly before they can hold us up taking it.

Sure enough, the game is only a couple of minutes old and

they're already repeatedly at it: standing in front of us after they've fouled us, stopping the quick free, wasting time, allowing them to get men filtering back.

There's a hop ball, it goes up and I win it but Michael Murphy fouls me and the ball spills. I spot Paul Murphy in acres of space and I'm looking to take a quick free but Michael Murphy still has the ball, under his arm, and won't give it back, acting as if he doesn't know what's going on. I know well what's going on though, he's trying to slow it down again, so as much to lay down a marker as anything, I slam wrestle him to the ground.

Everyone piles in after that. I look over at Marc Ó Sé and his nose is all busted. I'm thinking: *Jesus Christ, I'm after starting World War Three here.*

Next thing, there's an even bigger commotion down by their goal. When I arrive down Neil McGee is running off the field with his nose running red, roaring at Alan Fitzgerald, and the ref is flashing red at Alan. *What in God's name is after happening here?* It's not like Alan to bust a fella. It's only afterwards that I'll see the TV pictures like everyone else. McGee had a hold of Alan's hand as if he was trying to break his fingers. Alan had no choice but to lash out. If the umpires aren't going to do their job, you've to do what I learned a long time ago in Tarbert.

So Marc and McGee are replaced by blood subs and Alan has been sent off. Now Eddie Kinsella is calling myself and Michael Murphy over. I can live with a yellow, especially if Murphy's getting one as well; it'd have been worth it just to put down that marker and for this opportunity now to have a word with the ref.

"Eddie, they're trying to slow us down taking the quick free.

There's five minutes gone and all you've been doing is throwing the ball in."

Again, I'm calm when I say it. I've learned from watching the likes of Darragh Ó Sé how to handle refs, though I'm not quite as good at it as him. Darragh was a master at it; he'd fuck them when they needed to be but he'd plamás them too. They're human beings at the end of it all and they're usually not going to react well to being roared at.

It works here. Eddie leaves the two of us off with warnings. He throws the ball in between the two of us again, I win it, and thankfully this time we're able to move it on and play a bit.

Now that we're down to fourteen men, we've to work our arses off, right across the field as they move it over and back. We're still pushing up; there's no point in just getting bodies back against Donegal because they'll simply gather up some steam in their own half and rip right through you with runners coming from all angles. There's lots of communicating and passing men on. "I've got him, Bryan! Track seven!" It's a very tricky period for us but we ride it out and begin to get on top.

There are flashpoints all over the field. Two of our lads, Shane Enright and Denis Daly, are shown black cards. Then Leo McLoone is sent off for them. With both sides down to fourteen men, we push our lead out to 0-7 to 0-2. Donegal are deliberately avoiding kicking the ball out towards me, probably having seen how myself and Bryan did well against Down, but I'm getting on a lot of ball in general play and distributing it well. But three minutes before half-time, I pick up a yellow card for an awkward tackle on Ryan McHugh. Then in our last attack of the half, I'm wide open for a point but try to loop a fist-pass into young Pàdraig O'Connor who is straight through on goal.

I pride myself on my decision-making and my handpassing but I misjudge this pass and it's easily intercepted.

I'm disgusted with that and back in the dressing room at half-time I apologise to a couple of fellas. They tell me not to worry, to keep it going, but while I'm on the treatment table in the side room, getting some ice from Ger Keane for a bang on the leg, I'm still cursing myself.

Éamonn comes in and spots me.

"Kieran! Take your point!"

"I know, man," I nod sheepishly. If I was the manager I'd be telling me the same thing.

When he addresses the group, he just tells us to keep it going and to try to run at them. Move it through the lines. It might be easier to use our half-forward line more now that we're playing against the breeze; when you have the wind, you can tend to kick over your half-forward line.

Bryan speaks. I chip in as well. They'll have a period of dominance at some stage, I say. It's how we react to that which will determine if we win or lose the game. Dig in, work your bollix off and it'll turn again for us.

They have that period of dominance straight away. Neil Gallagher is on at midfield for them now and they kick four points in as many minutes to level it, one of them from Gallagher after I stand off him too much. *I have to win this kickout if it comes near me. This is the adversity I talked about at half-time; time to walk the talk now, Star.*

I go up and grab it one handed and pass it off. I keep running, all the way into their D where Bryan picks me out with a quick free. I spot Peter Crowley storming through the middle and lay it off to him and Peter finishes it to the net.

That settles us. We kick on from that. Donncha Walsh fists over his third point. Bryan lands another couple of monstrous frees. I'm still working like a dog, pushing up close on Gallagher after that point he kicked. Maybe if I was from a weaker county I'd mind myself more, trying to last the seventy minutes, but with the bench we have I use all my energy up.

With twelve minutes to go Johnny Buckley comes in for me. So I go from player to cheerleader and a nervous one at that; just before I came off Michael Murphy banged in a goal to bring them back to within three points. I'm down on my honkers outside the dugout, shouting on the lads, and thankfully they see it out. Gooch lobs over a point to make it 1-13 to 1-8 and then Eddie Kinsella blows it up.

I shake hands with the Donegal lads. A few years back Neil Gallagher rang me when he damaged his shoulder and I talked him through the rehab work I did when I'd a similar injury; he couldn't have been more thankful. I've had horses of fun with Michael Murphy and Neil McGee in Australia with the International Rules team. But that doesn't mean I'm not going to throw them on the ground if I feel it's necessary.

Today it was necessary. The media no doubt are going to go to town on this game and lambast us for going over the top but today that's exactly what we'd to do; we'd to leave the safety of our own trenches and go over the top. We went to war and won it. Last year we took some stick after another battle against Dublin down in Killarney. And maybe we were affected by that talk because we didn't play with that edge again for the rest of the year and it cost us in the All Ireland final.

You don't really celebrate wins in the league, other than maybe winning a final. But without it being said, there's a real sense of satisfaction back in the dressing room. Fellas are clasping hands, looking each other in the eye and nodding, as if to say: That was a good shift we all put in today for the green and gold.

In the first half we were down to fourteen men but we carved out a four-point lead. When Donegal wiped that out and had a gale-force breeze at their backs with half an hour to go, we still found a way to win. We had each other's backs. There was a bit of temper in fellas. They were going to the point of fighting without throwing a punch, with the understandable exception of Alan Fitzgerald. The quiet fellas were talking, communicating. Everyone stepped up. The spirit of Banna Strand was there.

As pleased as I am with my teammates though, I don't wait around for the team meal. Instead I slip away. It's Mother's Day and I want to be with Hilary, Mom and Lola Rose, especially as most evenings last week I was either out training or away up the country with work.

We go back to the house, order some pizza and sit around the TV. Laochra Gael happens to be on and it's the first showing of the one they've done on Declan O'Sullivan.

And at one point watching it, I'm thinking: *Jesus, Declan would have loved that there today*. There was a bit of him in all the boys. They played like winners. Warriors. Aggressors.

CHAPTER 6

ME AND RUS

'Donaghy had the face of an eleven-year-old boy, yet he had huge hands. And he cursed all the time – he said it was "a massive fucking steak"'

Rus Bradburd, Paddy on the Hardwood

I N THE LATE SUMMER OF 2002, I GOT A CALL from a man I had never met before. An American, Rus Bradburd, was the new coach of the Tralee Tigers. "I heard you're the best young basketball player in Kerry," he said, "and I'd like to see if you'd be interested in playing for the Tigers."

As a kid I would have bitten his hand off but now I was nineteen. Because of the constant struggle for sponsorship, the Tigers had dropped out of the Superleague a few times since I was that starry-eyed young fella watching them win the league in '96, so it wasn't like playing at that level had remained a fixed goal of mine. Certainly not with the Tigers anyway. I was playing for the other club in town, St Brendan's, which had the much stronger youth structure and an adult team with which I was getting plenty of court-time and enjoying a great social life, down in The 'Hound after every game, a sort of hoops version of the Stacks C team.

I still went to most Tigers home games but it was nearly all Americans on the court. Ricardo Leonard now qualified as a Bosman because he'd married Teresa. They'd a Canadian point guard who also qualified as a Bosman because he had a British passport. On top of that you'd two professional Americans.

Now I was never good at maths but even I knew that left only one spot in the starting five for an Irish player. And at the time Micheál Quirke was one of the best players in the country while John Teahan, one of the stars of the '96 league-winning team, was tougher than an old boot.

So I was processing all this in my head when this American on the other end of the phone said, "I tell you what, let me take you to dinner. You pick where. As long as it's not McDonald's."

That got my attention. Money was short and I'd yet to meet a

Yank who didn't like McDonald's. I suggested my favourite spot – the Brogue Inn. When I say my 'favourite', I'd only ever had dinner there twice; I couldn't afford more than their big breakfast. My thinking was to put the squeeze on this new coach for a fine meal and end any notion of joining the Tigers.

I met him outside the Brogue. He wasn't anything like what I expected. The guy apparently had been an assistant coach for fourteen years at Division One college level in the States. Eight times his team had made it to the NCAA March Madness tournament. He had successfully recruited Tim Hardaway, a famous five-time NBA All Star. I had this vision of a polished, well-dressed guy, the kind who'd be fitted out in a smart suit with the hair laced with Brylcreem. This guy was small, scrawny and scruffy, wearing a tattered pair of plain black trainers, while his hairline was heavily receded. If he'd been sitting instead of standing outside, I'd nearly have thrown him some change.

We went inside and before he could give me his sales pitch, I made sure to get in my food order. The highest-priced item on the menu was the 25 euro T-bone steak. The great Bill Kirby, the owner of the Brogue and a great Stacks clubman, was on.

"I'll have the T-bone steak, Bill. With extra spuds as well as the chips, that'd be great."

"Eh, just the soup for me, thanks," Bradburd coughed.

That made the new coach even odder in my eyes. Soup?! It would be years later I'd learn he had only €30 on him, that he hadn't counted on me ordering so much.

We made small talk for a while, him explaining that he'd taken a sabbatical from the States to come to Ireland to write a book of short stories and learn to play the fiddle. Once the food came, he got to the point.

"I think you should play for the Tigers. You'll never reach your potential with St Brendan's because they're not in the Superleague."

I nodded casually while chewing my steak. It was delicious.

He continued to do most of the talking. I'd get to play, he said. All the Irish guys would. Only I had to get fit to be able to play as hard as he'd demand. "I've heard you love your nights out," he said. "You'll have to cut down on that."

"No bother, boy," I said, munching on the extra portion of chips. "I've been off the drink for six weeks."

I knew there wasn't a chance he was going to play all his Irish players. His bench would be like any Tigers bench in recent years, a group of male cheerleaders for Ricardo and the other Americans. At tops I might get three or four minutes a game.

This Rus mightn't have looked like an American coach but he could bullshit with the best of them. At least I'd got a massive fuckin' steak in the Brogue out of him.

I DON'T know why it was six weeks I said I had been off the drink. It was just a figure that came into my head. There was no truth to it, anyway. And for the next six weeks I was on the gat almost every day.

That September I'd started a Post Leaving Cert course in town, Health and Leisure Studies, with a possible view to getting into Tralee IT proper the following year. At the start I was well up for it: I'd all my books, my highlighters, the different coloured pens all packed and in their proper place. But after a few weeks I couldn't be bothered getting out of bed to go in and listen to someone drone on about health and leisure. I'd only go in to play basketball with the school team or head straight to Horan's and start drinking cans of cider at two in the day, playing pool, before heading out with the college crowd at night.

At the end of those six weeks I went down to catch the Tigers' first home game of the season. They were playing Killester, one of the top teams in the country with four American-born players over 6'4" as well as some of the best Irish players in the league. Tralee were without Ricardo who had blown out his Achilles tendon and Micheál Quirke because Kerins O'Rahillys had a big match the following day. That left me curious: what Irish players might the new coach stick in?

The answer: all of them.

I'd never seen a coach in the Irish league use his bench so much, certainly no Superleague coach the Tigers ever had anyhow. Aidan O'Shea started. Aidan was an old teammate and could shoot the three, but he was 5'6" on his tiptoes. Then Kevin O'Donoghue, who was barely an inch taller, came in for him. Alan Keane, another player I knew from The Green, swished four three-pointers right in front of my seat. My friend Andrew Dineen was sitting beside me. "Jesus, sit still will you?!"

"I am still! What are you talking about?"

"Sure look at your leg! It's bouncing like mad!"

I looked down and saw he was right. I was wired. I couldn't get this idea out of my head: *I'm better, taller and quicker than all these guys and here they are playing in the Superleague.*

All night I was expecting Killester's superior talent to tell. But in the final minute Kevin O'Donoghue hit a shot from the top of the key to seal the win. As the crowd flooded the floor afterwards, I slipped away quietly, unable to bring myself to

The Greyhound where the team were all bound to be. Instead I headed straight home and went to bed, only I couldn't sleep. I had to call that Yank first thing in the morning.

This time I did most of the talking, telling him I'd get up to speed with the rest of the team quickly enough. "I've been off the drink for six weeks." Christ, I'd said it again.

Bradburd wasn't impressed. He laid into me, without raising his voice. "Oh, so you've missed the first six weeks of practice, then you see the Tigers win, and now you want to jump on board." He'd be running it past the other players if it was okay for me to join. If they objected, I was out. Even if they were fine with me joining the team, Bradburd wasn't going to play me until I'd trained with them for a month.

He also noticed that evening in The Greyhound that everyone greeted me as Star.

He scoffed. "That's another thing. You've never even made a basket in the Superleague. I'm not calling you 'Star'!"

The next day the players voted that it was fine for me to become a Tralee Tiger, and that first week in with them I trained hard. But even though they had a big do-or-die Cup game against Denny Notre Dame the following weekend, Bradburd held true to his promise and didn't play me. The Dublin side would edge it, and watching on from the bench in my street clothes, I was disgusted, knowing I could have made the difference.

A few weeks later we had the same opposition at home in the league. Bradburd threw me in and gave me the job of guarding Lennie McMillian.

I was seriously pumped about that. Lennie had been there back in the '80s for the basketball explosion in Cork. In the '90s I had grown up watching him often put on a show in the

Complex as well as win four Cups on the telly. He was in his forties now, but still a fresh, lean, crafty player that could hugely influence a game at this level.

By the end of the first quarter, one of our Americans was in foul trouble. I'd have to guard one of their even taller and better Americans, the legendary Anthony Jenkins, but again, that was fine with me. I began poking him in the stomach as he'd shoot, pulling his jersey under a rebound. Bradburd would say afterwards that he could see the surprise on the faces of the Notre Dame Americans; who was this kid grabbing rebounds, knocking down shots and stealing the ball off them?

We ended up beating them and once the buzzer sounded, I went mad, as if we'd won a championship. I'd been buzzing all night. The crowd in on top of you, Eye of the Tiger belting over the PA, going up against the likes of Lennie and Jenkins; this was what I had dreamed about as a kid.

What made it all the sweeter was that there was a huge cheering section from St Brendan's, including my old coach, Charles O'Sullivan. I felt as if I had two coaches that night, one on either side: the ever-loyal Charles, urging me on, and this American character Rus, who was strangely growing on me. That night we all headed to The Greyhound where Aidan had a free bar for the team, but eager to impress my new coach, I only drank water until he headed home and I could party properly with my new teammates.

That night I crashed over at the Americans' place, something I would do over the following weeks. The Bosman, Barnaby, was moody, someone who didn't want to be in Ireland any more, but the two Americans were great to hang around with.

Chris Thompson was what Americans would describe as

a real stand-up guy, the kind his college coach would allow babysit his kids. Chris was limited offensively, but he was a brilliant rebounder and worker. The two of us would die laughing at each other, him with his great southern Louisiana drawl and me with my fast Tralee accent which must have sounded like Japanese to him at times.

The other American was another Chris: Chris Davis. In many ways he was the opposite of Chris Thompson. He was a very talented player and scorer but hardly the most dedicated. Fag butts littered his window sill while empty beer cans rested on his bathroom sink. But at 6'7" with his Rasta dreadlocks and a killer smile, the birds were all over him and I was happy to pick up any bits that fell off the tree.

I'd happily contribute to the number of empty cans around their place. During the week we'd knock down cans of cider, watch some TV, then hit whatever nightclub was busy.

On Tuesdays and Thursdays it would be Horan's: college nights. Wednesdays would be Benners nightclub. Fridays we'd usually take it easy with a game the next day but then after a home match it would be Spiral's following a few pints in The Greyhound where during the week Aidan would have some lunch waiting for us, as long as we woke up before 2pm.

Mom wasn't happy about this lifestyle at all. A week or so before Christmas, I called over to the house for the first time in about a week.

"Where have you been?! We never see you! You're not working, not studying, what are you doing?! I heard you're out every night with those black fellas! Then sleeping all day, probably!"

"Mom, they're my friends! Anyway, I'm nineteen! I can do what I want!"

"Well, you know what you can do so? Pack your bag and get out of this house!"

"Oh yeah? You know what? Fuckin' fine! I'm out of here!"

I charged up the stairs, stuffed some gear into my duffel bag, and was gone.

After a couple of days I had cooled down a good bit. I hated being angry with Mom and her being upset over me. I'd say it was our first row since the first few months after Dad had left the house. We'd as good a relationship as a mother and a son could have. I was her little angel and she was my rock.

Of course, that's what it was all about. Here was her little angel, the fella who, when all his friends were drinking in the town park, wouldn't go; now it seemed he was drinking every night. Now those Americans were taking her little baby away from her.

I didn't fully appreciate that at the time, but I did have enough cop on to know I'd acted the bollix and had to patch things up with her. So I called her. "Mom, I'm sorry, look."

She was also sorry for losing her temper. She asked how things were over in the apartment and how the Americans would be spending Christmas. "Look," she said, "instead of them being by themselves, they can come up to our house."

So that December 25, 2002, the Donaghys and the two Chrises had a Christmas like no other they'd had before. Nan was inside in the living room, chatting to the two boys about what Christmas is like in Miami and Louisiana. She even touched Chris Davis's dreadlocks, declaring, "That's a lovely head of hair!" When Mom brought out the dinner, the two boys called for us all to hold hands and close our eyes while they said grace. For a moment I took a peep around the table, and I could see Conor, on the verge of giggling, but Mom and Nan were loving it, at peace with the two Chrises and the world.

After that, I'd call around more to Mom and Nan, but I'd still decided to move in with the Americans. The Canadian Bosman had fecked off to play in Iceland, so that left a spare room in the three-bedroom apartment. I'd squatter's rights while the two Chrises with their grace before meals had made the move easier in the eyes of Mom. Besides, I was the only teenager starting in the Súperleague, and probably the Tigers' best Irish player now. And the best players got free accommodation, right?

The day after the Castleisland Christmas blitz, Chris Thompson was let go. We needed more scoring. A Dublin club were already interested in snapping him up but Chris wanted to go home to his girlfriend and little baby. I think I was more devastated about him leaving than he was. I'd grown very close to him and to this day the two of us are still in touch.

The big upside to Chris's departure was the player who'd be taking his place. Rus called me aside at training one night and whispered, "We're getting Antoine Gillespie!" It was the first time I'd seen the man smile in a month after a few tough, narrow losses.

I gave him a fist bump. "Great stuff, Coach." As if I knew who Antoine Gillespie was.

Rus did though. He'd recruited him from the same Chicago playgrounds that he'd spotted Tim Hardaway and taken him down south to the University of Texas El Paso where he'd smash all Hardaway's scoring records. Gillespie would become a legend there, being spotted dribbling through campus, weaving around the light poles at night. Rus was sure with his amazing shooting touch and work ethic that he'd make the NBA.

Gillespie would just miss out on the NBA but he'd go on to have a very respectable career in Europe. In France he was making six figures annually, until he did his groin and his team signed another American. So when a desperate Rus happened to call him, Gillespie was more than happy to come to Ireland. His groin had healed and Ireland was the perfect opportunity to show he was fine to play with some team in France.

Gillespie's first morning in our bachelor's pad, I found someone pounding my bedroom door. "Get up, man, let's go to work! C'mon! Get dressed!"

I half-opened one eye and popped open my phone. Fuck's sake – it was only 8am! I pulled the covers over my head, wishing your man would just go away.

But Gillespie wasn't having it. He walked straight into the room and kicked the leg of my bed, shook my arm. "Hey, let's go! Get your lazy ass out of bed!"

So I dragged myself out of the *leaba* and then he dragged me to the Complex, even though I was the one who knew where it was. "We can't get in here," I'd protest when we got there. "We have to book the practice time."

But Gillespie didn't care if the hall was booked or locked – he was getting in his workout. And this wasn't just a shootaround – everything he did was with intensity and a purpose. He'd snap the ball out to you. Shoot! He'd rebound, fire it out again: Shoot! After sixty shots my arm was wrecked. A few weeks later we'd a session where he'd put up over five hundred.

Our first Superleague game after Christmas, I got to see just how much hard work pays off. We were at home against league leaders Star of the Sea from Belfast and Gillespie went off for forty-five points.

I'd never before played with someone who seemed so in the zone. With a minute to go he made a shot from five feet outside the three-point line to give us the lead for the first time. With their last possession Star's Bosman, Scott Summersgill, tried to get a shot off, but I kept with him all the way down the floor and then rose up to block him. Once the buzzer sounded, I ran straight to Gillespie and jumped in his arms.

After that I was his shadow. In the morning we'd put up shots or lift some weights. In training I'd insist on guarding him because that would make me better, even if he left me muttering curses as he sank shot after shot. I'd even buy one of those Peruvian wool caps with the earflaps like he had.

It just showed you how impressionable I was back then, which meant I was still open to being influenced by the other American in our apartment.

Whatever about being the opposite of Chris Thompson, Chris Davis was definitely the opposite of Gillespie. Gillespie wasn't a natural; I don't think he ever dunked a basketball in his life. But he'd shot a basketball millions of times. That's what made him so good. He was a workaholic, an early bird, a self-made player. Chris was lazy, a night owl, surviving off sheer natural talent and athleticism.

At weekends Chris and Gillespie would party together with me in the middle. But on Monday it was back to the pro life for Gillespie while Chris would stay in chill mode, beginning every day – when he eventually woke up – with a Marlboro Light.

After Chris missed a training session after sleeping it out, Rus had enough: he wasn't going to play him in our next game, an away match against Denny Notre Dame.

So, you're Chris Davis, in Tralee on a wet winter's Friday

evening, with no game now the next day. What would you do? What else but ask young Donaghy: hey, how about we hit the town? And sure what else am I going to do but head out with him? Chris mightn't have been a great professional but he was a great guy, great fun, and this could be our last night out together.

So Chris and myself are inside Benners, downing brandies, having a great laugh, until I check my watch and see that it's 4.30am. Better go: I've a bus to catch and a game to play later on. So I slip out the side door, knowing Chris in a nightclub is well able to fend for himself, and head back to the apartment. I stagger in to bed and try to set the alarm for eight o'clock…

Sometime later, I stir. *Hey, what time is it? Where's my phone?* I can't see it anywhere; all I can see is some bit of daylight peeping in under the blinds. *Jesus, it's bright already! Where's my fuckin' phone?!* I frantically look for it, finally finding it beside the pile of clothes by my bed.

Forty-eight missed calls. All from one person – Rus Bradburd. He must have been ready to fire a rocket through the wall. I'll later learn he'd been throwing stones at my window after having no joy with the doorbell, all the while with the team bus running outside.

That must have been at just after eight. It's now almost nine. *Right, what am I going to do?* I do what every basketball player has at some point: just throw on a T-shirt, a tracksuit and two boots.

I call our captain, Kevin O'Donoghue. He says they're half-an-hour from Limerick but that they'll be stopping off there for some breakfast. Okay, I'll get a bus. I sprint to the station about a thousand yards from the apartment. Anything leaving for Limerick or Dublin? There's one going in five minutes. Perfect:

how much? Sixteen euro, he says. There you go. Onto it, gone. I get into Limerick and see the team bus and your man Rus is there, fuming. He's got a bottle of water and a banana in his hand and as I walk up the aisle of the bus, he slams them into my chest in disgust, half-bursting the banana.

So we get up to Dublin, join up with Gillespie and our hired American for the night, Mike Trimmer. We actually start well. Alan Keane drains a couple of three-pointers. Then Super Dave Cronin checks into the game.

Now most nicknames in basketball are just as they suggest. Earvin Johnson was known as Magic because he was magic. Michael Jordan was Air Jordan because it was as if he could fly. There's a bit more irony at work when it comes to Super Dave. He isn't super. He's anything but. He's about 5'6", can't jump and wears these huge goggles. But Rus loves him. We all do. He lives for the team, never misses a training session, and because we're so stuck for players, he's called on now.

So he catches the ball just outside the three-point line. Their towering American, Randall Mounts, is running out to block him. But Super Dave manages to get his shot off and it finds nothing but net. A surge of energy shoots right through my chest. *Fuckit, this is on! We can beat these boys! Let's go!* I'm high-fiving Super Dave back down the court, we're digging in, making stops, making plays. Kevin O'Donoghue and Liam Culloty come up with big shots and with a few minutes to go we're only four down.

Rus calls timeout. I flop myself down on the bench like a heavyweight boxer at the end of the eleventh round. My legs are totally gone. Rus is going through such and such defence that we're now supposed to be going into but all I want is water.

I'm slugging down these paper cups of the stuff like I was slugging brandies the previous night when I spot Super Dave with another cup in his hands. Just as he's about to pour it into his mouth, I grab it. *I need more of that.* And I drink about half of it when just as I'm handing back the rest of it to Dave, Rus gets up off his knees and flings the paper cup right into my face, splashing me and the first three rows behind our bench.

"Okay, big boy!" he shouts, getting nose to nose with me. "You want to stay out all night and party?! Well, let's see what you can do with the game on the line!"

And of course, I hadn't the heart to answer him back. Or the legs. We ended up losing by twelve, when if I had anything at all, we'd have pulled off the shock of the season.

That night I'd piss Rus off even more, deciding not to travel back with the team and instead go out again with Chris Davis, who was up to see his girl in Dublin and hang out with some other American ballplayers. But after a while as I was there in the club, seeing all the women flock around Chris and his friends, it occurred to me: *What the fuck am I doing here? Jesus Christ, what am I doing in general?*

I got the train home the following morning and it was one of the loneliest and most sobering few hours of my life. It dawned on me: I couldn't continue like this.

"Fuckin' plumbers are out of work all over Ireland!" Donaghy hollered. He must have done some research. He quoted some unemployment statistics. Soon they began shouting at each other. It was hard to hear a young man

use the f word around his mother. That was something I
didn't miss about college coaching: managing personal
problems, babysitting, calling moms. But for some
reason I didn't mind with Donaghy.

Rus Bradburd, Paddy on the Hardwood

GETTING – or at least holding down – a job was proving
beyond me.

After I stopped going into the health and leisure course, Mom
signed me up for a plumbing apprenticeship. First day out on a
job, the senior plumber traced two lines on a concrete kitchen
floor and told me to drill down that channel so some pipe could
be fitted in underneath the sink. As far as he was concerned, it
was a prick of a job, easy, so he left me to it while he headed
away to do some proper plumbing.

So I stick the Kango drill into the ground. VROOM! Down
she goes, only instead of putting it in at an angle, I plonk it
straight down and the thing gets stuck. I'm there for hours,
trying to get it out, only I can't and there's no-one to help.

Eventually, after kicking the shit out of the thing, I manage to
get it out but by the time your man comes back, I've only about
two foot drilled. He looks at me. "Is this all you've done?!"

I told him about the drill getting jammed. He thought I was
having a laugh. When I told him no, I was serious, he stormed
out, so with that, I basically walked out on the job and the
apprenticeship as well.

Then I got part-time work in Celsius clothes store. John
Murphy, a big Stacks man, gave me the break but starting at
nine in the morning didn't suit my social life. I'd sleep in and be
too embarrassed to go in to work. John was the understanding

type but one day he sat me down and just said, "Look, Kieran, I think we're better off parting ways."

"You know what, John," I said, "I think you might be right." And at that, we shook hands.

To be honest there were a couple of other partings back in those manic, confusing few weeks that I was a lot more cut up about.

A few days after my night out in Dublin, Gillespie headed back to France. Another team over there were offering ten times what the Tigers were paying. "Sorry, kid, I have to go," he'd tell me when he called round just before his cab came.

I was heartbroken; he'd become like a big brother to me. The following night, I couldn't bring myself to go to training.

The next week then Chris Davis was an hour late at practice. That was it for Rus: he fired him on the spot.

You would have thought that was the Tigers pretty much goosed, and in a way, we were: we wouldn't win a game the rest of the season. Then again, we had lost seven of our previous eight games anyway. But what we were learning under Rus was you fought and you fought until the buzzer went. If you ever found yourself thinking, *Fuckit, I quit, I'll wait 'til the next one*, something in you had been broken as far as he was concerned. There was so much more to be said for thinking, *I'm going down fighting, no matter what.*

There was one game we had down in Cork where we were trailing by fourteen points with fifty seconds to go. Rus called a timeout. "Right, let's get it back to ten."

At the time I thought it sounded silly and pointless, but the following day, after we'd get it down to eleven, I thought about it: You know what, our leader didn't quit when things were bad.

And I felt that was the way I was wired too; my impulse was to fight, on my back if it came to it.

In those last few games, our playing rotation was totally different to what I pictured at the start of the year. There was no Ricardo. No Canadian Bosman. No Quirke. No Teahan, who missed most of the year with injury. Two different Americans. But with the likes of Kevin O'Donoghue, Liam Culloty, Super Dave and myself, no-one gave us a hiding. Even when we lost by a point to the Killarney Lakers – the only time I lost a Super-league game to our local rivals – I was proud to be a Tiger.

I'd especially miss Kieran Donaghy. He could be a headache but his struggle to mature – on and off the floor – typified the Tigers' season. Coaches are supposed to energise players but that somehow worked in reverse with Donaghy. His exuberance had the effect of a strong cup of tea... I needed Kieran Donaghy.

Rus Bradburd, Paddy on the Hardwood

AFTER that first meeting in the Brogue and that massive, expensive steak, Rus and myself would often sit down together throughout that 2002-2003 season. I'd pop in at lunch to his place. On his way to training he'd call over to my mother's house where he'd always resist Nan's offer of an Irish coffee but never the scones buried in fresh cream. He was especially glad to call over after I'd followed some advice Gillespie gave me the day he was leaving. "Man, move back into your mom's. You haven't earned a free place of your own."

Rus would return to coach us the following season; once the club had secured a sponsor, Horan's Healthstores replacing Kellogg's Frosties, there was never any doubt.

He got a bit of a land when he arrived back. He called to the house around lunchtime where Nan welcomed him in and the pair of them had their usual chat, pot of tea and scones. After a while he asked if she would mind if he went upstairs and woke me. She proudly informed him that he was five hours too late: I was working, a regular Monday-to-Friday, eight-to-five job, in the new Supermac's in town, owned by Mick O'Dwyer and run by his son, John. Thanks to their generosity I now had shifts that allowed plenty of time for my sport.

I had also been working hard on my game. Gillespie told me before he left: Keep developing your game and you'll be a top player. At first when he had left I felt hurt, even betrayed, but I came to realise that he left me with a great gift: the importance of hard work.

All these years later and I'll still say it: I don't know if I'd have made it with Kerry only for Antoine Gillespie. Yeah, I was always likely to get a spot with the Kerry Under-21s at some stage. But on a team like that, everyone is twenty, twenty-one. There's no senior figure, there's no Gillespie who knows what it takes to carve out a professional career for a decade, work on his game every single day and still be able to look out for and guide others.

That offseason it was like I was thirteen again, out in Mom's backyard practising the shot Seánie Burrows had shown me, only this time I was working on some moves and drills of Gillespie's and developing a jump shot like Rus had recommended. Up to then I was basically just a set shooter from the perimeter;

my feet wouldn't leave the ground which left me open to being blocked by better defenders.

Rus would nail it when it came to recruiting our professionals for that second season. Brandon Mason, someone he'd recruited for New Mexico State, was excellent at creating his own shot off the dribble. And he was fiery, a great man for the chest-bumps; Rus rightly figured that he'd spark well off someone like me.

Damond Williams, another former player from New Mexico State, had the purest shooting touch. In one game against UCC Blue Demons he'd have the perfect shooting night, making every shot and free throw to finish on thirty-four points. Then when Damond didn't want to come back to Ireland after Christmas, Rus just signed Travarus Bennett to replace him. Bennett had been the defensive player of the year in the famous NCAA Big Ten conference two seasons earlier, playing with the University of Minnesota. I've never shared a floor with a better defensive player than Travarus.

Probably the best signing of the lot was Chris Bracey. With his contacts in the NBA's farm league, the CBA, Rus had heard about this 6'5" guard from Chicago that was the owner of an Irish passport because his grandparents were from Roscommon.

As good as any of our professionals then was Micheál Quirke. He was a monster in the middle for us and at the end of the season would be voted best Irish player in the league.

That 2003-2004 campaign, we'd go from having the worst record in the country to having the best, winning sixteen of our twenty regular-season games. But that didn't make us league champions. The title would be decided on a playoff format, similar to the Final Four in American college hoops.

It was down in the Mardyke in Cork, where we'd beat Star of the Sea in our semi-final. Our final opponents were Killester.

Our one concern going into the weekend was the fitness of John Teahan. His back had been at him and he'd to undergo physio twice a day from his wife Marie, a sister of Maurice Fitzgerald. Midway through the second quarter of the final, he went up for a layup only to get bashed by Damien Sealy, one of the smartest and most hard-nosed players in the league. Normally when Teahan would get knocked to the floor, he'd bounce straight back up, a bit like that relentless, metal-liquid fella in Terminator 2. Teahan didn't move. Quirke had to lift him to his feet while Rus called a timeout.

Rus squatted down in front of Teahan like a cutman before his bashed-up fighter.

"John, are you alright?" he asked, waving his hand in front of Teahan's glassy eyes, even slapping his cheek.

No response.

I splashed some water in his face. "Come on to fuck, Teahan, boy! You going to let them do that to you?!"

Teahan swayed from side to side in his seat. Looking back, it was a clear case of concussion. But I didn't know that then, all I knew was we needed him back out on the floor, so I took a whole cup of water and flung it at him.

That jolted him, but again he said nothing. Our stats man, Padraig Locke, the same Flourisher who years later would keep a parking spot for me near Austin Stack Park, was vigorously rubbing his shoulders while Rus started to issue some instructions about what we were to do on defence.

Next thing Teahan raised his arms, pushing Quirke and Bracey aside, rose to his feet and let out an almighty roar.

And after that, I roared, and then all the lads did.

It wasn't any motto or slogan, it was much more primal than that. It was the best timeout I was ever in, and watching Teahan limping and grunting his way to the free-throw line and knocking down his two shots, I knew we couldn't be beat.

At half-time we were fourteen points up but Killester would be a tough nail to hammer. With four minutes to go our lead was down to single figures when I cut out to the wing to take a pass from Teahan. Sealy came running towards me. I threw a head fake and he flew right past me. Then, instead of driving straight to the basket, I took two hard dribbles to the left and pulled up for a jump shot...

If ever there was to be a film made of that season, this would be the part where everything slows down: I'm hanging in the air, my eyes fixed on the basket. An open-mouthed Rus follows the flight of the ball. My mom is in the crowd, slowly, anxiously, rising to her feet... This is the moment, this is the move Gillespie put me through in our morning workouts, and which I'd repeated tirelessly over the summer.

The ball spins and it spins and it spins...

Swish!

And then the film explodes back into full speed. Rus punches the air: The kid, he did it! Mom is smiling, standing and clapping in the stand. Super Dave and Kevin O'Donoghue spin their towels above their heads. I fist-pump my way down the court, and then turn round to pick up Sealy, only to see the other Killester lads giving out to each other. *We have them, boys; We have them.*

A few minutes later, we did: 69-54. The Tralee Tigers in the space of a season had gone from last to first.

At the time it was the most euphoric moment I'd known in sport. Running over to Mom and Nan in the crowd. Chest-bumping Mason, and hugging and slapping all my other team-mates and, of course, Rus. Then our captain John Teahan was called to the podium for the presentation. Only he refused to go up. He insisted Kevin O'Donoghue should accept the trophy.

Kevin had been our captain the previous season, a season that nearly broke us but instead was the making of us; before learning to win, we first had to learn how to lose. Over those two years so many players had walked in and out the door yet Kevin hadn't missed a single night of training. It was a lovely touch from Teahan. Rather than raising the trophy, he grabbed Rus from behind and lifted him instead.

Rus had his own unique idea of celebrating the moment. In America when they win a championship, it's a tradition to cut down the net. He produced a pair of scissors. Ready?

Kevin O'Donoghue had a worried look. The gym's caretaker wouldn't appreciate it.

Quirke agreed. We'd get arrested.

"Fuck the caretaker," I said. If he gave out about it, we'd post him a new net.

Later that evening the bus rocked up to The Greyhound where Aidan was waiting to serve us. The first through the door was me. Hadn't it been six weeks I'd been off the drink?

LATE that night in The Greyhound, Rus cornered me. He was going back to America for good. He'd loved his time in Ireland and how it had helped him fall back in love with basketball, but now was the ideal time to leave here and coaching, and start his new life with his fiancee Connie.

That was the first thing he'd tell me. The other was that I'd be heading to the States as well. He'd often told me I was good enough to get a scholarship to a Division One college. Now a couple of coaches he knew were happy to take a look at me. As a gift, he'd bought me a round-trip ticket to Chicago. I'd be heading out with Chris Bracey and staying with him there for three weeks in preparation for a tryout with Loyola University-Chicago, a school with big Irish connections and which had even won the NCAA championship back in the '60s.

So I go over to Chicago, stay with Chris and his brother. The whole city seems to know Bryan Bracey. A second-round NBA draft pick, he's gone on to make huge money playing in the best leagues in Europe. He has this massive, growling, brilliant white Yukon Denali SUV, with its darkened windows and huge chrome-rimmed wheels. The speakers in the back boom like something hanging off the wall in a nightclub, while at night, neon lights glow under the jeep. He even lets me ride it around the block and I feel like I'm starring in Pimp My Ride. Unreal.

For the most part though it's Bryan behind the wheel with Chris riding shotgun. My second morning there they say they're taking me to Holy City. They share a knowing laugh. If I can handle the streetball there, the tryout at Loyola should be a breeze.

So we're in our ride, going through this part of town, and I realise I'm not in Tralee anymore, Toto. Either side of us are derelict tenements, boarded up, graffiti everywhere. Gangs of men, young and old, litter every corner, drinking out of paper bags. Even the Alsatians are going around in pairs.

Bryan pulls the jeep in at the side of a street. He's going in to a store to buy some energy drinks; you want to come in? Chris jumps out but I take a look at the store with its steel cages, barricaded like a prison, and decline. I slink across the backseat of the jeep, praying the tinted windows are doing their job.

Finally, after what feels like forever, the boys come back out, drinks in hand, and on we go. We park outside what looks like a church. A couple of kids are hanging by the street corner. Bryan throws them fifty bucks and tells them that if anyone messes with his wheels, they'll find him in the gym.

Next thing, I'm bounding up this rickety steel staircase bolted to the side of the church, Bryan and Chris behind me. At the top of the stairs there's a huge steel door. I open it and it makes this creaking sound like at the start of Michael Jackson's Thriller.

In front of me I find thirty black men staring back at me, one of them with the ball under his arm, having stopped dribbling there in the middle of the game.

Then they see the Bracey brothers either side of my shoulders, the game resumes and we take our spot on the stage behind one of the hoops, waiting for our turn to play.

On the floor the centre of attention is this one shooter. He must be pushing forty but he's making everything he throws up. Played D1 in college, the Braceys inform me, an All-Conference player in his day. "That's Mayor," says Bryan. "Hey, you guard him."

So it's our turn to play and I shuffle up to the guy. He starts laughing. "You lost, White Boy?!"

First time he brings the ball down the court, I'm waiting for him at the top of the three-point line, only he pulls up five feet outside it and drains it.

Next time down, he shouts, so everyone can hear. "Come on, White Boy, don't be scared!"

So I push right up on him, sticking my forearm into his back. He bump hops all the way down to the three-point line, then chops down on my arm with his fist. I back off – *Fuckin' foul!* But this is streetball: no refs, so no blood, no foul. He slides back outside the arc and sinks another three.

"Hey, Bracey," he shouts going back up the court, "where'd you find this white bitch?!"

Steam is coming out of Chris's nostrils. He shouts over to me that he wants to defend that guy next time down.

"No way, man," I say, "I got him."

Mayor looks to chop me with his fist again, only this time I'm ready for it and dodge it. He keeps backing me down, slamming his shoulder off my chest, but then just as he goes to bump me again, I move back, dart to the side, and get a touch of the ball. He falls on his arse, the ball breaks loose in the open court and I'm onto it in a flash. I speed dribble to the far basket and with the adrenaline pumping, I ram it through the hoop as hard as I can and swing on the rim. BOOMSHAKALAKA!

On my way back running past Mayor, I put my index finger to my mouth.

All the guys on the stage rock back, raising their arms and knees: Damn! White boy's talking shit to Mayor!

We'd own the floor for the next two hours. As we were leaving, Mayor came over to me. For a moment, I braced myself. *If he swings, I'm in trouble; we're seriously outnumbered here.* Instead, he broke into a smile and with a deep voice, said, "What's up, White Chocolate? Hell of a run, kid." Then he slapped me a five and gave me a hug.

Walking back outside, I felt invincible. We jumped into the jeep, everyone around knowing better than to mess with the Bracey brothers' ride, just like everyone in the church gym now knew better than to mess with their friend, White Chocolate. Riding and bumping with our boom-box blastin', the same guy who had slinked across the backseat a few hours earlier rolled down those black-tinted windows. And then I let out the biggest, most joyous yell any white boy has ever roared passing through the streets of Holy City.

THE following week I'd have that workout at Loyola. The gym was the complete opposite of that old gym in Holy City. Everything was huge and shining bright – the fibre-glassed boards, the locker rooms, the floor of the four courts side by side. Walking in there was a lot like seeing what was on the other side of that creaking door in Holy City: *Christ, am I ready for this?*

With Loyola's season just over, it was basically just a scrimmage. I played really well and afterwards the coaches shook my hand. "Good run, Kieran, we'll be talking to you." The impression I got was that there'd be a scholarship there for me.

We all know the end of this story: I'd never see the Loyola campus again. The following semester they wanted another look at me but things by then had changed.

Being realistic about it, my grades would never have been good enough to go straight to Loyola. I'd have had to go to a junior college first and although Rus had a few good ones lined up for me, I declined.

Rus and myself remain great friends. There's not a week we're not in touch and I don't get to enjoy some more of his wit. Every few years his job as a college lecturer in English writing allows him to come over to Ireland for a semester or two, and every Halloween he'll stay in my place and be part of the coaching staff at my Be A Star basketball camp I run for kids.

Sometimes, over a glass of wine on the kitchen table, he'll say he still can't believe I turned down a chance to play in the States, that if I'd four years of practising twice a day to go with my athleticism, competitiveness and basketball smarts, I'd have made it to the NBA, or at least made very good money playing in Europe.

I don't agree with the NBA part, and personally think Micheál Quirke would have had the better college career. But sometimes I do think and even regret how more financially secure my family could be if I'd played in Europe. With my Irish passport and Bosman status, I could have played in one of the better leagues.

But back in the summer of 2004, I didn't chase Loyola, enquiring about that scholarship.

I'd started going steady with Hilary, the same girl I'd met back in 2001 out with Gooch and the rest of the minors but had let fall between my fingers; I wasn't going to let her go again.

I was making money working, something a college player couldn't do for at least a few years.

And things were beginning to happen with Kerry.

UNDERDOG

Austin Stacks Park, Tralee, 11/12/2004

"Kieran Donaghy is going to be a very serious footballer. Kerry can't afford to lose him as he will be the finest fielder in the game if he sticks to football"

Mickey Ned O'Sullivan, Underdogs manager, December 2004

AUGUST, 2003, AND WHILE THE STANDS AND terraces of Fitzgerald Stadium are empty, down on the field I'm full – of fire, energy, confidence. I've just kicked three points off Darragh Ó Sé in the first half of a game between the Kerry seniors and the Kerry Under-21s that I'm playing with. Two of the points were bombs from outside the 45; with the other, I tore past him and fisted it over the bar. I'm competing well in the air, getting the better of him in general. The way I'm feeling, I couldn't give a shit that he's the best mid-fielder in the country. At half-time just there, our manager, Jack O'Connor, was delighted with me. "Keep it going, Donaghy." And that's exactly what I plan to do here.

So we're back out on the pitch. Jack takes up his position in front of one dugout while Páidí Ó Sé strides further up the line and assumes that familiar pose: collar up, chest out, feet spread, hands on the hips. In the middle of the field his nephew lines up for the throw-in while across from him, I'm all set for the re-start as well.

Next thing just after the ball is thrown in the air, I'm on the fuckin' ground, holding my jaw, and Darragh's tearing up the field, nowhere to be found near the scene of his crime.

Looking back, I should have expected it. While Jack was com-plimenting me in our dressing room, down the corridor Páidí was probably tearing strips off the wall and out of Darragh. There was always going to be a reaction from such a proud player and clipping me in the jaw with his elbow was his way of clipping my wings.

It basically worked. I was rattled for a while after, and though I would still tear into him, I was hardly motoring as well in that second half as I had been in the first.

I didn't let it pass. "That was a dirty dig, Darragh," I said, the next time our goalie was stepping back to take a kickout. He just shot me a look that said, "There's plenty more where that came from, young fella."

Leaving Killarney that day, I was still in good spirits. The fact that Darragh started hitting me meant that he rated me. Going home in the car with our captain Mikey Collins, I started to dream beyond the 21s, that maybe I could go on and play for the seniors.

As it would turn out, later that month I couldn't even make the starting fifteen of an Under-21 team that would be beaten by Waterford in the Munster final. Jack went for a midfield pairing of Séamus Scanlon, who was getting some game time with the seniors that summer, and Paddy Kelly, who'd also got the nod ahead of me when we were minors. I only got to come on with five minutes to go, just before Shane Walsh would fist a goal that gave Waterford football one of the greatest wins in its history. But as embarrassing and disappointing as that defeat was, I knew I had another year at Under-21 and that I was progressing nicely as a footballer.

Twelve months later I was in training with the seniors. Jack was now their manager and with the way I was going with the club and the 21s, he called me up after the Munster final. A few weeks later he'd picked me for the match-day panel for the All Ireland quarter-final against Dublin.

That was the time I roomed with Dara Ó Cinnéide. Dara was a hero of mine since '97 when the county won its first All Ireland in eleven years. After they'd beaten Mayo, myself and Andrew 'Crazy 8s' Dineen swarmed onto the pitch, spotted Cinnéide and chanced our arm by asking him if he could get us into the dressing room. We were only fourteen at the time and he didn't know us from Adam, but we told him to say to anyone who asked that we were his cousins. Dara went along with it and so we got to see celebrations that no other supporters could, like a naked Maurice Fitzgerald jumping around with the cup.

Now, seven years later, I was rooming with him the night before an All Ireland quarter-final. At half-nine he closed the curtains, switched off his light and motioned for me to do the same with the TV remote. "Big game tomorrow, Kieran. We'll get a good night's rest now."

In my head I was going, *What?! Are you serious? I'm a half-twelve, one o'clock man. No way, man!* But sure what could I say to him? He was the team captain and I was a rookie, away with the team for the first time. Looking back, I should have just gone down the corridor to someone like William Kirby, a Stacks clubmate. But I was new to it all and for all I knew maybe this was how all Kerry players prepared before a big game. So while Cinnéide was fast asleep within minutes of turning off the lights, I was left there, bored out of my mind, staring at the ceiling, twiddling my thumbs; no iPhone in those days.

That early night's kip worked nicely for Cinnéide anyhow; the next day he kicked five points and the goal that swung the game. I didn't get on myself but it was an unreal experience just being there with the seniors on a big match day. The bus in with the wailing siren and garda escort. Warming up in front of a packed, heaving Hill. Looking over at Darragh Ó Sé at half-time, the steam coming off him like a race horse at the end of a Gold Cup; I nearly felt like throwing a bucket of cold water over him. All day I couldn't help feeling, *This is where I want to be, this is what I want.*

I'd make the match-day squad for the semi-final against Derry too, but was dropped for the final against Mayo. A week or so out from the match I breezed in to Seàn Hussey, who always fits the suits for the Kerry team. He went red after checking his sheet of paper a few times.

"You're not on my list, Kieran."

And at that I went red as well.

It was only at William Kirby's wedding a few months later that Jack O'Connor would apologise that I didn't learn directly from the management that with Séamus Moynihan back fit, I was the man making way.

I'd end up watching the game from the Canal End, the same end in which Gooch scored his wonder goal. I was delighted for Gooch and the lads after the couple of very tough seasons they'd been through, but I was disgusted to miss out on it all – the train up, rooming with Cinnéide or whoever, the banquet, and above all, that All Ireland medal.

What made it worse was that Darragh had been out injured for that final. Although he was always going to be included on the match-day panel so he could get his medal, I would have thought with him out, I would have been moving up the pecking order of midfield options, not down. In the last trial game I had got the better of Micheál Quirke. Years later I'd learn from Micheál that Jack had told him a couple of weeks out from the final that he'd be starting. He was in the gym every day with Pat Flanagan, he was playing alongside Kirby in every training game. But then Jack changed his mind after that trial game and moved Eoin Brosnan to midfield. How could that week in training cost both Micheál his place on the team and me my spot on the match-day panel?

Management instead favoured John Cronin of Legion, from the same club as the selector Johnny Culloty. In fairness to John, he had been there from the start of the year and deserved his medal. But the way I saw it, Johnny had obviously fought harder for his clubman than Ger O'Keeffe had for me. So when I got a call to play for this reality TV team, the Underdogs, in a live televised match against Kerry before the end of the year, I saw it as a massive chance to prove the selectors wrong, and that the next time suits were being fitted and medals were being handed out, I would be on the list.

The Underdogs had already been training for months. The team was made up of players from all over Ireland who had yet to play a senior league or championship game for their county. The manager, Mickey Ned O'Sullivan, being a Kerryman, spotted that I still met that criteria.

He'd felt his team were struggling around the middle of the field, so about five weeks before the game against Kerry, they drafted in myself and Pearse O'Neill from Cork.

We played a few challenge games, including one against Limerick in which I did very well on John Galvin.

That night then the truth is if I wasn't playing for the Underdogs, I'd have been playing against them, and I'd have had as much of a point to prove. Kerry had five of the team that had started the All Ireland final while players like Micheál Quirke, Declan Quill, Padraig Reidy and Ronan O'Connor were like me, panellists looking to break onto the team proper in 2005.

The evening of the game, the team met in the Earl of Desmond hotel on the outskirts of Tralee. Then, as we got onto the bus to take us into Austin Stack Park where 6,000 people and the television cameras were waiting, the bus suddenly went pitch dark: the lights were switched off and this familiar voice came on over the speakers.

It was our selector, Micheál Ó Muircheartaigh, except this commentary was different – he was calling a game that had yet to take place.

"And the Underdogs, they're three points down with five minutes to go against Kerry, but they're still fighting away, they refuse to go away! And here with the ball is Kieran Donaghy. The Austin Stacks clubman goes past one man, he goes past two men. He gives it into Barra Ó Muirí. The Armagh man has it, he shoots… he scores! And the Madraí are really rolling now! They have the All Ireland champions on the rack!"

And on it went, with Micheál name-checking every player on the team, from Kenmare's Hugh Murphy in goal, to our corner forward, Daniel McCabe from Down, with sound effects from the crowd and all to go with it. By the time we arrived at the ground we'd come from behind to beat Kerry by a point. Barra Ó Muirí beside me had tears coming down his cheeks. The hair was standing on the back of my neck. I'd never come across anything like it before. I've never come across anything like it since. It was literally ahead of its time, a visualisation if you like, brilliantly put together by Mickey Ned and of course, the genius of Micheál himself.

And that's exactly how it would pan out – just as Micheál had written it – the Underdogs would win, scoring the last three points of the game to win 3-11 to 2-11, after extra time. You could see how massive it was for the lads and I was delighted for them. For six months they'd been travelling most weekends from all around the country for this one game, this one break. Lads like Mairtín Ó Cinnéide, our captain and full back, a Dub who wore a scrum hat on the night because he'd been concussed a couple of times in the lead up to the game. Garrett Britton, a half back from Donegal: as tough as nails. Stephen Wallace, from Ardfert, who'd kick 2-2 on the night.

For a lot of them that would be as good as their experience of senior inter-county football would get. I think Barra got another trial with Armagh, he was a classy little number eleven, but at the time they were loaded with class forwards. Last I heard, he was a local Sinn Féin representative.

Sometimes you'll have a bit of banter with a few of them on Twitter. A couple of years ago I bumped into our wing forward, Philip Brady from Cavan, at a golf classic in Adare Manor and we had great craic over a few beers. On the tenth anniversary of the game, the lads all met up for a reunion, only I couldn't go because the Stacks were getting ready for a Munster club final. But if there's another one in 2024, I'll be there.

I WAS playing very good football into the end of 2004. I got to put down something of a marker against Kirby and Quirke in that Underdogs game and the same month the Stacks had an epic county league final against Crokes. We were two goals up with a couple of minutes to go, only to let it slip, but as galling as it was to lose, I was now routinely dominating games at mid-field.

The following spring Jack handed me my league debut. It was against Dublin, in Austin Stack Park. I started at midfield along-side Ó Sé – Tomás Ó Sé. Sound man, Jack, thanks a million! He decided we'd "try something different", with the two boys swapping their usual lines of the field: Tomás at number nine and Darragh at centre-back. For the first twenty minutes the three of us were all over the place until Jack put the two boys back in their normal positions. That steadied things and we finished the first half very strong to go into a seven-point lead. I was buzzing, the big Tralee crowd cheering on their local man.

I trotted out for the second half, taking up my spot for the throw-in. Ciaran Whelan was behind me: an absolute ox of a man with serious footballing ability. My uncle, Brian, had me well steeled for this match. Earlier in the day he had told me, "You'll be hit harder today than you've ever been hit. Get straight back up. Don't let them see you were hurt." Five minutes into the game, Whelan caught me across the mouth under a kickout. I could taste the blood in my mouth. I spat it out and looked over at Whelan. "You'll have to hit harder than that!"

"Don't worry, bud," he said, "I will."

Well, he was a man of his word. Once the ref threw the ball up for the start of the second half, Whelan just ploughed through me with his knee into my back. Then he caught the ball, stormed downfield, played a one-two and stuck it into the top corner.

After I finally picked myself up off the floor, I was floundering out there until, midway through the second half, Jack yanked me. With the game on the line, this was no place for boys, only grown men. And so Kirby, who had been my man of the match in the All Ireland final the previous September, came in to save the day for Kerry.

My contribution for the rest of that league would be just a couple of appearances coming off the bench, but I couldn't really complain. The team played some brilliant football, just missing out on a league semi-final spot on scoring difference. I understood the pecking order: that Kirby, as long as he was free from injury, was still the best midfield partner for Darragh. But with the basketball season now over, Quirkey and myself would be competing with a few others to be next in for either of them.

A huge moment for me was that year's Munster final. With twenty minutes to go on a baking hot afternoon down in Páirc Uí Chaoimh, Jack threw me in. It was a very tight game, decided by a brilliant goal from Declan O'Sullivan, and Jack trusted me enough to put me in there with the game in the melting pot. I didn't let him down, setting up a point and getting through a lot of work around the middle.

And yet it could have been a disaster. The second I jogged onto the pitch, Noel O'Leary came over to personally welcome me to what Cork-Kerry clashes are all about.

With my juices pumping and maybe because of the way I had been introduced to the big-boys league by Ciaran Whelan a few months earlier, I lowered the shoulder and ran through him as hard as I could.

Next thing O'Leary went down, clutching his face, and the referee was calling me over.

Jesus Christ; ten seconds into my first championship game with Kerry and I'm going to be sent off. Thankfully he had a good read of the situation and showed me just a yellow card. But I sometimes wonder what would have happened if he had shown me red. My championship career with Kerry could have been over before it had even started.

I'd still leave Cork that day with a big red face on me. In just those twenty minutes out on the field I got completely sunburned. Afterwards I had to sit in the dressing room with ice

packs pressed to the side of my head, trying to staying conscious. I'd hardly ever before played in such scorching heat, and
never in a match played at such a pace. For the first five minutes
I could barely breathe. But I'd survived that heat and Jack had
gone with me in the heat of battle.

He'd bring me on in our next game as well: against Mayo in
the All Ireland quarter-final, my first time getting game time
with the seniors up in Croke Park. I'd also come on for Kirby
in the closing minutes of the semi-final, a thirteen-point win
over Cork. That was three straight games now that I had been
brought on and I couldn't wait to come on in the final against
Tyrone.

This was the game and opposition that all of us in Kerry had
badly wanted. A chance to avenge 2003, a chance to put two
All Irelands back-to-back.

The team was now fitter, cuter, more hardened; ready this
time for their defensive set-up and all the dark arts a few of
them weren't afraid to dish out.

Then they went and outplayed and outsmarted us again.
With me rooted to the bench for the lot of it, watching Chris
Lawn catch three high balls for them around their square in the
closing minutes.

I'm not saying I should have been in at full forward; I hadn't
played there all year for club or county. But if I had been on
the field, I'd have been drifting in there, I'd have been in underneath it, contesting it, winning it, at least once anyway.

The dressing room afterwards was the most devastated I'd
seen up to then. The deathly silence. Fellas in a daze looking at
the ground, having given everything they had but no prize to
show for it. And I was there thinking: When it came to it, Jack

and the lads didn't see me as someone who could help Kerry win the game. *That's another year gone without getting my hands on a Celtic Cross. Will I ever get one?*

Who was to know what would happen after that?

CHAPTER 8

'C'MON!' I SAID!

'One evening I get stuck into a kid called Kieran Donaghy. I'm waiting for him to show me some bit of drive. "Kieran," I say to him, "you're fucking around in this panel for two years, getting bits and pieces. You're half this and half the other. What are you going to do about it?"'

Jack O'Connor, Keys To The Kingdom

Coming out of my cage
And I've been doing just fine
Gotta gotta be down
Because I want it all...

SATURDAY, AUGUST 5, 2006, AND ON THE TEAM bus I've The Killers on my iPod and Armagh on my mind.

This is it. This is what I've always wanted. My first championship start in Croke Park for Kerry. It could all open up for us today. It could all end for us today...

...And my stomach is sick
And it's all in my head...

The last day, against Longford, I was a bundle of nerves. In the warm-up my stomach was doing somersaults. I'd to ask our team doctor for something to help it settle down, telling him it must have been something dodgy I ate but knowing well it was because I was about to be thrown in at full forward for the first time ever in a Kerry shirt. As it turned out, I managed to do just fine but that was against Longford, in Killarney. Armagh, in Croker, is a different ball game altogether.

You can feel the tension on the bus here. All week the whole camp has been on edge. We can't lose this. Not to these northern boys. No fuckin' way. Not again. Not after 2002 to them. Not after 2003 and last year to Tyrone. Nobody seems to remember that Kerry beat Armagh in 2000 in the semi-final. Or the All Ireland the boys won in 2004 when neither Tyrone nor Armagh between them showed up for the showdown. Lose here today and all everybody will do is ram it down our throats that we couldn't beat the Ulster teams, that we didn't have the bottle or fight for them.

I didn't play in any of those games but I'm a Kerryman, and I've a bit of personal history with some of these boys as well.

A month or so after last year's All Ireland final, I got called up to play for Munster against Ulster, above in Crossmaglen. The selectors were obviously stuck for players, because not only did they start me when I'd yet to start a championship game for Kerry, they stuck me in at full forward.

It was an intimidating environment up there: the barracks overlooking the pitch, the helicopters hovering around, and a couple of thousand people up on the banks urging Ulster on to sow it into these boys. Down on the pitch it was hostile as well.

I was being marked by Kevin McCloy from Derry. Tough operator, fair operator; he'd hit you hard but there was no nastiness, no bullshit, no guff from him. It was a bit different with some of the lads playing alongside him; Enda McNulty at corner back was throwing a few jibes my way. Before half-time I won a high ball and was pulled down, and as the ref blew for a penalty, I gave an oul' fist pump. Declan Browne's shot ended up coming back off the post before they cleared it away. As the play swept down the field, McNulty shouted across the line.

"McCloy! Break that fucker's legs!"

McCloy said nothing.

I said something though. "Yeah? Why don't you come over and do it?"

Obviously I knew he didn't literally mean what he said, that he only wanted to rattle some lanky kid he'd never seen before. But I wasn't going to take any shit from him, otherwise he'd walk over me all day, every day.

So McNulty came over and we wrestled to the ground. Fists were thrown and as he was getting up, I felt his knee on my chest. The ref came over and as I stood there with a cut eye and he stood there with a burst nose, a red card was shown to us both.

The two red cards were later rescinded and McNulty would be free to play in the final, but coming back down in the car with Ger O'Keeffe and a few of the lads, I was seething, talking about how some day I'd get my own back on him.

Today now could be that day, but fuckit, it's going to be a battle. Armagh are just after winning their third Ulster title in a row. They've the best defensive record in the country and the personnel of that defence are mean as well. McGeeney. McNulty. And Francie. All week all everyone is talking about is how will Donaghy do up against big bad Francie Bellew, a modern, Ulster version of Kerry's own Paddy Bawn Brosnan as Micheál Ó Muircheartaigh described him on the radio.

> *...'Cause I just can't look, it's killing me*
> *And taking control...*

Fuckit, these boys are hardy bastards.
This is where you get shown up, Star.
You're not playing Longford today.
Maybe these northern boys do have it over us...

And then I see it. Appearing on the horizon, towering above the old tenements of the Dublin inner northside. Croke Park.

My adrenaline pumps. My nerves go from worry to excitement. Goosebumps pop up and run along my arms.

I look outside the bus window and see Kerry supporters with their green-and-gold jerseys and flags making their way in.

Mom and Hilary will be heading in now. And Aidan and Uncle Brian. And Dad…

I look around the team bus. Séamus Moynihan is here. He looks nervous too, but he's here. Darragh Ó Sé as well. And Tomás Ó Sé. Marc Ó Sé. Paul Galvin.

And right across the aisle in the other second-last row of seats: Gooch. For God's sake, man, you'll always be fine when you have him alongside you.

Fuckit, bring it on! Bring them on! Can't wait!

I turn the music up full blast.

> ***…Destiny is calling me***
> ***Open up my eager eyes…***
> ***'Cause I'm Mr Brightside!***

JANUARY 29, 2006, and it's the same ol' story. One step forward, one step back.

It's half-time in the McGrath Cup final on a freezing Sunday down in Páirc Uí Rinn and after being one of our best players the week before, Jack's told me that's my lot for today.

So I'm there in the dressing room with Tom O'Sullivan who they've also told is finished for the day. Everyone else has just filed back out for the second half. I look at Tom. He looks at me.

"Fuckit," he says in that typically breezy way of his. "I'm off home anyway."

"Me too!" says I.

So we shower, get changed and walk out the door.

Of course, I wasn't thinking at all. For one, Tom worked and lived there in Cork; home for him was only a few minutes away. I was there like a spare prick outside the ground until I called Aidan and informed him we were leaving early, that he was giving me a lift home.

And Tom was an established player. Jack would put his behaviour down to Tom just being Tom, a bit of a rogue. I hadn't that kind of credibility and leeway.

Sure enough the next night at training, Jack had a stern word.

"Kieran, does this mean every time I take a fella off, he's going to feck off down the town?"

I nodded, apologetically. That's when he laid into me about whether I was serious about this thing. If I was, he'd give me a fair crack in the league.

I pretty much parked the basketball for the season after that. If I was to establish myself on the starting fifteen with Kerry, I couldn't be rushing to or from some Superleague game or training session with the Tigers. I'd to save the energy, be focused, for the football. With Kirby having retired, there was a spot there for me in midfield if I really went for it.

In fairness to Jack, he was as good as his word. He didn't hold that strop down in Cork against me, and the following week for the opening of the league, he started me, in Tralee against Mayo, at wing forward, to see if I sank or swam. After I swam, he'd me in every game of that league.

A big one was the league semi-final against Laois in Killarney. In all the earlier games, the opposing team would have their main midfielder taking Darragh; Darragh then would get the better of him and I'd usually beat their second fella. With Laois there was no weaker link; Noel Garvan and Padraig Clancy were one of the best midfield pairings in the country, each as good as the other. I ended up on Garvan, an All Star nominee the year before. Their keeper Fergal Byron kicked everything down on top of us, trying to keep it away from Darragh. They saw me as a possible mismatch, but I cleaned up.

Darragh was a dream to play with. He was just so commanding, so crafty. He'd set the tone for everything. If we needed someone to do some bullying he'd be the one in throwing punches for us. If there was a lull, if the other team was beginning to get on top, he'd sense it and before maybe a kickout shout over, "C'mon, Donaghy, we need this one now!"

It was also the way he'd say it. He wouldn't be making a big hoopla about it. He would say it with a sense of urgency but never a sense of panic, clenching his fist, making you want and believe that next ball was yours.

In the league final against Galway down in Limerick, we were three points behind at half-time. I was saying to myself, *Fuckit, I'm struggling here.* Darragh came over to me in the dressing room. "Listen, we're doing fine. We're not getting bate. Don't worry about it. We need a big second half now out of the two of us, we'll get stuck in and win the throw-in."

And that's what happened. We went on to win by eight points.

But I was bringing something to the party as well – legs, freshness, and through my basketball, a defensive presence and awareness that might not have been there before.

In that league final Galway had some very dangerous forwards: Pádraic Joyce, Micheál Meehan, Derek Savage. If they were left one on one, they'd skin you. So any time the ball would go in over the top, I'd drop back and leave my own man. Meehan might have the ball, looking to take on Tom O'Sullivan, and next thing, I'd be running over. "Put him this way, Tom!"

The year before when Ciaran Whelan put me on my ass and then stuck the ball in the net, his route to goal opened up for him like Moses with the Red Sea. Everyone just stayed on their own man because it was every man for himself.

I'd a different mindset coming from the basketball. If someone scored on John Teahan, that was a score on us, on me; I could have left my man on the opposite wing, sagged to the middle and helped John out. If someone then fired the ball over to my man, another Tiger would move over to him and the rest of us would rotate accordingly.

Help defence is what we'd call it, and that's what I was now bringing to Kerry. Tom O'Sullivan and Marc Ó Sé loved it. Afterwards in the dressing room in Limerick, they both said to me: Christ, Star, if you can keep doing that, it would be mighty.

I flew it again in the first round of the championship against Waterford, even kicked two points, and motored well the next day against Tipperary. I was chomping at the bit for the Munster final against Cork, especially with it being in Killarney. My time had finally come. Everything seemed to be going to plan.

Then after a crazy, hot day in Fitzgerald Stadium, that plan went out the window.

I see Kieran Donaghy walking out towards me on the sideline.
"Hey, Donaghy! Where are you going?"
"I got sent off."
"What did you do?"
"Nothing."

"Nothing?"
"I swear to you. Nothing."

Jack O'Connor, Keys To The Kingdom

THE only reason I got sent off in that Munster final was because of another sending off that day. I can't think of any other reason why.

In the opening thirty minutes we were under the cosh. Cork were playing with the wind at their backs and with fire in the belly and five minutes before half-time they were 7-1 up. But I was doing alright, having really settled after making a great catch over my old Underdogs teammate, Pearse O'Neill.

I was mad for more work, so after we'd got it back to three points just before the stroke of half-time, myself and Paul Galvin were tackling Anthony Lynch as he was coming out with the ball over by the stand side down by the scoreboard end.

Joe McQuillan blew for a foul, but to stop Lynch taking a quick free, I stood in front of him, poking at him, half-hoping he might react and the ref might throw the ball up.

Lynch swung back his elbow. I managed to get my head out of the way but I could feel the wind of his swipe so strongly, I ran the palm of my hand across my jaw almost to check I hadn't actually been hit. *Did you just throw an elbow, you prick? That could have broken my jaw, man!*

Did I try to get him sent off? No; if I did, I'd have dived on the ground, clutching my face, instead of standing there, feeling my jaw.

Did I still make a bit of a meal out of it, hoping the ref might show a yellow and give a jump ball? Yeah.

Did I feel sorry that Anthony Lynch was shown a straight red?

No. I wasn't ecstatic about it but I wasn't sorry for him either. Whether he hit me or not, he had still swung the elbow towards my face. In the rulebook that's a straight red, harsh or not.

But then early on in the second half I was booked for backing into Ger Spillane and then ten minutes later again shown a second yellow for a harmless tackle on Nicholas Murphy. It probably wasn't even a foul, let alone a yellow card, but Jack had warned us at half-time it was only a matter of time before the ref would make it fourteen men apiece.

The game would end up ten points apiece. Because I'd also picked up two yellow cards in a league game up in Tyrone, that ruled me out of the replay in Cork. As much I thought I'd been hard done by with that second yellow card, I was prepared to serve my suspension.

Then on the Friday before the replay, we learned that Cork had successfully appealed Lynch's suspension on a technicality. I was raging. I was desperate to win another Munster medal, this time as a starter, desperate to hold my place on the team.

That Saturday morning I was straight on to Jack who was straight on to our chairman Seán Walsh: can we do anything for our man? But there was no joy. It was too late. Cork had pulled a stroke and on the Sunday they'd pull another one over us, beating us by six points.

That was agony, being there, only able to hand out water to fellas and then sit and watch helplessly as Cork with their chests out kicked points from all angles towards the end, each one greeted with a massive cheer from their crowd. A section of ours booed Declan O'Sullivan when he was taken off, which sickened me. Our whole season was unravelling and my mind was scrambling. *We'd to take the long way to an All Ireland now.*

The wrong draw and we possibly wouldn't even see Croke Park. I possibly wouldn't get back on the team with how well Tommy Griffin went in midfield.

That was the darkest hour.

But what is it they say about the darkest hour and the dawn?

The whole mantra for the week is Donaghy. Either he works or we sink.

Jack O'Connor, Keys To The Kingdom

THE day after the game in Cork, Jack rings. He wants to try me at full forward the next day. He'd mentioned something to me in passing alright up in the Hayfield Manor Hotel after the match, but I didn't know if he was serious about it. After his phone call, I now know he's very serious about it.

In fairness to Jack, himself and Séamus Moynihan played a blinder at that team meeting in the hotel.

Jack said that the knockers would be really out in force now, claiming that the team was flat and finished and that things were poisonous in the camp. Jack told us to ignore the noise, fuck the begrudgers, stick together and it'll turn for us.

Moynihan reminded us that at the end of the day we've only lost out on another Munster medal. A lot of fellas in the room have lost count of the number of Munster medals they have. It's All Irelands we want. The draw was made while we were on the bus to the hotel. Longford in Killarney. Perfect game to get us back up and running. Win and we're back in an All Ireland quarter-final, in Croker. It's all still there for us.

Jack knows though that things need shaking up. That's why he's ringing me. Our play, he says, has become too laborious and lateral and the ball isn't sticking inside. We need a ball winner in the danger zone. Me.

He's obviously remembered last year's county championship when the Stacks put me in at full forward against our closest rivals, Kerins O'Rahilly's. I caused some mayhem in there alright, doing well against the O'Shea brothers, Morgan and Barry, former Kerry players, over the course of two games.

But that was at club level. In my head I'm thinking I'm not a good enough footballer to play number fourteen for Kerry in the championship. That's a spot for the likes of Dara Ó Cinnéide, John Crowley and Maurice Fitzgerald; or a Declan O'Sullivan, Mike Frank Russell or, if necessary, a Gooch now, fellas used to having 1-5 after their name in the paper. I'm not that calibre of scorer or player. Never will be. You can maybe transform a basketballer into a midfielder for Kerry. But full forward for Kerry? I'd nearly feel like an imposter in that shirt.

I don't say that to Jack though. I say I'm on for giving it a try.

The following night in Fitzgerald Stadium after a light recovery session, Jack tells me and Marc Ó Sé to stay behind and brings us down to the dressing room end goals. Myself and Marc take up our spots around the edge of the square. Jack goes over by the right wing with a bag of balls. He tells me to make a few runs and just look to win the ball, nothing else.

In fairness to Jack, he's a beautiful kicker of the ball, deadly accurate. He pings a couple of high diagonal balls into me. I manage to hold Marc off and grab them. He plays in a few low ones then. I dart one way to shake off Marc, then break the other way to get out in front.

"Alright, that's it," Jack says, and tells me I can go in and get togged off while he calls Marc over for a word.

Jack will later say they both liked what they'd seen. That Marc was pleasantly surprised by how fast and agile I was.

So the next night I'm in there being marked by Mike McCarthy, the best full back in Ireland. I manage to break even with him, possibly better. I'm winning the ball, laying it off to Mike Frank and Gooch or whoever is playing alongside me.

After that, all Jack can talk about is getting the ball into Donaghy. Seán O'Sullivan, Declan O'Sullivan, Darran O'Sullivan – high diagonal ball into Donaghy that he can attack, got it? Paul Galvin, same for you. He has them constantly doing drills in which they've to bomb the ball into me.

He's even fucking Tomás Ó Sé out of it whenever he comes sallying up the field, looking to play a one-two or to kick his own point. "Cut that shit out, Tomás! We get it to the half-forward line and we get it into Donaghy."

I'm uncomfortable about that. The whole thing is revolving around me, this lanky basketballer who's never even played a McGrath Cup game at full forward.

A few days before the game I ring Jack. "Jack, just so you know, if this full-forward thing goes pear-shaped and then you take me off, I'll be disgusted with you! I was going well all year at midfield! So if there's five balls kicked in and I don't win any of them and then I see number 14 up on the board…"

Jack tells me not to worry. All I have to do is to try and get my hands on the ball. And if I have no joy with that, he'll bring me out the field. "Relax. Either way, you'll be grand."

I can't help it though. The day of the game we're doing our warm-up in the back pitch and as I see the crowd streaming in, my stomach is in knots. I'm thinking it must have been funny chicken we ate a couple of hours ago. I'm going to throw up.

My head is spinning as well. Hot day, big crowd, all here to cast judgement on Jack's Great Experiment – novelty act, more like it. That's what I'm thinking. Because I'm afraid they'll say what's been said of almost every gangly fella that's been thrown in at full forward and didn't win the first couple of balls: "Take that big useless donkey off!"

I can hear their voices in my head, their groans from the stand. And I can hear and feel my stomach growl again.

I go over to our team doctor, Michael Finnerty. "Need something for this stomach, Doc. Must have been something I ate."

He says he'll give me some Motilium and hands me two tiny tablets. I fire them straight down the hatch.

Ten minutes before the game now. Jersey's on, warming up on the main pitch, and the stomach has settled. The head's slowing down too but it's still racing fast enough. I look up the other end of the field, scanning to get a glimpse of my man, something I've done since I was playing with the Under-12s. What does he look like? Big? Rough? Slow? Most of the time it's been a number eight or nine I've been looking out for. Now it's a number three.

I finally spot him. There he is. Barry Gilleran. Looks strong, tall enough, though I'd say I've an inch on him. Doesn't seem the most rugged fella. No convict, like. Will play it hard but fair, I'd say.

Almost time now. We start jogging down to the dressing room goals, the wind at our backs. Good, we'll be playing with the wind. And as I get closer to the edge of the square, these other, positive, thoughts come over me. *Jesus, the pitch is immacu-*

late; the groundsmen must have been out cutting the daisies with scissors. The sun is shining, you've your lovely brand new gloves on. And look at who you've playing alongside you here. Gooch in one corner. Mike Frank in the other. For God's sake, man, all you've to do here is win the ball, lay it off to them and they'll take care of the rest. As Jack would say, relax. You'll be grand.

Sure enough, two minutes in, Séamus Moynihan plays in a ball that bounces in front of me and I manage to tap it down into the path of Mike Frank for the opening score of the game.

Five minutes in, Darran O'Sullivan dashes down the wing over by the stand side, then stops, shimmies, comes inside and shapes up to kick with his left leg, about sixty yards out from goal. Already, even after only a couple of weeks at training here in Fitzgerald Stadium, I know what to do; once he checks onto his left, that's a trigger for me to step one way and then go the other to get a few yards on my man.

The ball Darran's launched is like a scud missile coming at me. I'm following it with my eyes. It'll take everything for me to catch it. But with the tip of my fingers and thumbs, I manage to leap up and grab it. I have it over my head. I bring it down, spin around. Barry Gilleran and another defender are drawn towards me. I can spot this gap in front of their goals that Eoin Brosnan is running into. I pop it over my shoulder off to Eoin steaming through. And Eoin slips it into the net.

After that my confidence is through the roof. After seventeen minutes we've already racked up 3-2, with me having a hand in every score. I even manage to kick a point myself. The fourth official puts up his board for a substitution and in total contrast to my fears before the game, it's not my number that goes up: it's that of Barry Gilleran.

The following night when I'm watching The Sunday Game with Hilary, she says how tough that must have been for him, his whole family and what seemed like the whole of Longford down to watch him; it was the biggest game of his life up to that point, just as it was for me. And as she says it, I have this sense of sympathy for the man, gone in seventeen minutes.

But that's the following night, on the sofa at home. At the time, out there on that field? No sympathy, no mercy. *Good luck and goodbye. Next man. Next ball. Keep it coming!*

By the end of the game, Brossie has finished up with a hat-trick. I've had a hand in 4-4 of our 4-11. Would have been 5-4 had keeper Damien Sheridan not made a fine penalty save.

I'm buzzing. I'm away. I'm Mr Brightside.

Afterwards I spot Donaghy in the sunshine outside the dressing room, surrounded by journalists and chatting away happily. A young player talking to journalists? What next? I leave him there, though. His positive nature is infectious.

Jack O'Connor, Keys To The Kingdom

AFTER the game the media all want a word with me. The Sunday Game name me Man of the Match and I say, great, Mom will love the bit of Waterford Crystal. In my own mind though I'm already thinking of another little prize that would look very good around the place, namely in the driveway.

On the Monday I'm on the phone to Billy Naughton, who runs a Volvo car dealership in Tralee. I'm hoping he's seen the morning paper and all the 'A Star is born', 'The New Bomber' headlines. Because the 'New Bomber' wants a new car — sponsored, free. I'm sick of going around in my Vauxhall Astra, the wheel nearly falling off any time I go over 100 kilometres an hour, and rattling away as I pull into training while Darragh Ó Sé glides in and parks by me in his automatic Renault Laguna.

"Billy! How's it goin'?! Yeah, yeah, thanks very much, went very well. Actually, Billy, that's why I'm calling. I've had two crowds on to me this morning about giving me a car. But look, I know you, and how far you go back with Hilary's dad…"

There's been no-one onto me about a car. But who knows what will happen next year or even next week? Armagh and Francie Bellew could beat us up a stick and there'll be no more 'Star Struck' headlines and no sponsored car then.

Billy tells me he'll go talk to some people and see what he can do. In the meantime it seems like the whole country is waiting to see what I can do against Francie Bellew and Armagh…

…And my stomach is sick
And it's all in my head…

JESUS Christ, I'm going to be taken off here.

It's coming up to half-time and Kerry are losing and I'm losing the battle with Francie. Fuckin' nothing's going right; well little enough anyway. And Paul Hearty, their keeper, is happy to let me know it. He's constantly shouting out to Francie but I'm the target audience.

"That's it, Francie, you have him bate up a fuckin' stick! Sock it into him!"

And Francie is — in that unfussy, crafty way of his. Most full backs, they'll pull your jersey and the officials can see the jersey being stretched. Francie has me grabbed by the shorts! There's no visible give there and I can't move. Whenever I've protested to the umpires, they don't know what I'm on about. And Hearty is knocking great enjoyment and mileage out of it.

"Go on, Donaghy, you big soft basketball cry baby!"

My Tyrone parentage even gets a mention, again hardly intended as a compliment. But it's more my own voice than Hearty's that's tormenting me now.

This isn't your day. This isn't for you.

This is where you get shown up, Star.

You're not playing Longford today.

A ball came in towards me under the Cusack Stand, down by the Davin End which we're playing into. I was out in front of Francie, and spotted that if I got it, Galvin was outside me and I could pop it to him before Francie could plough me over the line. But I got too far ahead of myself; I was making the pass before I even got hold of the ball. It ended up going through my hands and trickling over the sideline while I fell over, looking like a new-born foal.

Francie then quickly took the sideline ball, popping it to an orange shirt, and a big roar went up from the Armagh support in that section.

Another time Seán O'Sullivan got the ball and I looked to go backdoor on Francie, darting behind him towards goal. Seán's the sweetest passer of a ball I've played with but I knew from the moment it left his foot that he had undercooked it and that

Honoured: Receiving the 2006 Player of the Year award in the company of hurling king Henry Shefflin and Taoiseach Bertie Ahern

On the charge: Bursting past Ciaran Whelan as we beat the Dubs in a classic semi-final in 2007

Faith from the fans: A lot of people expected me to fall flat in 2007 but Pop Lynch, a friend from Tralee, had his banner ready after I scored a second goal in that year's All Ireland final

'All we have to do is...': Having my say in a Tigers timeout in the 2008 Superleague final in Limerick, one of the sweetest wins of my career

Twin towers: Tommy Walsh and myself were flying going into the 2008 All Ireland but the McMahon brothers and Tyrone clipped our wings

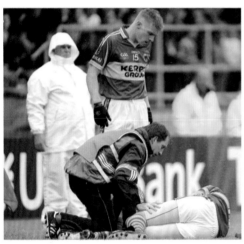

Break it like Beckham: In 2009 I broke the metatarsal bone in my foot – twice – but still made it back for the All Ireland final

Real lift: I got a bit carried away after the 2009 final – and so did Darran O'Sullivan, over my shoulder

Down and out: The 2011 All Ireland final was one of my proudest performances in a Kerry shirt – and one of my most devastating defeats

At last: My dad often wondered what I'd look like in a Tyrone shirt. Sadly, this win over them in 2012 came just months after his passing

Pride of Kerry: In the Melbourne Cricket Ground with Tadhg Kennelly, Eoin Liston and Tommy Walsh in 2011 (left); in the same series I got to play alongside Armagh legend Steven McDonnell

My boys: Aidan O'Mahony and Paul Galvin have been there with me and for me in good times and bad: like after I captained Kerry to winning the 2015 Munster final (above left), winning the 2013 Munster final (above right), a trip to Pearl Harbour (bottom left) and then for the minute's silence for my late father in 2012 (bottom right)

War and peace: During a game I will fight you to win. After it, as Tommy Freeman and Michael Murphy among others could tell you, I'll congratulate or commiserate with you

Banter: Having the craic with Dublin legend and international rules teammate Alan Brogan

Game for a laugh: Starting a water fight (top) and sharing a joke with James O'Donoghue and Bryan Sheehan (above)

Glove-hate: The Dubs on the Hill love to hate me but if I was full forward for them I'd be one of their favourites. Here I am with a Hill 16 hero and friend, Dublin Gerry

he big day: My boys Vinnie Murphy, brother Conor, Daniel Bohane and Micheál Quirke on a
edding day stroll with me in 2013 before I married my beautiful bride Hilary in Waterville, Co Kerry

Sun, sea and sand: I just loved every team holiday we were lucky enough to go on, including this one in Jamaica in 2009

Kings of Flamingo Park: With Tommy, David, Jack and Barry John after we beat Miami's finest streetballer, Curtis Joseph, and his crew

Lightning Bolt: Striking a pose with sprinting superstar Usain Bolt in Jamaica. It's good to see him wearing the right colours!

Hello ma'am: I was invited to meet Queen Elizabeth II with Henry Shefflin, Declan Kidney and Big Jack Charlton

Magic moment: Face to face with basketball hero Earvin 'Magic' Johnson

even if I changed direction, it would hop straight in front of Francie. Sure enough, Francie took it into his chest, and as he came storming out with it, I could only chase from behind and try to tackle, fouling him in the process. I lost the plot with Seán over that – "Put it in over the top, man!" – but seeing me angry made the Armagh crowd even bolder and louder, like an army of Paul Heartys. *"That's it, Francie, you have him bate up a fuckin' stick! Sock it into him!"*

I have had some joy, I have tried to hang in there. About fifteen minutes in, Darragh punted in a high diagonal ball towards the other wing with Francie hanging off me and Kieran McGeeney doubling back. I managed to grab it overhead, put it under my arm and charge down the wing, horsing elbows into the pair of them until they fouled me and Gooch swung over the free.

A few minutes later Aidan O'Mahony pumped in a ball that I managed to deflect into the path of Mike Frank who popped it back to Galvin for a point. But fuckit, I'm still struggling. *We're* struggling.

McGeeney, though he's wearing number eight, is sweeping back, cutting out ball into me and the rest of the full-forward line. At the other end of the field, McDonnell and Clarke are on fire. They've just combined for another goal and a point. They're up 1-7 to 1-3 and everything is in their favour.

We've to make a change here, only I fuckin' hope I'm not it. I know Declan O'Sullivan has to come on soon, but Jesus, *give me 'til half-time at least, Jack. Please.* Gooch comes jogging across. "Hold tough. All you need is one chance and you'll take it. Hold the head. Just keep going."

Fuckit, fair play, Gooch. That's what I need to hear, not Paul Hearty and the little demons in my head.

Entering added time now for the first half. A ball floats in. I knock it down to Gooch and he kicks it over the bar for a point.

Then Seán O'Sullivan plays in another ball from the wing. It's perfect. I palm it down to Gooch and he fires a shot at goal, only for Hearty to save it. It rebounds to Mike Frank. He rifles another shot. Hearty makes a brilliant save – to be fair, he's a great keeper – but he can only push it over the bar.

Instead of being two goals down, we're only two points down. We're the ones with momentum now.

Jack is upbeat at half-time. "Fair play to you, Donaghy. You could have turned your hole to it, everything was going against you, but you're after getting us two points there."

I'm mad for more road now. We all are.

We start the second half like men possessed. Darragh wins the throw in and drives right through the centre to set up a point for Seán O'Sullivan.

Tomás fires in a ball towards me. David Coldrick spots that Francie is holding me on the edge of the large square. Yes! Finally! I turn and applaud Francie and Hearty as he says something else back to me. Mike Frank taps over the free. The game is tied.

Next ball – game-changer. It changes everything…

…Destiny is calling me…
Open up my eager eyes…

Paul Galvin gets in a massive hit, the ball breaks and next thing Seán O'Sullivan is running down the right channel. He's not looking to bomb this one into me though; I can tell by the way he's shaping up he's going to go for a point. Tough shot, especially kicking into a slight wind. It could well drop short if he overpulls it. If he does, I want to be underneath it. So I spin off Francie and drop to the back post.

It's floating in. Starts dropping, dropping…

I leap and grab it over Francie who doesn't even get off the ground.

I slip to my knees. Francie's still between me and the goals. I bounce back up. He gets right up on me. Close. Too close. I throw him a back-to-goal move, like I would in the basketball down in the low post. Fake to the endline, then swivel to the middle. I manage to shake him off with my left hand. I bounce the ball with my right. I can see through the corner of my eye Hearty coming off his line.

I blast it. Past him. Into the net.

I hop over him.

And then I turn around…

I know, I know: if a hundred other Kerry forwards got that goal, the hundred of them would all have just run off, at most maybe jumping up and punching the air.

But I'm not all those other Kerry forwards. I've a message for Paul Hearty that I want to deliver up close and personal, that after all his shit talk, I'm the one still standing while he's the one having to pick himself up off the floor. I lean down and stick my face in his.

"Who's crying now, baby?!"

Not me.

…'Cause I'm Mr Brightside!

Donaghy's goal was a statement. Most of the time I'd try to keep calm on the sideline but I let out an old yahoo when I saw Donaghy. It felt like being set free.

Jack O'Connor, Keys To The Kingdom

YOU are your people. Especially when it comes to this game. Out there in Croke Park, you represent them, you are them, and a part of them is in you.

At the same time that Jack is having his little yahoo, so is Gene Moriarty of Kilcummin. A grand-uncle of mine. A brother of Nan's. A son of Eugene Moriarty and a nephew of Dee O'Connor who were multiple All Ireland winners with Kerry, a tradition I'm trying to follow in now.

Gene would be a bit of a rogue, at least compared to his late brother-in-law, Seán Mac Gearailt, Nan's husband. Sometime in the late '70s they went to a Munster final in Cork. Seán, being the conscientious school teacher, insisted they be in an hour before the minor game to secure the best seats in the house. Gene wasn't impressed, waiting all that time under the hot July sun, especially when he could have been in a pub with some of the lads, but his mood picked up when Kerry won both games. Once the final whistle in the senior game went, he jumped straight to his feet.

Seán tapped him on the leg. "Sit down, Gene," he said softly. "Let the crowd out and we'll go at our ease."

So Gene had to sit there and wait. Just as they finally got up to leave, he spotted a fantastic homemade Kerry peaked cap on the seat next to Seán. Lovely, he thought, and straight into the pocket it went. Out came the school teacher in Seán again. "Gene, put that back! The owners could return for it!"

So like the scolded schoolboy, Gene put it back, only once Seán looked away, Gene stuffed the hat back into his pocket.

On August 5, 2006, Gene still has that hat. He's worn it at every Kerry game he's been at since. So he's watching his grand-nephew grab a ball in front of Hill 16. Then he sees the young fella shake off Francie Bellew and fire the ball to the net.

And with that, Gene Moriarty leaps up and lets out such a yelp, he flings his beloved cap high into the air.

He'll never see it again. He's had his last moment with it. But what a last moment, and afterwards even Gene has to have a little laugh at how somewhere high above him justice has been finally served by that proper gent, Seán Mac Gearailt.

You are your people…

After the goal, I want to let out a bit of a yahoo myself, and not just to have a go back at Hearty. So as I run back out like a hundred other Kerry forwards would have done in the first place, it just comes out of me…

Back in the days playing with the Cs in the Stacks, Aidan's young fella, Tommy Stones, had something of a personal catch-phrase. Whenever he'd score a goal. Or like that time he was shouldered into The Greyhound after playing against Lispole with a broken collarbone. "'C'MON!' I SAID!"

Tommy would have picked up that line from Ed O'Connor. Ed was one of the older lads on the team, the corner forward before I came along, and would look out for me even after I took his place. He was a Chelsea fan like myself and Tommy. So when we'd be down in The Greyhound watching Gianfranco Zola bang one in, the three of us would be thumping the counter, roaring, much to the annoyance of Donie the Silver Fox: "'C'MON!' I SAID!"

So when I run back out, pumping my fist, after sticking it past Hearty, that's what comes screaming out of me.

"'C'MON!' I SAID!'"

You can take the boy out of The Greyhound but you can't take The Greyhound out of the boy.

Every group of fans needs a bit of a hero and I suppose Donaghy has taken on that mantle. He has lit up the place. He has lit us all up, to be honest. He has an infectious enthusiasm about him that has given us all a lift. Even the older players would tell you he's done that.

Jack O'Connor, August 2006

MIDWEEK in Tralee and the foot traffic is busy in Q Sports, the place where I work for my friend Wayne Quillinan. With people who want to buy, people who want to browse and mostly people who just want to have a chat with me here by the counter.

"A great win Saturday," says the man with a peaked cap, though not Gene's.

"Ah, it was," I nod. "Great stuff altogether."

"Ye showed Armagh afterwards. You put manners on Francie!"

"Ah, Francie's alright. Good fella."

"Darragh was powerful."

"Powerful. But everyone was. Nineteen fellas there who played, they all did a job. Savage stuff."

"Ye'll beat Cork the next day now. No bother to ye."

I stop to look up from my paper work.

"Jesus, weren't you in here after the Munster final telling me how useless we were? Didn't Cork beat us in the Munster final? We'd no chance a month ago!"

"But ye've come..."

"Look, we'll get nothing easy. We'll do our best. See how it goes."

He gets the hint.

"Ah, yeah, I know. I know. I'll head on, Kieran."

"Alright. Good man."

I smile. He's one of the good ones. And it's better that there's an air of positivity about the place than the doom and gloom that was there a few weeks ago.

In the camp itself the mood is buoyant. I'm in my element, bouncing off all the lads, in a way I couldn't last year because I wasn't on the team.

There's Séamus Moynihan, the legend. Soon, we all know, he'll be retiring. A few nights before the Longford game I threw my arm around him. "Just four more games with you, Séamo! That's all I want from you!" It's become our own private little joke which I keep telling after every game.

Gooch is teaching me all the subtle arts of full forward play, staying out on the field with me after training.

Before training, Seán O'Sullivan is kicking beautiful long diagonal ball into me like he's been doing in games.

Declan O'Sullivan has been brilliant, regularly calling me after training on his way back to south Kerry, telling me how well I'm going. Even though he's not starting at the moment, he's still being a captain, looking out for fellas like me.

Paul Galvin's the same. Constantly encouraging me, cajoling me to push for more. "Donaghy, don't you stop 'til you get what you want!" We don't even have to say what that 'what' is.

There's something else though I've wanted that I've now got.

That sponsored car I asked Billy Naughton for after the Longford game?

It's all mine now after the Armagh game.

That's how much neck I have and that's how quickly my life is changing this summer.

It's a brand new Volvo S40. A spaceship compared to my old yoke. Just got it there the morning Billy's own son Peter is being married in Cork, so I'm driving up with Hilary to the wedding in it. Jesus, she has serious horsepower. Sailing here. Cruising. Lovely.

We're only five miles out the road, just at Farranfore, when I see a siren flashing in the rear mirror. Fuck!

The Garda comes over. I try to roll down the window but I don't know which button it is. Back windows are sliding down instead of mine. Jesus, he's going to think now I've been drinking as well.

"Do you have any idea how fast you were going?" he asks.

"Not a clue," says I. "Tell me."

"153kph," he says.

"No way," says I. And I mean it. There's no way I knew I was opening it up like that.

I explain the situation. Heading to a wedding. New car. Just getting used to her. No idea of her power.

And then I get an idea of mine. He lets me off with a warning. Then he says to take it easy on that road to Cork – but not to take it easy on Cork in Croke Park.

I'm as good as my word. I'm man of the match in that semi-final. With Graham Canty out injured, Cork move Derek Kavanagh back on me. He's tall and he's strong but I'm more comfortable in my new position than he is in his. While I only kick one point myself, another seven or eight come off me and we win 0-16 to 0-10.

Just one more game, Séamo.

THE Friday morning before the All Ireland and I have to head to the sea, I have to get away. My head's wrecked again.

I finished up work a week ago. After the semi-final it was bedlam in there; streams of people were coming in just to have their fifteen minutes of chat with the guy having his fifteen minutes of fame. By the time of the game it could have completely drained me and even distracted me. Wayne has been great to me but last week we decided we'd leave it altogether. I'm on the verge of glory here so to hell with anything that could mess it up.

So I'm on Banna Strand where I like to go in the lead up to big games. Just to breathe in the fresh air, walk along the shore and let the cool water seep between my toes and calm the mind.

At the moment it is full of doubt and even guilt. On Tuesday I missed training after coming down with the flu. I went in to training, ready to grit the teeth and get through it, but Jack took one look at me coming in. "Jesus, what's wrong with you?"

"Nothing. A small bit of flu. I'll be grand to do a bit."

Straight away he whipped out his phone and called Doctor Dave Geaney. "Donaghy has the flu. Get ready whatever medicine he needs. He'll see you in fifteen minutes."

So I stopped off in Castleisland to see Dave. He took my temperature, gave me antibiotics.

The last two days I've spent in bed. Taking my medicine, drinking plenty of fluids and playing plenty of PlayStation: Tiger Woods, ISS Pro Evolution Soccer, NBA Live. I've needed something to distract me because I've been kind of panicking, the thought of my season being derailed at the last moment.

I'll go out now on Sunday, stink the place out and they'll all say, "Ah, Donaghy, no bottle. Came to the big game and he bottled it."

I'm still feeling a bit weak but I want to see how I am. I'm out here with Uncle Brian. Brian is like a confidant, a minder. At least twice a day he'll ring me, asking about training, how I'm feeling. We go for a jog and have a bit of a kickabout. I'm wrapped up well, the hoodie of my tracksuit all knotted up. When we hop into the car, Brian has the heating on full blast and I'm sweating buckets.

At home I hop into a lovely, warm shower, get changed and I'm not feeling too bad. But then that evening I take another turn. On Saturday I'm going back and forth and whether it's all in my head or not, I don't know.

I head up to Dublin with the team and that evening we have a light workout in Westmanstown. After only four runs I'm fucked. I go over to Doctor Dave. "Dave, there are silver stars going round my head. My legs are like jelly."

He reassures me I'll be fine. How long is it since I last ate?

And sure it turns out I haven't eaten since the train five hours ago, there being no protein shakes en vogue in 2006. I go back to the hotel, get three breasts of chicken with some pasta into me and it's literally what the doctor ordered. After that I'm fine. I feel great. Perfect. Ready.

I've decided I'm going to enjoy this final. I might never play in another one and I've dreamed about this since I was a kid.

I'm going to soak up the atmosphere in the parade. Look out for where my family are. Keep the head up. Stick the chest out.

The whole team is primed for this one. Declan is back in the starting fifteen, leading us out. He had to get in somewhere, the way he was flying in training. Eoin Brosnan is the one to lose out. Brossie has scored four goals in our last three games. That's how ridiculously strong we are at the moment.

Five minutes in, Declan shows Mayo and the rest of the country what we've been seeing in training. He storms through the middle, plays a one-two with me and kicks it to the net.

Two minutes later Tommy Griffin punts in a ball from way out the field. In 2004 against Mayo, Cinnéide and Crowley caused murder under the high ball. Now I'm in there and Jack has made it clear to me he wants for Mayo to have that sense of déjà vu.

I grab the ball overhead in front of David Heaney. I back into him. He gets right on top of me. Again, too much on top of me. I just bounce off him and spin. I hold him off with my left hand and hop it with my right and I blast it…

You are your people…

When I was a kid and would see Uncle Brian's car pull up across the road after the journey down from Dublin, I'd run out to him. "C'mon, Big B, I'll be Kerry and you'll be the Dubs!"

He'd say he wanted to get a cup of tea and a sandwich first but I'd pull on his sleeve and drag him into the back garden. At the bottom we'd an old turf shed with a corrugated iron roof. Its wall was the goal. I'd place the ball on the penalty spot. Brian would be the goalkeeper and commentator, John O'Leary and Micheál Ó Muircheartaigh rolled into one.

"And it's a penalty, it's a penalty for Kerry! Who's going to take it? Kerry

are two points down and time is up. Surely this is the last kick of the game! I can tell you that Jack O'Shea is going to take it…"

And God bless Big B, Kerry would always win the All Ireland, though at times an initial save by O'Leary would mean there'd have to be a retake of the penalty because of some unseen infraction. I'd run in with the good news to Nan.

"Oh good man, Keek," she'd smile. "A goal for Nan!"

And then better than any All Ireland final banquet, she'd let me have the first pick of her buns and a lick of the delicious mixing whisk from her Kenwood chef mixer.

It's something she's said all through the years. Before going out to play with the Cs: Get a goal for Nan! Same all the way up: Did you get a goal for Nan?

Most of the time I didn't. And nearly all the time she wouldn't be there to see for herself, being wheelchair bound with her bad hip. But today, for the first and only time in her life, she's in Croke Park, up in the disabled section high in the Hogan Stand after being wheeled up there by my Uncle Ciarán.

So when that ball flies past David Clarke and into that net down by the Davin End, I wheel off in celebration, thinking of only one thing. I point up to my second mother: Mary Fitzgerald nee Moriarty.

A goal for you, Nan.

THE rest of the day is like a dream. A nightmare for Mayo but a dream for us. After ten minutes it's 2-4 to no score. David Brady – another natural midfielder – is called from their bench to mark me and he fights like a warrior but later he'll say his role's more like being sent in to look for survivors. After twenty-five minutes Gooch also finds the net to make it 3-6 to 1-0. Mayo rally before half-time with a couple of goals but a few points either side of the break pushes our lead back out to double figures.

It's a procession from there on in, one I can enjoy. I get to actually take in the fact we're going to win an All Ireland without the stress of not knowing which way it will go. Near the end I kick a second point off Brady, this one from range. It's just our day. It's just my summer.

On the whistle a wave of green and gold sweeps the field. A friend, Johnny Boona, manages to find his way to me and grab me in a headlock, breaking his watch which scrapes my face in the process, though I'll only realise what happened later that evening from the sting I get putting on my aftershave. "ARRRGGGHHH!"

In the dressing room afterwards, everyone's just floating. Later I'm talking to reporters when I spot Tommy Griffin, who had a stormer in midfield, strolling down the corridor, cradling Sam.

"Hey, Tommy, watch that!" I shout with a smile. "That's precious!"

Tommy grins back with the big thumbs up.

We get back to the hotel and I'm there in my room with Hilary, hardly able to comprehend what has just happened. I'm sitting on the edge of the bed in my suit for the banquet, about to put on my shoes, and I just flop backwards, clutching my face, stretched out.

"Are you alright?" Hilary asks.

"I just can't believe it, Hils."

I've won an All Ireland. With Séamus Moynihan. There's no

more games with Séamo now but he has his fourth All Ireland and I have my first. Eighty years from now I'll still be in a team pic on some wall of the Kerry side that won the All Ireland in 2006...

If they'd given us our medals up in the Hogan Stand that evening as they really should, I don't think I'd have left the room that night; I'd just have stayed there, turning it over and back, marvelling at it, trying to take in that it was real.

But it was.

It was magic but it was real.

CHAPTER 9

ALWAYS ANOTHER GAME

'Many will ask what are management feeding Kieran Donaghy. He was running around like a young fellow from one goalmouth to the other. And the chance to see again the class of Colm Cooper is enough to make a visit to a Kerry game worthwhile, especially his confrontation with the Dublin defence'

Eugene McGee, Irish Independent, April 11, 2016

S O ONCE MORE WE ROLL INTO THE DARK underground of the coliseum, ten years on from that summer of 2006.

A lot has changed for me and Colm Cooper since then but one thing has not. We still share an unspoken ritual. We both sit across from one another on the second-last row of the team bus; me to the left and, on the other side of the aisle, him to the right. For years I'd Séamus Scanlon immediately beside me but since he went I just sit alone, by the window, while Gooch sits over by the opposite window, by himself. And all the time we'll wait for everyone else to move out – even the boys in the back row – before he'll rise to his feet and I'll let him out first.

As I say, we've never spoken about it; like a lot of things between us, we don't need to. But ever since that game against Armagh and Francie, I never move until he moves. I always wait to follow him.

Why? Because if you're walking out behind him, you always have a chance. I don't know if he feels that bit more secure knowing I have his back but I know for sure that I feel massive confidence entering the lion's den with Colm Cooper right there in front of me.

Today we play Dublin in our first league final since 2009. Back then when we beat Derry there were only 20,000 in Croke Park. Today there'll be 82,000. Everyone wants to see this one after what happened last September and how we've responded since.

There's a lot of talk about how I'm going. 'Rejuvenated' seems to be the word everyone is using. I'm definitely thriving playing out the field. In other years it's been tough, stuck inside at full forward on soft pitches in the pissing rain, waiting and waiting for ball to come in. In this year's league I haven't had to wait; I've been able to move around and get on it.

What Éamonn really likes is the intangibles I'm bringing, the stuff that nobody notices but that he does. Communicating with fellas, making sure we're holding our shape, passing men on. The week after the Melee in Tralee with Donegal, we were up in Castlebar. Another dogfight. I thought I was diabolical in the first half, fumbling ball and giving it away, but the next night when Éamonn was showing us the video clips, he said that I set the tone for the day with how I double-backed on Aidan O'Shea to help Mark Griffin and cut out the danger.

Our next game up in Clones, I kicked a couple of long-range points with the outside of my boot but what pleased Éamonn the most was once more my workrate. The One Percenters he calls them, plays that can't be measured on the scoreboard or even the stats sheet, though my stats and GPS readings were very good that day against Monaghan. I led the tackle count with eight. I had the second most possessions with thirty-six. I was second as well for distance covered, 11.5 km. Only the Ironman that's Donncha Walsh got through more.

Another huge plus for us is the form of Gooch. He destroyed Roscommon here the last day in the semi-final. Making plays only he can make because he sees plays only he can see.

His spatial awareness and game smarts are just incredible. One year when we were out in camp in Portugal, we had a soccer game at the end of the week. The way he played, I honestly think with a month's training he could play in the hole for Liverpool. Not that he'd keep Coutinho out of the team, but that he could play there and you wouldn't be wondering, "What's your man doing out there?"

When Jack threw me in at full forward back in '06, Gooch kind of took me by the hand. We never had a big sitdown in some coffee shop; we just went out there onto the field and went through how this thing could work. "Hey, listen, if I have the ball here, then you go there. And then if you get it here, look, I can…"

It'd become almost telepathic. I might be struggling in a game and he'd just give me this look, maybe gesturing with the hands to stay calm, be patient, stick with it. Other times then he'd shoot you this stern look which told you something needed to change and that it had to happen right now.

He's deep. While I'm open, he's guarded. I'll hug you. I could tell you at two o'clock in the day that I love you. I might say to Gooch, "God, Colm, you're fuckin' flying lately." He'll never say that to me. But the day we beat Mayo down in Limerick, he sought me out on the pitch. He knew there'd been serious pressure on me that day, that I'd gone from the wilderness to suddenly being our number one option. When he found me, he shook my hand and looked me dead in the eye. As if to say, "Fair play, big fella. You delivered when Kerry needed you most."

He's a great man to go out with. We could be in South Africa, just the two of us, drinking strawberry daiquiri cocktails, and we'd lose all track of time, just chatting.

Whenever the two of us are drunk, the talk always turns to basketball. I remember playing against him in a first year tournament back when I was in The Green and he was in the Sem in St Brendan's. He was class. The football kind of took over after that but to this day he'd be into his NBA as much as me, raving about some play by LeBron James or Steph Curry.

One year we were out on a team holiday in San Francisco, drinking in a nightclub on North Beach, talking hoops again by the counter. Next thing I turned around and he was gone. I looked around everywhere inside, couldn't find him, so eventually I headed for the exit. When I got my bearings outside, I spotted Gooch about two hundred yards up the street in some heated conversation with four black fellas.

When I arrived on the scene, the tallest of them went, "Hey man, take this guy away! He's crazy!"

Gooch was there to him. "No, c'mon! You and me! Right now! One on one! Let's go!"

Your man looked at me again. "Told you. Bring this dude home."

Gooch looked at me, then pointed over to a tattered basketball court in the distance. "None of them will take me on one-on-one, Star!"

He turned back to the boys, especially your man. "Hey, tell ye what so – me and Star will take ye on two-on-two!"

Well the four boys broke down laughing. All the time they'd thought it was a fight Gooch was itching for, not a game of ball. But with it being two in the morning and brothers not always having a basketball by their side, ready to scrimmage at a moment's notice, they let it go this time.

I've often played the Gooch one-on-one – in golf. If we played ten times, he'd beat me five times and I'd beat him five times.

Back in 2011 himself and Eoin Brosnan from the Crokes and myself and Daniel Bohane from the Stacks had a heated fourball series. With our two clubs wearing the same colours, we christened it the Black and Amber Cup. They beat us in Killarney, then we beat them in Tralee. The deciding eighteen holes were in Fota Island where we had our training camp before that year's All Ireland final. With two holes to play, myself and Bo were two down. But I made a putt on the seventeenth to bring it to the last and then Brossie fluffed a four-footer that would have won the match for them. Well, you should have seen the face on Gooch and how embarrassed and apologetic Brossie was to have let him down. Eoin's a fine golfer yet there he was, "I'm sorry, Gooch! I'm just shit at golf!"

We could have shook hands on the eighteenth green and left it at that: good game, good craic, all friends, no losers. But no losers would have meant no winners and that wouldn't do for me or Gooch, so we agreed that we'd play the first as a playoff hole. Everyone was so nervous, it was like the Ryder Cup.

Myself, Gooch and Eoin were all up by the green in two but Bohane was fifty yards back on the fairway after getting into trouble off the tee. So the three of us were there eying up our next shot when Bohane walked up to his ball and pitched it straight in. I picked up my ball and sprinted down the fairway, hugging and slapping Bo a high five, completely forgetting that if either of the boys chipped in we were heading for a second playoff hole. But they both missed, and later on I'd learn that on the way home in their car to Killarney, Gooch didn't say a single word to Brossie. He was still fuming about that four-footer on the eighteenth that cost him the Black and Amber Cup.

That's the thing about Gooch: he wants to win – at everything. I hate losing. Fuckin' hate it. But I can accept it. After a while anyway. But while the rest of us will have a week of hell after losing a championship game in Croke Park, for Gooch it will be a whole winter. He loves Kerry and its history and tradition and puts enormous pressure on himself to uphold it.

This last winter was a rough one, which is one reason why today is a big one for him. It's a big one for all of us. Another shot at the Dubs and to break this winning streak they have against us here, and to set us up nicely for the summer.

Twenty-five minutes into the game, Gooch leaves Philly McMahon grasping at thin air by selling a dummy and curling it over the bar to put us up a point. It's an outrageous bit of skill, one that will prompt Andy Murray's mom Judy, who is in attendance, to tweet that Colm Cooper is a "wizard". But straightaway their Cooper, Johnny, comes up from corner back and kicks a score of his own to cancel out Gooch's.

That's kind of the story for the rest of the game. For anything we do, they have an answer. Before half-time they quietly shift into another gear to go in at the break 0-10 to 0-8 ahead. We hang in there even though Peter Crowley is the only fella playing out of his skin and we're still only two down with twenty minutes to go when a third different Dub in the one passage of play checks Mahony off the ball; Aidan duly clips Johnny Cooper and is sent off. Even after that we're still only trailing by four with sixty-seven minutes gone on the clock and a good bit of injury time to be played. I'm in at full forward now and Gooch comes over to me. "We just need a score to get it back to three. Go out and tell the lads to just settle down and get the ball in our hands." But just as we both take off running to rally the troops, one of the lads fails to read Brendan Kealy's kickout, Paul Flynn pounces and rattles the net. Gooch and I catch each other's eye and we know: That's it for today. It's done. Dublin strike for another goal and a couple of points and by the end they've won by double figures.

It's deflating. We approached the game as if it were championship. We felt we'd our homework done, that our prep was bang on. I picked up a head cold the week of the game but fuckit, I've played with that before. I still covered more ground than anyone. But now I'm wondering if it was stupid ground I was covering, trying to be everywhere but being nowhere.

Early on I got a good block in on Dean Rock but after that I didn't get on enough ball. I was trying to drop back and help out our defence but then Denis Bastick would pick up ball on the wing and I'd have to run out to him and I was kind of stuck in no-man's land.

Five minutes before half-time I was moved to full forward. I don't know if it was because management were unhappy with how I was going at midfield or they just felt it was worth trying to maybe nick a goal heading into the dressing room, but anyway I was put in there. As this high ball came floating in towards me down by Hill 16, Cian O'Sullivan started backing into me. I knew the ball was going over his head so I held my ground for a second and then sprung off him as he backed some more into me and I rose up to catch the ball. Next thing Eddie Kinsella blew his whistle. Free out.

I was fuckin' furious, slam hopped the ball and everything. I shouldn't have done it, I'm losing the mental battle when opponents see me losing the plot like that, but I was just so frustrated. If that's a push in the back by me, then Eddie and every other match official should take a look at what I and other big men like Michael Murphy and Aidan O'Shea have to put up with whenever the ball is in the air.

After the game Éamonn uses strong language to reporters about how hard it is for me to get a free in and around the square even though opponents are hanging off me.

To be honest though, there's a lot more we could have done to help ourselves. We just have to work out how.

HALF-TEN the morning after the game and I'm having breakfast with Hilary in a Killarney hotel when I get a text. Gooch: **Well, LeBron, where are you?**

I text him back. **In town. Where are you, Steph?**

A basketball thing again. LeBron's a huge man; Steph Curry's a scrawny, skilful fella. Already I know how this day is going to pan out. A lot of hoops talk because there'll be a lot of drink. I tell Hilary, "I'm going to be out with Colm for the day." She understands. Last night we went out with most of the team and fellas were visibly hurting, especially Mahony having been sent off, and it's still not easier in the morning for someone like Gooch. On days like this he needs me.

I meet him in this favourite haunt of his, the Speakeasy. Grand spot. The barmen are gas with gas nicknames: Box, Snack Box and Hard Man. Gooch asks me what I'm having. I tell him I'll have a brandy and Bailey's to settle me.

He looks at me. Are you sure? It's only half-eleven in the morning!

I nod. Yeah, I'm sure.

He gives Hard Man a shout. "I don't believe I'm saying this, but can I have a brandy and Bailey's for the big fella?"

Hard Man turns around and sees who has arrived. "Oh, Jesus Christ…" It's going to be a long, hard day, this one.

A few hours later the pair of us go out the back and try to solve the problems of our world. Just trying to figure out ways to get better, to attack them better and what we do with their kickouts. To be honest though, I don't really want to go into it.

"Look, Gooch, there's enough time to be dealing with it, and you and me with drink inside us aren't going to fix anything here. We've just got to go back training harder."

We change the conversation. See that Cavs game last week? And off we go, talking hoops while on the gat. At six o'clock he bails out and heads home. That's usually my cue to head back to Tralee but Mahony and Kieran O'Leary are on their way in.

I'm not to know it but it's my last night out with Kieran as a Kerry teammate. The following week he's one of the lads let go when Éamonn culls the panel for the championship. I'm gutted about it. Classy player and an even better friend. He was the captain in 2014. Everyone goes on about the goal I set up for James O'Donoghue in the drawn semi-final against Mayo but that left us still a point behind; it was Kieran who kicked the equaliser; that was the biggest clutch play of the year. He's been a great servant for Kerry but the last few years he's struggled with an Achilles injury and his job in Liebherr has involved serious hours, meaning he could often miss a week's training. Something had to give or someone had to go, so Kieran's gone.

So is Tommy. I'm just as cut up about that. Whenever he came onto the team in 2008 playing alongside me, I kind of took him under my wing a bit like Gooch did with me two years earlier. I don't know if I've ever been prouder of a teammate than when he tormented Cork in the 2009 final. But then he went to Australia to chase the professional dream. He was a huge loss to us so when he returned eighteen months ago, no-one was happier than me. But it just hasn't worked out.

He's now going to just focus on the club. Maybe that's what

he needs. Maybe that's what he needed all along, to get a lot of club football into him instead of going straight back in with Kerry. I can see him still offering the county a lot in the future, but sadly it seems I've played my last game alongside him.

The Friday after the Dublin game, some of us are at Bryan Sheehan's wedding, including Tommy. It's down in a lovely spot in Cromane and the girls all love it but for those of us with club games the next day, it can be tough drinking water all day listening to punters breaking your chops about the league final.

When we arrive at the reception I spot Marc Ó Sé being cornered by some local with yellow fingers from the fags. I can tell Marc is trying to move him on.

"What do you want, big fella?" he shouts over to me.

The one thing poor Marc has going for him is he doesn't have a club game the next day; he can drink away.

"A pint of water, Marc."

So Marc bolts for the counter, leaving his friend with yellow fingers trying to latch on to me.

"Ye let yerselves down badly at the weekend," he says.

"Ah yeah, yeah, we did," I nod, looking everywhere but at him. "Not good enough at the weekend, no."

"Jesus Christ, them fellas are like Heffo's Army!"

It's quite the art, trying to be ignorant in as polite a way as possible dealing with situations like that, but it's one you learn to pick up if you're going to cope with being a Kerry footballer. The trick is to move on the conversation – "It's a lovely day outside, isn't it?" Either the chat moves on or you move on. Otherwise you'll just go insane.

Look, it's going to be like this for a while. Even Marc's brother, Tomás, was critical of him and the team in his column in the paper. People are going to write off the team and they're going to compare the Dubs to the All Blacks, let alone the great team they had in the '70s.

But as players we look at it differently. Yeah, this is a serious Dublin team. The best opposition I've come across, bar maybe the Tyrone team of 2005. But I don't think they're better than the team we had there in the late noughties. I think that Kerry team would take them. I think this Kerry team can take them. We're going to need to have everything right and have a plan in place but we've Paul Geaney to come back, James O'Donoghue to come back. Fellas like Mahony and Marc will be bulling for another shot at them. Dublin will be talked up now to the heavens, they'll blitz Leinster and probably whoever they meet in the All Ireland quarter-final but if we take care of our business and meet them again at the end of August, we'll give them a serious fuckin' rattle.

AT the weekend we go back to our clubs. The Stacks are playing Dingle in the club championship semi-final in Annascaul. I arrive there nearly two hours before throw-in. Normally I hate getting to a game so early, too much time to kill, but I need to get some physio and band work in on what seems like a dead leg I picked up in Croke Park just before half-time.

A few minutes into the team warm-up, I'm bending my knee and sliding my feet in a tackle drill when bang! – torn quad. I go up to our manager, Stephen Stack. Fuckit, I'm gone.

With five minutes to go, I go back up to him on the line. We're two points down. We've had two men put off. Greg Horan, our county Under-21 star, has done his cruciate. Pa McCarthy, our speedy wing back, has done his groin. Denis McElligott, our corner back, has done his groin. Daniel Bohane couldn't line out at all. I might be one of the walking wounded but the way I see it, right now that makes me fit enough to play, especially with Pa staying on to hobble about at corner forward. I say to Stephen to stick me in at full forward beside Pa. Shane O'Callaghan was killing Dingle in there in the first half but they've since put a sweeper in front of him. I'd occupy the sweeper. Play Calla about ten yards in front of me and that'll get him back on the ball.

So I hobble on, up alongside Pa who's also on one leg. The next minute a high ball is lumped in. I catch it, back into my man and spin onto my right leg only to be dragged to the ground. But because I make some contact on the ball as I'm falling, the foul isn't clearcut enough for the ref to give a penalty.

Deep into injury time now. Still two points down. For some reason their keeper goes long with the kickout. Wayne Guthrie catches it out on the wing, is fouled and pumps the ball in to me. The Dingle lads are around me like a swarm of fuckin' bees but I manage to get my hands on it, swivel and handpass it over my shoulder to Calla who half-volleys it. It seems to bounce on the line before one of the Dingle lads clears it but we protest to the umpires anyway that it was over, and maybe because he felt we probably should have got a penalty, he reaches for the green flag. Goal! Game over! We've won!

The Dingle lads are going ballistic remonstrating with the umpires and ref, but us, we're just ecstatic. For a moment I forget my leg is shagged. Pa too. We're all hopping about the place like we've won a county final. That night we head to The

Greyhound, all the girls as well, and we have a massive sing-song. Now Croke Park last Sunday seems some distance away.

That's the beautiful thing about sport. Just when it hurts you it can always lift you because there's always another game.

Tomorrow I'll have to go for a scan and see how bad the tear is but right now tomorrow can wait. All again is well in the world. Everything again is possible.

CHAPTER 10

THAT SECOND ALBUM: WHAT'S THE STORY, SUNDAY GLORY?

"Donaghy is the key. If he stays healthy and keeps his feet on the ground, he'll transform Gaelic football. You can have all the tactics in the world but with his hands and his athleticism, he'll be very hard to stop"

Jack O'Connor, October 2006, upon stepping down as Kerry manager

I'D LIKE TO THINK I DIDN'T CHANGE AS A person after the summer of 2006 but my life definitely did. Ahead of that year's All Ireland semi-final, I was still working in Q Sports, spinning basketballs and selling adidas shoes in my tracksuit bottoms. In 2007 I was being paid to wear those adidas shoes while at work I was wearing a suit, shirt and tie as a business development officer with Ulster Bank. I was asked to so many award nights, I'd the road to Dublin worn down. I was even going up there in helicopters. Well, this one time anyway.

That winter after we won the 2006 All Ireland, five of us were invited by a couple of property developers to come up with the Sam Maguire to meet their family and some clients and friends. So in the morning they sent a chopper down for us – myself, Gooch and the three Ó Sés – and flew us to this mansion near the airport. We met their family, posed for loads of photos, enjoyed the Midleton whiskey they generously kept pouring into our glasses. Then we were brought to some bar where again there was a big welcome for us. By the time we got the chopper back at six o'clock that evening, the Famous Five were well on it. When we landed back in Farranfore, it was like Scattering Day at Puck Fair. Marc shot straight out and ordered a taxi to Dingle. Gooch and myself headed into Tralee on the tear in another taxi. Darragh then got some lift home from someone he knew, leaving poor Tomás stranded at the airport bar all on his own.

That wasn't the half of it though when it came to that Darragh fella that day. A few years later, shortly after Darragh had retired, I bumped into one of the developer's sons and we had a great laugh about that morning in his dad's house with

Sam, drinking whiskey. Then he said, "You got your few bob for that, you did?"

I was bemused. "No. I didn't."

He goes, "What?! I'm sure my old man gave Darragh a few bob to give to all of ye!"

The next time I met Darragh and mentioned it to him, sure he just rocked back that big head, rubbed his hands, and gave that big laugh of his.

And I suppose that episode with the helicopter in a way said a lot about me back then. I was literally going up in the world, but with a rogue like Darragh around, I still had some more to learn about the ways of that world.

AS much as my star had risen in 2006, I was well aware going into the following season that people, especially the headline writers, were waiting for this Star to fall.

It's one of the reasons why I didn't go on the All-Star trip to Dubai that January. It wasn't just that the Tralee Tigers were in a National Cup final; I wanted to get in a really good pre-season so I could attack the league with Kerry. I couldn't wait to actually get back playing football instead of just fuckin' talking about it as I had that whole winter at all those functions.

On top of that, we'd a new manager, Pat O'Shea, after Jack stepped down a few weeks after the All Ireland, and I wanted to make a good early impression. It would be fair to say I then went and did the exact opposite. I got sent off in our opening league game, an away loss to Mayo. Then in our third game I was put off again, this time for a straight red card.

We were playing Fermanagh away. They were wiring into me from the start, poking me in the arm, kicking me in the heels. A few minutes before half-time I kicked a wide and running back, out one of them thundered into my back. I flicked out my leg, out of sheer petulance, making your man stumble, and with it being right in front of the ref, sure that was me gone.

I walked straight off the field and to the dressing room, only to find it locked and no-one around to open it. Bad news for that dressing-room door – I took two steps back and kicked it open like some cop in a film. I slumped down and held my head in my hands, not believing the two things I'd just done. Some steward came in, yelling about what had happened to the door, but since there was nothing I could say to justify it, I just stayed sitting there in my own silence, my head almost touching the ground, even after your man finally turned and headed off.

After the game though Pat had plenty to say, in front of everyone, in that same dressing room that now needed a new door handle. About how some fellas were going on as if they were too big for all this and felt they couldn't be touched. He didn't name anyone but we all knew he was talking about me.

He wasn't afraid to name me to the media though. "It's obviously disappointing for the team," he'd tell reporters. "At the end of the day Kieran's a high-profile player and he has to recognise the responsibility that goes with that. He's a great guy and a super footballer but he needs to be more disciplined."

Pat was spot on but at the time it was a hard thing for me to hear; ever since I started sport, the worst thing you could ever tell me was that I'd let down my teammates. A bit of me was still pissed off with him, but the penny began to drop that things had changed and I'd have to change with it.

That would be the last straight red card of my career because that's when I worked out that it's better to be the aggressor than the reactor. Whenever I kicked a score or a wide, I wouldn't be facing the goal and allowing some back the chance to run in and dunt me a shoulder and then have me reacting; instead I'd be turning around and hitting him the shoulder before he ever got a chance to do it to me.

The only thing was it would take some time to put that strategy and that shoulder to use.

Just when I got back from suspension, I went and did my AC joint in a game up in Letterkenny. I was causing wreck in the opening twenty minutes when I went to handpass it to Mike Frank, only for a Donegal lad to run into me, causing my hand to go across me and pop my joint out over my shoulder. After being out for one month through suspension, I was now out for at least two months with injury. Disaster.

Another inconvenience about the injury was the Tuesday after that match I had a job interview. A few weeks earlier I had met with a Listowel man called Seán Healy who was very high up in Ulster Bank and wanted me to come work with them. We met in the Listowel Arms and talked about the job for about half an hour and then football for two hours. Seán was Kerry to the core and as we got up to leave, he told me that the job was practically mine; I'd just first have to do an interview with both the regional and branch manager. So on the Tuesday morning after the game in Donegal, I rocked into the interview with my arm in a sling and wearing this hoodie I'd still on from the Sunday night since I couldn't put on a suit.

I leaned back into the seat. Well, what I thought might be a nice chat ended up being this big, formal interview. What can you bring to the bank? What can you bring to the team? What kind of people's person are you?

And all the while I was there thinking, *What's with all the questions, like?!*

As it turned out, I did get the job; a fortnight later I started working for Ulster Bank. The first few weeks I had to do an induction course up in Dublin. It was mind-numbingly boring. The only thing that kept me going was that at five o'clock we'd be finished and could go for a few drinks together. The first night I took the class to Coppers. We ended up there the second night as well. And the third…

I'd say by the end of the second week the ones who interviewed me for the job would have loved me. My classmates definitely did. What kind of people's person was I? What could I bring to the team? Free entry into Coppers, that's what!

THERE was another connection with the bank I'd made by then. A few weeks after the All Ireland final in 2006, Hilary's father Frank rightly identified that I could do with a bit of guidance to deal with all the offers and requests that were coming my way. He made a few enquiries and then brought me to meet a man in Killarney called Eddie O'Donnell, a Tipperary man based in Cork. Eddie was a retired branch manager in Ulster Bank and had been helping Seán Óg Ó hAilpín.

I went along, expecting to meet Jerry Maguire's twin brother, a slick, fast-talking operator in his twenties or thirties. Next thing I was being introduced to this gentle, slight, hunched-over sixty-something man with silver hair combed over to the side, wearing a cravat. But right from that first meeting I clicked with Eddie and all these years on he's still a great friend and advisor.

He'd look after my diary. He helped me to say No to things, otherwise I could have been using up too much time and energy that I needed for my football.

He also made sure that I was taken care of properly by the various corporate brands that were approaching me. In the summer of 2006, a sales rep came into Q Sports and offered me a couple of free pairs of Nomis football boots to wear playing for Kerry. Sure I was delighted; at the time Nomis were a really cool, expanding Australian sports company and the boots were beautiful: kangaroo skin, black and gold; the curl and grip I got from them was unreal. But in 2007 that same rep wasn't back to me, offering me a few quid to wear them. Adidas were though, so I signed up with them, Eddie having negotiated the deal.

'What drives me? Knowing one medal doesn't make a collection.'

Kieran Donaghy, Kerry footballer, Car ad campaign, 2007

ON the eve of the 2007 championship I was rolled out to the media at an adidas event. Back then I used to feel a bit out of my depth at that kind of thing in the company of the other brand ambassadors: Alan Brogan, Conor Mortimer, Mattie Forde, Micheál Meehan, Owen Mulligan, along with Galvin and Gooch.

They were all incredibly skilful footballers, all able to throw dummy solos and bomb it over from forty yards, in most cases, with both feet. I didn't have their tricks. Compared to them, I was a bit of a one-trick pony.

The big question at that gig then was whether I was going to be a one-year, one-hit wonder. I had never heard of Second Season Syndrome before, at least not that term, but that was the line of questioning from the media. They spoke about sophomore slumps, about how in music it's common for acts to struggle with "that difficult second album"; was I finding it difficult?

It annoyed the shit out of me, the angle they were pushing, but I suppose it was fair enough. It was what the whole country was wondering. I was even wondering it myself. That was a real fear I had: how do I match 2006? How am I going to have four games as good as that again and win an All Ireland? No team had won back-to-back All Irelands in sixteen years. All I had done to that point in 2007 was play one good game, get injured in another, get sent off in two and miss the rest.

But another part of me was confident – and determined – that it would come good for me, that I'd turn it around. The injury would heal. My shoulder would get stronger. I'd get more football into me. I was a championship player. I was a big-game player. They talked about second albums but back when I was growing up, mixing tapes and listening to Atlantic 252, Oasis were the main men. That scene in Father Ted where Father Damo asks Dougal, "Which one do you prefer? Oasis or Blur?" Well, I was Oasis. That season Ric and the Tigers won the Superleague, all you heard on the radio were hits from their second album. Wonderwall. Roll With It. Don't Look Back in Anger. Champagne Supernova. *Someday you will find me...!*
Classic after classic.

Well, the league was over. No point in looking back in anger. Just roll with it. We'd see then where that would lead me and where you might find me.

'For those who persist with their Second Season Syndrome drivel, they need only look at Donaghy's performance. He kicked two great points, went through an amount of ball and was top class. The Kingdom Munster Final Rating: 8'

OVER the years there were basically two kinds of matches we'd have against Cork in Killarney. One was where they'd be the better side for most of the game but we'd hang in and kick a few late scores to sneak a draw. The second then was we'd be way up midway through the second half, they'd make a huge late rally but we'd squeeze through in the end.

The 2007 Munster final was very much a case of the second. We were six points up and cruising but then Cork came storming back to level it and would have gone ahead in the seventieth minute only a shot of Derek Kavanagh's flashed wide after a slight tug of his jersey by Tomás went unnoticed by the ref.

We went up the field and I got a ball on the loop on the terrace side about forty-five yards out. Marty Morrissey in his commentary was going, *"Into injury time now. Who's got the gumption? Who's going to step up for Kerry? Will it be Donaghy?"* Sure enough, I did, without hesitation, and it curled over the bar. It was just the jolt I needed, to kick the winning score of a big game like that, and it proved I was more than just this big awkward bollix.

The Monaghan defence needed a bit more convincing though, or at least they let on that they did when we met them six weeks later in the All Ireland quarter-final. We were rusty from such a long lay-off while they were battle-hardened from all their scrapes in Ulster and were up for bringing more war to Croke Park.

The Mone brothers were in our faces from the first minute to last, Dessie on Gooch and John Paul on me. They were constantly nudging us, shouldering us in the back, elbowing us in the ribs, standing on our toes – exactly what you'd want from a corner back and full back, basically! John Paul wasn't lacking when it came to the verbals either.

"You're only a fuckin' one-year wonder!"

I was quick enough to hit back, of course. "Yeah? At least I am a one-year wonder! What the fuck have you ever done, only hang off me for the last half hour?!"

We were lucky that day. We were four points down with ten minutes to go but then a ball broke off me for Declan to finish to the net and a late fisted point by Tomás saw us scrape through.

That set up a semi-final against Dublin. My first two days in Croke Park with a Kerry football squad had both been against Dublin: the first as a minor in 2001, then when I was brought along with the seniors for the quarter-final in 2004. Each day lit a fire in me to want to play for Kerry on a stage like that but each day I was just a bit player; a used sub on a losing team, an unused sub the other time. It was like being backstage at a great gig in a big theatre. Now I was getting the chance to be centre stage in front of a packed house. That's where I wanted to be. If you beat Dublin in an All Ireland quarter-final or semi-final, it's as if you played two All Ireland finals that year.

I was being marked by Ross McConnell, another midfielder that had been converted into a full back. After the Monaghan game though, I wasn't going to just stand in there on the square. The ball in to me had been atrocious that day (it's been the story of my whole career at full forward: when we win, the high ball into Donaghy is a great tactic; when it goes bad, it's terrible!) and besides, McConnell was a giant of a man; my mobility was better than his so I made use of it. I hardly stood under a high ball inside that day; I kept moving about, getting out in front, taking him on, setting up scores.

Then Darragh had to go off with an injury to his hip. All of a sudden the call comes in from Pat: Kieran, out to midfield. Tommy Griffin is on for Darragh but I'm to go out and play as a third midfielder. I haven't played out there for Kerry since the previous year's Munster final but our *fear láidir* is gone.

I start crashing into everybody. Even Ciaran Whelan. Especially Ciaran Whelan. I get on a ball under the Hogan Stand and shoulder into him. Two and a half years earlier in Tralee he had put me on my arse but now I'm the one sending him reeling.

I'm doing whatever it takes to win: I'm fist pumping after big plays, I'm roaring at teammates about where they need to be, about that tackle or run they've just made for the team. In basketball I'm used to that level of constant communicating, only this is a much bigger playing area and there's the hum and the roar of 82,000 people to contend with. Before the end of the game I'm nearly hoarse and worn out from all the shouting, but still there's more to do.

At one point Shane Ryan is charging through. He gives a little feint and rounds me. If he takes another couple of yards he's bearing down on Diarmuid Murphy and it's a possible goal. So I make sure it isn't. I grab the back of his jersey and give away the free.

Years later it would be a black card but in 2007 it's still only a yellow, and I know that: that's why I do that, even though the next day my fingers will still be sore from literally clawing his jersey to prevent a goal. And from then on any time we play Dublin in Croke Park, I'll be the boo-boy of the Hill; I think that's where it starts, with that foul. So be it: just like that free in, it's a price I'm willing to pay.

Dublin come roaring back anyway. With five minutes of normal time to go they're back to within a point. Cluxton comes out from the Hill 16 end, toe-tapping the ball. He edges outside the D, still soloing, looking to see what's on. But what he can't see is me. I'm like a safety in American football, staying low, creeping up from the line of scrimmage. Next thing Declan pushes up on him, Cluxton has to kick the ball and it hops straight to me between the two 65s over by the Cusack side.

Now I'm the one with it, now I'm the one who has to use it well. I see Declan make a run to the corner. But fuckit, that's a forty-yard kick. A twenty-yard curler, that's easy. A thirty-yard curler, that's a tricky one. A forty-yarder, especially when you're that close to the sideline, that's a tough kick, no matter if you go with the outside of the boot or the inside or just kick it straight. I go with the inside of my boot– the percentage play. I kick it high, maybe a bit too high, but Declan takes it into his chest. The ball then goes through six different pairs of hands and over to the Hogan Stand side before Seán O'Sullivan fists it over the bar.

It's a brilliant passage of football, to work a score like that, from one wing to the other, under that pressure, but as it turns out, we have to top even that. Two minutes into injury time Dublin again have it back to a point. Murph bombs it out on top of Darragh who has come back on. Whelan fists it away but it bounces to me. I ride a couple of tackles through the middle and pop it to Darragh. The ball again goes over to the Cusack side. And then we again work the ball over to the Hogan side, this time going through eight pairs of hands, not just six, and this time it's Declan, not Seán, O'Sullivan who slots it over the bar, kicking it off his left on the run. It's a score only a great player, and a great team, could have come up with.

That was one of the great days, the great games, and personally, one of my best performances. I didn't score, I didn't win man of the match, but in terms of the decisions I made, the way I went about trying to influence the game in every little way I could, it's one of the games I'm most proud of.

The final against Cork was the ultimate Can't Lose game. Galvin said it in a team meeting the night before the game; "There's fellas in graveyards all over Kerry that beat Cork their whole careers but if we let Cork beat us tomorrow, it'll be like all their wins over Cork didn't matter. Even if we win the next ten Munster finals it won't make up for it. If Cork win the first All Ireland final between the counties, they'll have it over us forever. A hundred years of our history is riding on this."

That's probably why the first half was so edgy, the only difference between the sides being a goal from Gooch when, with his back to goal, he flicked a high ball from Séamus Scanlon over Alan Quirke and into the net. But then a minute into the second half, Ger Spillane was going across his own goal with the ball when I stripped him of it. Again, a lot of it comes from the basketball: you're trained to go after the ball. It's not done enough in football: fellas are more interested in slapping and hitting the man's arms, trying to half-foul and half-hurt him, instead of targeting the ball itself. So with my long arms and instincts from the basketball, I knocked the ball out of his hand and suddenly I faced an empty goal.

I couldn't believe all I had to do was just tap into the net. I was expecting Alan Quirke at any moment to come in from my blindside and absolutely kill me. But he never came; he'd gone out towards the sideline for a return pass from Spillane. And so, seconds later, I went celebrating the easiest finish of all time as if it was the greatest goal of all time.

Cork were reeling after that. Ten minutes later Eoin Brosnan went for a point from pretty much the same spot Seán O'Sullivan had against Armagh the year before. Again I went to the far post in case the shot dragged, which it did. I went up with Quirke and Michael Shields for it, got a fist to it, they crashed into each other and I just ran in and half-volleyed into another empty net.

I wheeled off with Gooch on my shoulder to our supporters on the Hill and raised two fingers to them, though I could just as easily have flicked the fingers around to the critics and doubters.

There's a second goal. There's a second All Ireland. There's your second album.

Back up on the steps of the Hogan with Sam, *that's where you will find me.*

CHAPTER 11

DANCING IN THE RAIN

"Life isn't about how to survive the storm, but how to dance in the rain.' If ever a picture was to accompany that line, it would be of Donaghy hugging Quirke. There are lessons there about the joy winning brings, especially after battling through challenges. You'd have thought they'd just won an All Ireland for Kerry. Oh wait – they had'

Pat Price, Evening Echo, March 2008

SIX MONTHS AFTER THAT GOAL CELEBRATION in the 2007 All Ireland final, I was again showing fingers to the terraces. Only this time it was just the one finger and it was in all the papers for all the wrong reasons.

We were a point behind in Castlebar heading into injury time when I went for a point out on the right touchline in front of a stand of 12,000 passionate Mayo fans. But the shot drifted wide at the last second and next thing, this piece of wood flew past me. I turned around in the direction it came from and there was this big old fella dressed up in a St Patrick outfit – the big hat and green cape and all on him – roaring at me, so without thinking, I flashed our patron saint my middle finger.

Earlier on I had been hit in the calf by a fifty cent coin from another section of the crowd, as was our goalie, Diarmuid Murphy. At the time I made light of it, handing the coin over to the umpire and joking that he could buy a packet of crisps with it. But now I'd been nearly hit by some piece of wood (a wooden spoon belonging to St Patrick that he used for his bodhrán, though he'd later claim some young fellas had taken and thrown it, something he'd condemn), just kicked a wide, and we were about to lose a second league game in the space of a month by a point.

I didn't think of St Patrick again once I arrived back in the dressing room but I was still so thick afterwards, I left the phone off until myself and Micheál Quirke stopped off in his car for something to eat in Gort. When I turned it back on, it was nearly melting with messages.

"I know, man," Micheál winced from across the table. "I didn't want to tell you 'til you had cooled off."

Some fella had paused the TV and taken a photo of me

showing my middle finger to the Mayo crowd. And it looked awful.

The following day I was up in Dublin for an Ulster Bank promotion, announcing a three-year sponsorship of the football championship. A great day to be wheeled out in front of the national media. On the stairs I met Timmy McCarthy who was high up in the bank at the time. The same Timmy McCarthy that screams 'DOWNTOWN!' doing the commentary of the Olympic basketball, the same Timmy McCarthy that was a hero of mine when he coached the Tigers to a Superleague back when I was a kid. So I was expecting a bit of love back from one of my main men in a time of need. I was there, all bubbly. "Hey, Timmy!"

Timmy shook the head. "Very disappointed with you yesterday, Kieran."

"Yeah, Timmy, but they fired a piece of wood at me!"

Timmy wasn't having it. "You let an awful lot of people down," he said, and kept walking. So I kept walking. If I had gone down in Timmy's estimation, then the feeling worked both ways after that little interaction.

Timmy wasn't the only person to tut-tut about my actions. I offered a public apology, but the GAA hit me with a one-match ban, ruling me out of our next league match against Laois.

As it turned out, it was a blessing in disguise.

AFTER Rus Bradburd returned to the States in the summer of 2004, I'd keep playing Superleague basketball with the Tigers, as tricky as it was to combine with the football.

The following 2004-2005 season we would build on the league we'd won with Rus by winning our first ever National Cup and reaching the final of the league again.

At the start of 2006 though Jack had really challenged me, telling me I couldn't keep being "half this and half that" and "messing around playing basketball". So after January, I barely played for the Tigers for the rest of that season.

An exception would be made for a midweek local derby against Killarney. Kerry were training on the back pitch in Fitzgerald Stadium and I had asked Jack if I could leave twenty minutes early to play the second half of the basketball game in Tralee. I had been going well and training hard with Kerry so Jack gave the nod.

I grabbed my bag and sprinted to the car. Fitzgerald Stadium to Tralee Sports Complex: estimated time, thirty minutes. I made it in seventeen. Lawless stuff; the old Opel Astra bounced all the way down the old back road. The car park was jammed so I just abandoned the car outside the door and dashed inside, still in my Kerry shorts with my muddy knees. We were nine points down when I arrived but we'd win by three. At least for one more night we could still claim to be the top dogs in Kerry.

That season had been a mad one. In the Irish league so much of your season depends on your Americans. Most years when we dipped into the lucky bag, we were blessed. In 2005-2006 we weren't. The club recruited a 5'9" guard called Eric Bush who'd played for the University of Alabama. He was a good ball handler but too small for the Irish league and wasn't exactly the coolest head or the best teammate.

We were above one night in Killester and he got into a massive running battle with Micheál Quirke. At the time Micheál was the best big man in the league, Irish or American. But Eric wasn't passing to him. He kept jacking up his own shot, probably trying to impress his girlfriend in the crowd. So Micheál said, in a fairly measured tone now, "Jesus, Eric, move the ball, man!"

Eric snapped back. "Fuck you!"

Next time down the floor, I passed it to Micheál who made a nice move but his shot went in and out. Bush roared. "Pass me the ball, man!"

Next possession, same story. After that, Eric wouldn't pass it to Micheál. A timeout was called. Micheál challenged Eric if he was intentionally not passing to him. Eric again told him he could fuck off. Next thing Micheál, who has nine inches on Eric, rose from the bench and started pointing the finger. "I tell you now, man, I'll mess you up if you keep talking to me like that."

Eric jumped up. "Alright, man, knock me out! C'mon!"

The rest of us then all hopped up to keep them apart. "Hey, guys, relax!"

Killester would blow us out of it and afterwards Micheál was prowling around the dressing room like a tiger waiting for a lump of meat. But Bush never came in. He had headed straight off with his girlfriend.

When the club chairman Terry O'Brien and the committee met on the Monday night, they decided that Eric should be withheld a week's wages for his misconduct. I called over to the apartment where Eric and the other professionals were living. Luke O'Hea, our Bosman, answered the door. I asked how Eric was.

Not good, Luke said. Eric had been sulking and drinking ever since he'd got back from Dublin. He's lost the plot.

I went into the living room. Eric was there slumped in his seat, playing PlayStation with a big spliff on the arm of his sofa.

"C'mon, Eric, man," I said. "The rest of us are going down to the Brandon. We'll lift some weights, have a swim, go into the Jacuzzi. You'll feel better."

Eric though had a different evening in mind. He held up the two items in his hand and declared, "Man, the heaviest thing I'm going to lift today is this joint and this control pad!"

So when he put it like that, we left it at that and went on without him.

When we got back, his mood was darker. Again I tried to reason with him, telling him to cool down, take his punishment, otherwise Terry and the committee would send him home.

But Eric wasn't listening. He was raging.

"Fuck Terry!" he said and went over to the kitchen drawer and pulled out a massive knife. "Tomorrow morning, I'm going down to the Centre and I'm gonna slash the four tyres of that motherfucka's van!"

Terry worked in the local Irish Wheelchair Association Centre and was wheelchair-bound himself.

Eric wasn't finished. "Then I'm gonna slash the four tyres of his wheelchair!"

I looked over at the other boys and they were all trying to contain their laughter. Then Luke gave a nod of the head: Best get the hell out of here, Star.

I'd never see Eric again; the next morning Terry fired him before he ever got a chance to slash any of his eight tyres. The last I heard of Eric, he had been arrested for being in possession of a firearm and some marijuana not long after he'd got out from serving some time for dealing cocaine. I don't know if he's back in prison now or what, but life didn't seem to get any easier for him after he left Tralee.

By the way, you might have been wondering, who and where was our coach during all of that?

Answer: Eric Bush was our player-coach at the time!

That's how crazy things were with the Tigers that season.

There had been some logic to it, though. The previous year we'd won the Cup with another American point guard as our player-coach.

Chris Craig had been recommended to us by Rus after playing at the University of Texas El Paso. He couldn't have worked out any better for us. He was a brilliant point guard while as a coach, he commanded our respect. Even though he was only twenty-three, if Chris told Micheál or one of the other Americans what to do, they'd do it.

Off the court, he was very likeable. He could get quite homesick and would spend hours up in his room writing letters, but every Saturday night after a home game he'd be down in The Greyhound, having a drink and a laugh with everyone else.

Two years after leaving Tralee, Chris was the youngest head coach in American college basketball. Then a Division One team snapped him up as an assistant. Rus and other people who knew their college hoops were saying he was going to be one of the biggest coaches in all of America. He'd a young wife and child. He seemed to have everything going for him. Then it all went wrong.

When Hilary and I married in January 2013, Rus sent some wedding pics on to Chris and other Americans who had played with the Tigers over the years. A few weeks later we got this crazy email back from Chris, telling us to leave our house near the coast and get to the highest ground. A tidal flood was coming and so was the end of the world.

Two years later, on the eve of the tenth anniversary of our Cup final win, Sports Illustrated would run a seven-page feature on poor Chris. It turned out that after an assistant coach of his died from a diabetic seizure, Chris lost all interest in coaching and became obsessed with the Bible and the Book of Revelations. He'd blog that Barack Obama was the Anti-Christ. He'd drive around Texas with a car sprayed in text from the Bible. Then he was taken to a state mental hospital after he was arrested driving to his daughter's school wearing a turban and robe following a big bust-up with his wife. Chris's mother suffered from schizophrenia and now Chris was showing similar symptoms. In September 2016 then he was arrested for threatening to blow up a school, even though his truck had no explosives.

It's hard to believe. An image I'll always have of him is just after we've won that 2005 Cup. It's a picture that made all the papers: I have my hand up for a high-five and Chris with his big grin slaps it furiously. At the time we couldn't be happier. We've won, we're winners, teammates, friends. But then that moment is gone and years later you're reading about him in Sports Illustrated, unable to recognise the man you thought you knew.

In 2007 when we won the Cup again our Americans were Dave Fanning, Wilder Auguste and James Mooney. Dave suffered from vertigo. More than once I'd have to carry him up the stairs to his apartment. It was one of the worst things I've ever had to look at, seeing his legs go from him and him unable to open his eyes. But as a player I'd rate him as one of the best Americans to play in Ireland since the rock stars of the '80s.

Wilder Auguste was an absolute beast inside. James was a

shooter from New York with a father from Clare. When James got married in the States in 2012, I was a groomsman. He's been over to coach at my basketball camp. We're on to each other every week. Some year I can see the Donaghys and Mooneys together in Times Square doing our Christmas shopping. That's how close you become with these fellas. Wins and losses come and go but there are friendships that last forever.

Another great fella was Luke O'Hea. Shit-hot shooter and one hard-nosed Aussie. After we won the Cup in 2005 we were in a bar when some fella by the counter made a comment in the company of his buddies about an American of ours, Roy Smallwood. Roy must have pulled one of their girlfriends or something because your man went, "Fuckin' niggers think they can do whatever they want around here!"

Luke was sitting across, in different company, but the N word pricked his ears.

He raised his voice so your man could hear him. "Sorry, what'd you say about my teammate?"

Your man now was a hardy-enough looking bastard. "I said these niggers think they can do whatever they want."

So Luke stood up. Your man stood up. Luke walked over. Next thing, BAM! Your man just crumbled to the floor. Then Luke turned round and sat back down in his seat, as if he'd just been to the jacks.

That was one of the reasons myself and Micheál still wanted to keep playing Superleague basketball: it exposed you to fellas from different backgrounds that you wouldn't meet by only playing football for your club or county. We were mixing with players who had gone through the college system in the States and had played professionally for years. Roscoe Patterson, and the way he'd take the young Americans – and me – under his wing, making us his famous fried chicken; one of the best teammates I've ever had. Luke O'Hea, Chris Bracey, Antoine Gillespie: model pros.

And we just loved the competition. Going up to Cork and entering a lion's den like the Mardyke Arena where the fanatical UCC Blue Demons supporters would be up in arms, heckling and cursing "fuckin' Donaghy and Quirke!" They hated us! Even in the basketball, that Cork-Kerry rivalry was there. Or we could be above in Ballina for a Cup quarter-final where people were falling out the windows squeezing in to watch the game and a guy in a big ostrich suit would be behind the basket trying to put you off taking a free throw.

Our own gym in Tralee was probably the best of the lot. If we were playing Neptune, Demons, Killester or Killarney, they'd be hanging from the rafters in the Complex. Even when we were on the road in some place like Limerick and there might only be a hundred people in the gym, it didn't matter: a James Mooney three-pointer on the buzzer for the win and we'd jump all over him, that beautiful winning feeling surging right through us again.

When I married Hilary, Micheál was one of my groomsmen. But as much as we'd hang out together after matches with the Tigers or All Irelands with Kerry, our friendship was really forged from all those times we went to battle together and what we'd do for each other to win. I'd be flying around, irritating and talking trash to some American, forgetting that where some of these fellas grew up you could get shot for talking like that. But all the time I had my big Quirkey, minding my back, ready to step in. "Hey, leave him off, man; he's okay." Or four points down with four to go on a Friday night in Neptune and we'd catch each other's eye: *Let's get this done, man.* The amount of scrapes we were in alongside John Teahan and somehow found a way to come on the right side: that formed a bond that is nearly impossible to recreate or equal anyway else or with anyone else.

But one win, one game, stands out from every other. When we're old men we'll still be boring the grandchildren about it.

And to think it wouldn't have happened only for St Patrick and his wooden spoon that day up in Castlebar...

It's not a stretch to offer that no trophy in Irish national league basketball in the last twenty seasons was more influenced by domestic players than last weekend's Superleague finals. There were stages when it could have been Donaghy, Quirke, Teahan and Podge & Rodge on the court. Somehow, they were making it happen. Somehow, they were not going to be denied. With forty seconds remaining, Donaghy needed to skip off the court, ducking behind an advertising placard, to vomit from exhaustion. Talk about giving it your all. Even breakfast.

Pat Price, Evening Echo, March 2008

WHEN Pat O'Shea became Kerry manager, myself and Micheál thought it would make our lives a bit easier, allowing us to play more basketball. Pat had played international and national league basketball himself. He knew how good the game had been for our football and to Kerry football in general with the quick hands and decision-making it gave fellas who played it. But if anything Pat was harder on us than Jack about it.

I can now see it from his side: he was trying to win the county a third All Ireland in a row and here were two of his players putting their bodies at risk every weekend in another sport. By getting suspended for my "provocative gesture" to St Patrick, I was free to play for the Tigers in the last weekend of their season, the Superleague finals, but Pat put serious pressure on Micheál not to play in it. Fair play to Micheál, he had the balls to stand by his decision and opted to play the basketball.

A lot of it was out of loyalty. He knew we hadn't a hope without him. A week out from the finals, our top scorer CJ Hadley broke his index finger and flew home.

Then on the Tuesday night our Bosman point guard, Paris Katsimpas, went over on his ankle in training which meant he was out. With the finals being in the University of Limerick, the club had been able to get Pete Strobl, an American released by Ballina, to play for us since he was going to be in the neighbourhood anyway with his flight home from Shannon. At 6'10" Strobl would help us on the boards but that was about it.

That's where myself and Micheál saw the storm as a chance to dance in the rain. Defensively we'd guard Americans, which helped save our Americans' legs for offence. Offensively we didn't mind letting them take most of the shots. If that kept them happy, that gave us more of a chance to win, and all the two of us wanted was to win. Now with CJ and Paris out, what better chance to show what we could really do on offence?

In the semi-final on the Saturday, we beat Neptune in a real battle. Our other American Chris Jordan stepped up with thirty-one, I had twenty-four and Micheál chipped in with eleven. But then in the final on the Sunday, Chris got into early foul trouble and had to sit out most of the second quarter. At half-time we were nine points down. Then in the third quarter Chris fouled out. That left us down to the bare bones: myself, Micheál, a thirty-eight-year-old Teahan, an American who'd score only three baskets for us, and a young back-up guard called Ger Myles. All this against a Killester side that had already beaten us in the Cup final a couple of months earlier. Almost any other team in the league would have packed up their bags and headed home there and then.

But that's where we brought out every bit of pride and defiance that was in us. Micheál's attitude was that we'd have won that Cup final if he hadn't fouled out. Now here in the league final it wasn't him who had been fouled out. He took the game over, nailing a couple of three-pointers. I drove down the lane to make a reverse layup. Teahan drained two massive shots in the corner. Ger Myles hit a three-pointer. Strobl pulled down some huge rebounds for us. We just all got energy from each other.

We could see their big American, Arnaud Dahi, was tiring from having to guard Micheál. I was pinning down their other American, Michael Bonaparte. With 2:30 to go, I blew past him to give us a two-point lead. Bonaparte came back down and hit a three-pointer but then Micheál went straight back and made a brilliant up-and-under move to put us back up one. Then I got a hand to a shot of Bonaparte's. It came off the rim, I gathered the rebound, was fouled, and knocked down both free-throws, leaving my hand in the air after the second, knowing just how big it was.

Seconds later the buzzer went. The man with the ball, Ger Myles, hurled it up in the air. We'd done it. 66-62. Donaghy on twenty-two points, MVP Quirke on twenty, and Ironman Teahan, another Irishman, our third leading scorer on seven.

I still have that match ball upstairs. It's one of my most precious possessions in sport, just as that embrace I shared with Micheál after the game, grabbing each other's heads, has to be one of the best moments I've had in sport. We fuckin' did it, man. We grinded it out. We found a way.

That final in Limerick would turn out to be our last dance. At the end of 2008 both myself and Micheál would undergo knee surgery. There was only so long we could keep playing the two sports and deep down, we knew there was no way we could top that win. The following summer of 2009 the club withdrew from the Superleague as there weren't enough local players coming up behind us. It's a shame the show couldn't go on forever, but the memories will. We'll always have Limerick.

I PLAYED some of the best football of my career under Pat O'Shea. In 2007 we'd win an All Ireland and I should have won an All Star; then in 2008 I'd win an All Star and we should have won the All Ireland. A lot of teams still didn't know how to cope with me while Pat knew how we could play to get the most of me. He was a great thinker of the game, very tactically astute. To me he was like a basketball coach, which I loved. He had us running sideline plays and everything. Really innovative stuff.

And I loved him in the dressing room before the big games. The way he'd be bouncing around on his toes, clenching his fist, reminding us that we were Kerry; that no matter what was thrown at us, we'd respond because that was our history. You could tell it was a huge honour for him to coach the county and he was able to get across to us about what a privilege it was for us to play for that jersey. He'd ask you to remember who bought you your first pair of boots or who took the first session you ever had down in your club field and how they were connected to what we were doing in Fitzgerald Stadium and Croke Park.

My relationship with Pat was ninety percent positive. But there were times when we didn't see eye to eye.

That summer of 2008 I was continuously struggling with my knee after landing hard on it during a game with the Stacks out in Dingle, rupturing my posterior cruciate ligament. In the lead-up to our opening championship game against Clare, Pat was putting the squeeze on me to train. "Well, Kieran, it's as simple as this: if you can't train, then I'm going to start Tommy Walsh, and if Tommy plays well, you mightn't get back in."

I was like, "Pat, that's fine. I can't play, so if you've to start Tommy or whoever, go ahead. I'm not sitting it out because I want to sit it out. I can't move properly. My knee is like jelly."

I made a big squeeze to play in the Munster final against Cork. But the stability still wasn't there in the knee. I went for a ball in a trial game and the pain shot through me again. *Oh my God, my posterior cruciate is gone and now I'm going to wreck my ACL if I carry on here.*

So I put up the hand. I'm gone – subs. And I hobbled off into the dressing room where I slammed my boots against the wall.

Pat landed in after me. He wasn't having it: he wanted me back out there. I don't know if he thought it was just in my head but he wouldn't relent.

And so for a quiet life, I did as he said. I went back out. The physio looked at it. "Yeah, his day is done." And then I went back in and togged off. But afterwards I was looking at Pat, wondering, *Why are you treating me like I'm a young fella that doesn't want to be here?* I was a Kerry senior footballer. I was hardly trying to dodge training when there was a queue of All Stars on the bench chomping for a starting place.

Cork would beat us in that Munster final but in our next game, a fourth-round qualifier against Monaghan in Croke Park, my knee felt better and Pat brought Tommy into the starting line-up. Right away he clicked inside with me and Gooch. I'd score the goal that ended up being the difference between the sides.

After beating Galway in a classic in the rain, we were up against Cork in the semi-final. They'd beaten us in the Munster final, partly because we switched off at half-time when we were eight points up and partly because they brought on Michael Cussen at full forward. He caused mayhem around our square.

For those couple of years all the talk and all the rage was about teams trying to find a big target man. Nearly every team at some stage tried one at full forward. Dermot Earley played a few games there for Kildare. Dublin experimented with Ciaran Whelan. In Fermanagh you had Liam McBarron, in Mayo, Barry Moran for a while. The same with Vinny Corey in Monaghan, Padraig Clancy in Laois. Almost all of them were natural midfielders, or in the case of Corey, a back. At 6'7" Cussen was about the most effective of them with how he went in that Munster final.

But there was something I had going for me over him and all the others – I was playing for Kerry. The fellas I had who could deliver the right ball into me – Tomás Ó Sé, Paul Galvin, Seán O'Sullivan. The fellas I had to dish it off to – Gooch, Declan, Brossie, and now in 2008, Tommy. Cussen and the others weren't surrounded by players of that class.

In the end it told in that semi-final when we beat Cork in a replay, myself, Tommy and Gooch all scoring a goal over the course of the two games. The only thing was that in the last few minutes of that replay, I had to go to midfield after Cork drew level, scoring 1-6 unanswered. I caught the next kickout and popped it off to Darran who went on a solo along the left wing before passing it across to Gooch for the winning goal. Whatever way I reached back to catch that ball and landed, I felt a nick in my knee and had to hobble off.

It left me with a bad run in to the final against Tyrone. I missed a few weeks of training and had to be heavily strapped to get through our last trial game. But I'd be slow to use that as an excuse. Once that ball was thrown up I didn't feel anything; the adrenaline carried me through. If anything, I was maybe too pumped for it. With all the relatives from Tyrone, a chance to win three in a row and avenge 2003 and 2005: the day I wanted to do most was one of the days I did the least.

In the lead-up we talked a lot about pumping the ball in to Tommy and myself, or the Twin Towers as everyone was describing us at the time. But something I've found with Kerry over the years is that if we obsess about something, then that's all we'll do. If our manager says, "Mind the ball, no turnovers", we'll go out and kick nothing up for grabs; we'll mind it all day. Then if we're told, "Pump it in, pump it in, pump it in," we'll pump it in – blindly. There were times in that first half when myself and Tommy broke to the wing but our half backs would still just lump the ball down the middle, Justin or Joe McMahon would break it, and Ryan McMenamin or Conor Gormley would sweep it up.

Pat told us at half-time to vary it and be less predictable, which we were, but when we went back out, straightaway we conceded a prick of a goal. We'd come back and even go ahead with fifteen minutes to go after Gooch played a quick one-two with me from a free over by the sideline. But then Seán Cavanagh kicked two massive points and Pascal McConnell made that save with his foot from Declan. That's what it hinged on, really; we were a stud away from three All Irelands in a row.

But again, credit to Tyrone. They went up the field and scored the next three points. They won every breaking ball in those last five minutes, probably because they'd seen us win it in 2006 and 2007 and had that bit more hunger. They were the best team in 2005 and they found a way to beat the best team in 2008.

A few years later when I was visiting the relatives in Omagh, I'd learn that Tyrone had sent someone down with a small camera to film what we were at. I cringe now at how naive we were, having our last trial game open to 4,000 Kerry fans; well 3,999 and one Tyrone man with his camera.

Losing hit me hard. I was a smarter, stronger, better all round footballer in 2008 than I was in 2006 and 2007 but I prided myself on being a big-game player and here I was after failing to deliver on the big day. I nearly doubted myself after it.

Then a few weeks later I found myself playing in the Melbourne Cricket Ground, one of the finest stadiums in the world.

Again, there was always another game.

CHAPTER 12

DIFFERENT RULES

AUSTRALIAN TV COMMENTATOR:
So Reilly, whose long kick goes
to full forward... Oh, Donaghy
[with the high catch and mark]!
CO-COMMENTATOR: Ah, the big man! The
banker! Comes back with two big mitts.
COMMENTATOR: What an impact
he'd have in our game!

Seven Network commentary of 2008 International Rules second leg

O F ALL THE THINGS I'D LIKE TO THINK I'VE achieved in my career, playing for Ireland in three different International Rules series is up there. Yet if there was anything better than playing alongside the likes of Stevie McDonnell, Benny Coulter and Tadhg Kennelly, it was celebrating with them. Trying to beat Australia wasn't always fun and games on the pitch but it almost always was off it.

When I think of it, there was something of a partying element to those autumn internationals right from the start.

A few days after Kerry won the 2006 All Ireland final, I got the call from the man I had been constantly compared to that summer. Eoin 'Bomber' Liston was a selector to Seán Boylan, the Irish International Rules manager, and the two of them felt with my ability to win high ball around the square I could cause the Aussies the kind of bother Bomber had in his day.

So the first weekend of that October, I had to go up to Dublin for the final trial game, even though on the Friday night a few of us were playing for Munster under floodlights in a place called Ballyforan in Roscommon.

Looking back, it was madness that we played in both, especially with our game against Connacht having gone into extra time, but this was still a time when a concept like recovery was largely unknown to the GAA world.

It must have been midnight by the time myself and Aidan O'Mahony arrived up at the team hotel. We were still spitting fire over the goal and the trip to Boston for the final that the goalkeeper had cost us, so we said fuckit, we'd go to Copper Face Jacks and let off some steam there.

So, free gat all night in Coppers for the couple of Kerry boys. At about 5.30 we sneak back in to the hotel. A few hours later we're back on a field with fellas chomping at the bit to make this Irish team. Bomber comes over to me.

"Jesus, Bomber, I've a dead leg from last night," I says, bending over, holding my leg so he can't catch the smell of drink off me.

"Yerrah, you'll be fine," he says.

So I'd to play away, marked by Kevin Reilly from Meath, and of course with the chance to take the scalp of the Player of the Year and play for his country, it was all of his All Irelands rolled in to one. He leathered in to me; I don't think I got a touch of the ball. He was a fantastic footballer but he hardly met me at my best that morning.

Still, I got the nod to start in the first leg up in Pearse Stadium in Galway. A Saturday night, under the lights, full house.

I was a marked man from the start. In Aussie Rules they've a specialist role called a tagger. He doesn't care where the ball is; his job is to faceguard you, knock you, push you, hold you, basically frustrate the living shit out of you.

Ryan Crowley was one of the best taggers in the AFL and was hopping off me all night and questioning my sexuality. So I'm there, pushing him back, even not knowing how far I can go. I don't even know the rules of this fuckin' game. Are there red cards in this thing? Can I punch a fella or what's the story?

Stevie McDonnell looks over at me. Stevie is well familiar with this game and its rules, and that, basically, there are hardly any.

"Donaghy! Throw a punch into that fella!"

Crowley hits me again. I feel like I'm fifteen back in Tarbert. I swing back the elbow but your man deflects it and belts into me again, goading me.

Next thing, Stevie just jogs across and with this sweetest short right hand, hits your man right in his big mouth.

Crowley's spitting blood and fire.

"Listen," says I, "just play the football now, boy, and never mind the bullshit."

"No fuckin' way!" he roars. "If you think that's going to stop me, you've another thing coming!"

And sure enough, it was worse he got. He hounded me for the rest of the night. Any ball that came near us, he was hanging off me and nothing was being called.

Thankfully, Stevie again had the perfect answer, this time giving it on the scoreboard, kicking three overs in the last quarter. When Joe Bergin got a goal near the end, I got a bit carried away. I went in for a hop ball with Barry Hall, the baddest man in the whole AFL. I was banging off him, talking shit to him. Maybe not a good idea, in retrospect. "You little cunts!" he snarled over. "We're going to sort ye out next week!" In hindsight, that wasn't an empty threat.

"Yerrah, yeah! Bring it on, boy!"

That night we went on a massive bender in Galway. All the team and all the girlfriends were out, buzzing with the eight-point lead we'd be bringing into the second leg in Croker.

At the end of that week we all met back up in the City West Hotel. I was looking forward to the game on the Sunday: 82,000 again in Croker, only this time with them all shouting for the one team, our country.

Then that Friday evening I was called in to a room by Anthony Tohill, who was one of the selectors, and team captain Kieran McGeeney who informed me that I was one of the three players that wouldn't be on the match-day squad. But I was to stay positive, rest up, and if anyone got injured in the warm-up, I could be in.

I goes, "Alright."

I'm thinking: *Taxi!*

The Sam Maguire is out in Leixlip. A great Kerry supporter, Luke Moriarty, is throwing a bash out there and a good few of the boys are up: Darran, Gooch, Mike Frank.

I pop up to the hotel room. Graham Geraghty is lying on his bed, elbows out, hands cushioning his head, watching TV. Sound fella, and classy player. He sees me slipping out of my tracksuit into a t-shirt and pair of jeans. I tell him the story and he gets a great giggle out of it. You mad hoor, Donaghy!

And off I went, to Leixlip, for another great night.

That Sunday, Barry Hall and his boys were as good as their word in Salthill. Or a lot worse, more like it. I'd to sit and watch my roommate Geraghty get stretchered off unconscious in the first quarter and Marc Ó Sé getting punched around the place by fellas 6'6". I'd have much preferred to have been out there throwing punches myself, telling them to pick on someone their own size, but maybe I was the lucky one. At one stage Galvin came off and sat down after being in some scrape.

"Am I sent off? Am I done now?" he asked out loud.

Someone shouted back. No. He was only gone for the remainder of the quarter; he'd be back in for the next one.

Well, the look on Galvin's face. It was like he was a journeyman wrestler in some school gym after being told there was yet another steel chair to be smashed over his head.

Once he took that bit more punishment, Galvin would call it quits when it came to International Rules, just like Tomás and Gooch the year before. But me, I'd want more.

IF the International Rules brought me somewhat down to earth after winning the All Ireland in 2006, then it would somewhat lift my spirits after losing the finals in 2008 and 2011. Escaping from the coulda, woulda, shoulda speculation and recriminations to instead head to Australia, see my brother Conor and play ball with and against the best players in both countries.

Our first week Down Under in 2008 the AFL and GAA held a function for both teams to try to create a spirit of goodwill and called us both into a room to spell out the lay of the land. There had been no series in 2007 because of the fallout from Croke Park. Things had been so bad that day, Seán Boylan had suggested at half-time that we not go out for the second half. It was made clear to us that if there was any repeat of that it would kill the series for good and no-one would ever get the chance to play for their country again.

The message was received. That 2008 series in my view was the best there ever was between the two countries; they were two very tight games with huge hits and serious tackles but without the hero-fighting crap that ruined the series in 2005 and 2006.

If that 2008 series showcased the game at its best, then it allowed me to see Seán Boylan at his best. What a man. Heading into that series I wasn't just dealing with the pain of losing to Tyrone but also the pain in my knee from a knock I had picked up in the semi-final replay against Cork. When I told Seán about it hobbling around one day, he brought me into this room and dimmed all the lights. "Right, let me have a look at it."

So he started rubbing his fingers around my foot and I'd feel this pop. "Oh, that's good!" he said. "That will get the circulation going now." And on it went, me lying down while he sat there like some Tibetan monk giving a physio session. He rubbed the back of my calf so hard I groaned but then I heard another pop. "Oh, that's very good!" he exclaimed.

After a while he then said, "Right, that will get everything moving now. You'll feel better tomorrow."

I was saying to myself going out the door, *Not a hope, Seán. This thing has been bothering me for the last seven weeks.*

The next day I went out training and felt like a new man.

The first leg of the series was in the Subiaco Oval in Perth. A brilliant setting for a match: a full house of 40,000 people for some Friday night lights football. I was hyped at the thought of playing there from watching the West Coast Eagles on the box over the years go up against the likes of Tadhg with the Sydney Swans; now here I was, on tour with Tadhg, playing in the Subi. I went in for every hop ball, set up a goal for Seán Cavanagh and in the end we got out of there with a one-point win.

We had a great night in Perth, Tadhg having lined up this hopping spot called the Pure Bar for us, but no sooner had we crawled into bed than we were up again having to catch a plane. The second leg was in Melbourne. Looking at the map, I thought *Not a bother, great, we'll be there in two or three hours.* The flight was fuckin' six and a half hours. By the time we got to where we were staying, it was about eleven at night.

We were out in this place called Apollo Bay, well away from the bright lights of Melbourne so we'd properly focus and prepare for the second leg. When we landed there, sure enough it was like a ghost town. But just as we were rounding a corner to go into the hotel, a few of us could see this bar inside. A few winks to some of the boys; say nothing but we could be in luck.

We arrive at the hotel and next thing Seán tells us to stay in and get to bed early, that we've had a long day travelling and need our rest.

I go up to the room with Finian Hanley, a good friend from the bank though he leathered the crap out of me a few months earlier in that famous All Ireland quarter-final with Galway played in a monsoon.

"Jesus, Finian, it's only just after eleven. If we go down there, it might only be for two hours, but it'd be a bit of craic, like."

So Finian's on for it. We have a quick word and wink with Joe McMahon. Joey is someone else who was thumping into me only a few weeks earlier in Croker but we're getting on like a house on fire over here, maybe because we've a connection going back to when we were kids; the two years I lived in Omagh, Joey was in the same class as me.

Now he's in the same bar as me, and Finian; we've just after slipping into our jeans and down the stairs and out the side door after everyone had gone to bed. The place is jumping. We're in our element. The barman learns we're over here playing footie against the best in the AFL and he keeps throwing the drink at us; vodkas and cranberry to beat the band.

The next morning, I drag myself on to the team bus to take us to training. Seán Boylan spots I'm struggling.

"Are you alright, Kieran?"

I rub my head, wincing. "Bloody journey yesterday, Seán, it's taken a lot out of me."

And maybe it's because Seán's from Meath, but karma makes it up to me after having to line out against Kevin Reilly in that trial game two years earlier dying with another hangover.

"Oh, this is only a runaround, Kieran," says Seán. "To get the lactic acid out of the legs. Tell you what, you go back to bed."

So off the bus I get, and as I'm walking off, I look back and see Finian and Joe out the window, sticking the finger at me. You poxy bollix, Donaghy!

Too right, boys. I give them a big grin and wave. *Enjoy your runaround!*

THE second leg in the MCG – that's the Melbourne Cricket Ground – was an unreal experience. Blasting a goal to their net. Kicking another couple of overs. And in the end, helping the team edge the game on the night, 57-53, to bring the Cormac McAnallen trophy back to Ireland.

I missed the 2010 series in Ireland with the Stacks getting to the county final, but in 2011 we were knocked out early, and after the hurt of losing the All Ireland with Kerry, I was all on for another tour Down Under.

Unlike rugby tours, we didn't have court sessions but we had a fining system in which I was Judge Dredd – police, judge, jury and executioner.

No-one was sacred in my eyes. Stevie McDonnell, who'd become the top scorer in International Rules history in that series: Wrong top in training this morning, Stevie. One hundred dollars – oh, that's a sickener!

Bomber Liston: wrong jumper at the function. Forty dollars.

Team trainer, Mickey McGurn: Terrible sunglasses, Mickey.

There was no escaping me. I was the Law. I'd be waiting in the lobby at breakfast for you to hand it over, and if you didn't have it, I'd just send you back up for it, simple as that.

The one person on tour that would really test my ruthless

streak was the president of the GAA. The day before the first test in Melbourne, Tommy Walsh and myself were in the lobby of the Grand Hyatt, waiting around before a debrief session. Next thing, Christy Cooney comes out of the lift in this woolly old Irish tracksuit and ambles over to where the two of us are sitting.

We make the usual small chat. "God, big crowd around down here," says Christy, but whatever way his jocks have gone quare on him, he gives his crotch a fierce scratch. Considering our eyes are at that level, it's hard not to notice but we try our best.

"Ah, yeah, Christy, it is. Say there'll be a good crowd at the game as well."

"Ah, yeah, if the weather holds up, there will," says Christy, giving another massive tug around there.

When he eventually moves on, myself and Tommy look at each other and break down laughing.

A few hours later we're on the bus back from our kickaround in the Etihad Stadium. Time to take the microphone.

"Right, lads, it's fine time…

"Darren Hughes – white and purple boots. Terrible combination. Forty dollars."

Big roar.

"Cads…"

Eoin Cadogan from Cork shoots up his head.

"Cads, wrong shorts again. That's fifty dollars. If you get it wrong once more, that's two hundred dollars! That's three times you've got it wrong already."

Another cheer. Ah, Cads!

Next thing, I pause, and shoot a look at Tommy. Will I nail Cooney or what?

Tommy gives me the nod.

Fuckit, I will so...

"Right, lads, we've a special one here. A really hefty fine. But if you witnessed what Tommy Walsh and myself witnessed this morning sitting on this low seat in the lobby of the hotel you would understand. Christy Cooney came over to us with our eye level at about his mid-section. And well, he proceeded to put on the biggest display of ball-scratching..."

The bus explodes. Even Stephen Cluxton is in stitches. I still haven't looked in the direction of our esteemed president but it's not like I can stop now...

"Lads, the biggest fine of the week has to go to an tUachtarain himself. Two hundred dollars for Christy Cooney!"

I catch him then with my eye and wink. "Sorry, Christy."

When we get back to the hotel, I'm outside the bus, waiting for my fines. First man over to me – Christy Cooney, with $200 in hand for the kitty.

"Ah, very good, Kieran! Very good!" he laughs, wagging his finger and head. "Fair play to you!"

And fair play to you, Christy.

That night in the Etihad we would hammer Australia, 80-36. It was one of their weakest ever line-ups while we had one of our strongest. Anthony Tohill and his assistant Kieran McGeeney tried to sell it to us that the series wasn't over and that after enjoying a good night in Melbourne, it would be heads down and no going out once we hit the Gold Coast to prepare for the second leg. But sure the Gold Coast is the Vegas of Australia; a few of us would take advantage the Monday, Tuesday and even for a few quiet ones on the Wednesday before taking the show off the road on the Thursday with the game on the Friday.

Then we blitzed the Aussies again before hitting the town again. I'd collected $2600 in fines and after bartering with a few bar owners during the week, got a spot where there was free food and drink the following day for our travelling party.

It was one of those evenings when it was just great to be alive. We'd a fierce singsong, with Bomber giving a show-stopping rendition of Leonard Cohen's Hallelujah. I'll take that memory to the grave: my brother Conor, who had popped down from Melbourne for the week to crash in my room and Karl Lacey's, there alongside me, Tadhg and Tommy, watching Bomber belt out each verse and all of us joining in at that stirring crescendo.

...It's a cold and it's a broken HALLELUJAH!
Hallelujah, Hallelujah, Hallelujah, Hallelujah

Back when I was in school, we had a teacher, Èamonn Walsh, who'd bring the TV in on a Friday morning whenever Ireland would be playing Down Under. Then another teacher, Liam Scully, would come in and we'd talk about the various players that had stood out. Anthony Tohill. Kieran McGeeney. Trevor Giles. Ciaran McManus. Ciaran Whelan. Séamus Moynihan.

If Liam or someone had told me back then that I'd follow those names, in that tradition, I'd have said he was off his rocker. But now I'm proud to say I'm part of that. Someone who got to beat the Aussie professionals in their own backyard.

Hallelujah.

CHAPTER 13

WHEN JACK CAME BACK

'Big calls in the week of an All Ireland final have become a staple diet for Jack O'Connor. But this week has provided his biggest conundrum yet. There has been a doubt over Kieran Donaghy's place on the team. It was unthinkable five years ago but now it begs the question: is the big man no longer indispensible?'

Colm Keys, Irish Independent, September 2011

E ARLY AUGUST, 2011 AND I'M IN THE HOUSE when the phone hums with a message.

It's from Jack O'Connor.

Hi Kieran. I'm not sure if you realise it but your place is in serious doubt for the next day. You don't appear to be properly focused at the moment. Constantly late, even for the warm-up in Croke Park the last day. I also told ye to stay away from golf and you didn't. I know you have some promotion duties but the number one priority is winning the All Ireland. The promotions will disappear quickly if that doesn't happen. I'm telling you this while you still have time to get your act together. Jack.

I'm there, *What?!* The last day in Croke Park against Limerick was a prick of a game. Over after twenty minutes. One of those ones where the game just goes dead, boys start soloing up the field, taking too much of it. In the second half there was barely a ball kicked into me; who's going to kick high ball in when you're up ten points?

'Late for the warm-up.' Yeah, by maybe twenty seconds, putting on my runners – after coming straight from the physio.

And as for the golf. The Irish Open was in Killarney last week. My buddie Mark Murphy, a pro on the challenge tour, got an invite to play in it. Jack didn't want us walking around, wasting energy. But Mark had got me tickets. I wanted to see him play. It wasn't like I drove to fuckin' Timbuktu to see it.

I don't even respond to the text.

Next day, another one.

Hi Kieran, name me some place that I can meet you tomorrow evening because I need to talk to you. Jack.

This time I reply.

Whatever suits you, Jack. I have physio from half-six but maybe half-five in the Brandon.

Another one back from Jack. This time more reconciliatory.

Sound. I might have been hard on you in that text. I'm leaving nothing to chance in trying to win this thing. Talk tomorrow. Jack.

I know, Jack. Me too. See you tomorrow.

And in many ways that little exchange after the 2011 All Ireland quarter-final sort of summed up our relationship his second time around. There was still a fondness and respect for each other but this time there was a doubt.

And while we'd nearly always give each other the benefit of that doubt, it just wasn't quite the same as what we once had.

A FEW months after the re-appointment of Jack as manager, there was another team holiday on the back of reaching the 2008 final under Pat. That was the great thing about a holiday like that one in the Bahamas; if you weren't celebrating winning an All Ireland, it was a great way to get over losing one.

A lot of the craic came from getting fellas out of jams and sometimes getting them into some.

After the 2006 All Ireland we were in Australia. One morning we were supposed to go to the zoo with the girls when I met Darragh, Éamonn and Galvin in the hotel lobby. They said to tell Hilary that we were going for a run first, but while I was up in the room, to bring a few quid. So I come back down, fifty dollars in the pocket of my Kerry shorts. The lads have ordered a taxi, and I'm guessing something's up, but they're still talking about going for this run. So we're going around Sydney in this cab for about twenty minutes when at a traffic light I cop the driver beside me is doing a lap of the place.

"Hey, man, we passed here ten minutes ago!"

I hear a few seatbelts pop in the back seat. Jesus, the boys are trying to leave the rookie here with the thirty dollars for the cab! But I'm on to it and just as the boys are probably nudging and winking at each other, I'm off, bolting up through Kings Cross.

I'd look back and see Paul and Éamonn running behind me, breaking their holes laughing, knowing Darragh was the one stuck last in the taxi.

We'd shoot into some bar and take up this table by the window. A little later then we'd see Darragh jogging up to the crossroads, winded, hands on his hips. Where the fuck have the boys gone?

But after leaving *an feàr laìdir* sweat a little longer, we'd put him out of his agony, tap the window and then slag him how late he was onto that breaking ball.

The holiday in the Bahamas at the end of '08 was a mighty trip. We were staying in a lovely resort called Atlantis Paradise Island. One night we wandered over the bridge, just the lads, and came across this strip of shanty bars.

So we go on a bit of a crawl and start tearing into what the locals call Bahama Mamas. And Oh Mama, they're pure rocket fuel. By the fifteenth bar, the county board rep, Mike 'Larkin' McCarthy, is on a table belting out The Town I Loved So Well, the locals looking on, not knowing what to make of us.

We don't want to stop now; we want to keep the night going. We hear about this nightclub. So we head on down, a bunch of white paddies, to find the queue is all black, waiting to go through this police scanner checking for guns and knives.

We're well on it now. I've been drinking with Micheál Quirke since I was nineteen and have never even seen the big man wobble. But just after we've gone through the security check and are walking up this ramp to the main door, Micheál collapses. Timber! I reach down to pick him up, and what's better, one of the bouncers helps me and escorts him in! After that, he's a new man, giving it loads on the dance floor, pointing and swaying from side to side, getting down, getting low.

To the window, to the wall!

We're the only white guys in there; the rest of the club, all you can see is eyes and teeth. And some of the locals have a problem with that mix. I'm up at the bar when one of the young lads shoots over. "Some fella is after telling Gooch, 'Get out of here, you cracker.'" We all know that's a racist term. Next thing Quirke is nose to nose with the next biggest fella in the club. Tommy Walsh, about the most sober of us, taps my shoulder. "We're all dead if this goes down."

So we usher Micheál away and start rounding up the boys. We try to make our departure look as breezy as possible, nodding thanks to the bouncers, as if we're coming out of a club in Tralee. But when we get outside there's still three or four of them following us, menacingly. There's not a taxi to be seen. How the fuck are we going to get out of here?

Next thing, this guy in a roofless jeep pulls up. The only seats are at the front but he has an open trailer at the back so I leap in, throw him twenty bucks. Atlantis! Get the fuck out of Dodge!

Boys are piling in on top of each other, even as your man starts to pull away. He speeds up and we're off when I look back and see Declan O'Sullivan bounding out of the nightclub.

I'm banging on the side of the door. "We have to go back!" Declan's the worst fella to leave behind because he could turn round to ten of them and say, "C'mon so!"

Your man makes it clear: We're not going back!

So we keep going, high-tailing it out of there like something from Mad Max, hoping Declan is somehow alive, when just as we're approaching Paradise Island this pick-up jeep with two girls at the front whizzes past. And swinging out of the back window is one Declan O'Sullivan, yelling and punching the air. Not just alive, but back before all of us, and with another story to help us through the hard winter's training that will await us when we return home to Jack.

'Donaghy's career to date barely extends beyond a wet week and he has produced just a few months of excellence as a Gaelic footballer. Other than that, he exists as some sort of media creation and in 2008 and 2009 he has been as relevant and productive as Frankenstein's monster. Jack O'Connor's monster, in truth. He has yet to become a real, live, Gaelic footballer.'

Liam Hayes, Sunday Tribune, July 2009

THE first few months back with Jack, it seemed like we just picked up from where we'd left off with him in 2006. The league of 2009 was one of the best I've had. Goals against Galway and Westmeath. A big performance in a tight game against Mayo. An equalising point off Denis Bastick up in Parnell Park after we'd been seven down to the Dubs. In the final then against

Derry in Croke Park I played very well when switched to mid-field and played the ball in for Donncha Walsh's winning goal.

But in that game I broke a metatarsal bone in my foot. That was me out for ten weeks. Then the team were well beaten in a replay down in Páirc Uí Chaoimh.

I was back for our first qualifier, above in Longford. The opening thirty minutes, it was just like 2006 against them. Myself, Gooch and Tommy were causing absolute wreck inside. It's often frustrated me since, the memory of that day, because I don't think we got the blend of small ball and the high ball as perfect ever again. For me it was the ideal way to play when I'm at full forward. Longford couldn't live with it. No-one could have with the ball that was being played in.

Shortly after half-time I went up for another ball from Seán O'Sullivan. Their goalie came out and I tried to flick it over him and their full back. They both fell on my foot. Right away I knew I was in trouble. That was one long, dark bus journey back. I'd my leg spread across the aisle, the foot wrapped in ice, dreading that was me gone for the summer.

On the Monday I was up in the Santry Sports Clinic. The scan confirmed the metatarsal was broken again, just in another place. The screw they'd put in to the bone had bent. The following morning I had surgery. They said it would take likely ten or twelve weeks for the foot to heal. Straightaway I was thinking, *Right. Ten weeks. It's July 13. August 13, September 13, the final is on the 20th. That's basically ten weeks. I could be back to come on in an All Ireland final.* After losing the year before and the way I had played against Tyrone, I wanted to get back there.

So that summer, I didn't give a shit about whether Gooch and

Tomás went drinking and that crisis meeting. All I knew was that the team was still good enough to get to a final. And that I wanted to be an option for Jack if they did.

It wasn't like I could go round saying that though. "Hey, Jack, I'll be back for the final." The team had ended up just about scraping past Longford that day. Jack had enough to be worried about than taking me by the hand and making sure I'd a rehab programme. But lucky for me, we had a trainer that year in Alan O'Sullivan who was willing to go to huge lengths to help me when he saw that I was willing to as well.

It's why that All Ireland medal of 2009 is worth more to me than the ones of 2006 and 2007. Because of all the visits to Santry plaguing Dr John McKenna, all the time wearing the space boot to speed up the healing process, and especially all the work I did with Alan to get on the field for those fifteen minutes against Cork.

The 6am sessions down in the Brandon with him and his stopwatch, bursting my hole on a rowing machine, barking out times.

Down on my knees throwing punches at his boxing pads, again to build up my fitness without putting weight on my foot.

Swimming a length, hopping out, doing twenty push-ups; then back in to the water, another lap, then nineteen push-ups; working all the way down until there was just one length and one push-up to do.

We'd head down to Poll Gorm, a little estuary out by the Tralee Golf Club, at seven in the morning with our dogs. He'd strap a belt on to me to keep me afloat while I jogged in the water up to my neck. He'd be there striding up and down the shore behind me, roaring. "You're slowing down, big guy!

HE CATCH:
hought my time
ith Kerry was up
ntil this catch
the drawn
emi-final against
ayo in 2014

Take that: My goal helped us through an epic semi-final against Mayo after a replay in 2014

Stand and deliver: A goal in front of the huge Cusack Stand helped me win another Celtic Cross

Hill 16 is Kerry only: James was happy with my finish and seeing Hill 16 full of green and gold was a special sight

Total support: With Gooch and Ger Keane. Ger got m through 2014 in many way

u are your people: Sharing a special moment and that winning feeling with my wife, Hilary (left)
d my Uncle Brian (right)

y hello, Sam: A selfie with four of the best,
m Maguire, Marc Ó Sé, Barry John Keane,
d David Moran in front of 20,000 Kerry
s in Denny Street, Tralee

All-Star again: Here with my third All Star, six
years after my second and after the critics had
thought I was a yesterday's man

Last rites: With Austin Stacks late president Fr Michael Galvin after losing the 2003 Under-21 county final

Heaven: Winning the senior 2014 county final and eventually getting my hands on a medal I was chasing for 14 years

Ah Bishop, great to finally meet you: With the Bishop Moynihan Cup after beating Mid Kerry in the county final. It had been 20 years since our last county title

Super Rockies: Stacks fans are unique, with a parade before big games. Here they marched into Páirc Uí Chaoimh for the 2014 Munster club final

Charlie's Angels: With Daniel Bohane and cousin and junior C manager Aidan O'Connor, the man who christened me 'Star'

Rain, hail wind or snow: My first day as Kerry captain, we'd beat Dublin in Killarney

Massive honour: I led my team around Croke Park for the semi-final against Tyrone in 2015

That's it: I thought the final in 2015 was my last time standing on the sacred sod

Golden girl: My daughter Lola Rose playing with my MVP trophy after the St Brendan's National Intermediate Cup win in January 2016

A Munster final in Killarney: Winning another Munster final in 2016 (left) was great but not the same colour and buzz you'd have playing Cork

Hanging on: We gave it our all in the semi-final against the Dubs in 2016 but were ultimately edged out

ok, Daddy!: Lola Rose was delighted to run about the pitch in Croke Park and I was happy ough to get out there as well to escape the dressing room which was like a morgue

Modern family: With Mom, Sarah and Conor at a Stacks social

Two mothers bless me: The two women who raised me. Nan was the family leader. She died while I was on the field and it hit me har~~

My worl~
Hila~
Lola Ros~
and I~
20~

You're slowing down!" That summer Alan O'Sullivan was my shadow. If I started falling, he was there to push me back up.

And Liam Hayes, with that lazy article which I cut out, drove me on as well; as if I'd done nothing in '08 or in the league, just because of a poor final and then breaking my foot twice.

I'd actually strain my groin in the final moments against Cork, going for a run to shake Derek Kavanagh off. But I stayed on and just kept running, trying to occupy Kavanagh and free up space for the lads. Then Tomás came up the field and kicked the insurance point and that was it. A third All Ireland in four years for me and a third All Ireland in four years for Jack.

2010 was a strange one. For the first time in seven seasons being involved with Kerry, we didn't reach an All Ireland final. We didn't even make the semi-final. On a wet, dour prick of a day, Down ambushed us in the quarter-final.

Earlier that summer we had one of our sweetest wins ever over Cork, beating them by a point in a replay after extra time in Páirc Uí Chaoimh. Gooch played me through for a goal like only he can. Ask all the best forwards in Ireland to fist it twenty-five yards, with their so-called weak hand, into a breeze, over Graham Canty, and straight into a guy's hands in front of goal – nobody else could have put it where he did for me to just catch and roll past Alan Quirke. Then against Down he put two more goal chances on a plate for me, only I fluffed them. There are three days I've felt I let Kerry down badly – the 2008 final, a 2012 Munster semi-final down in Cork, and that day against Down. You can miss one goal chance but not two.

Twelve months later, we'd win our All Ireland quarter-final. A routine win over Limerick. That's when I got that text from Jack about my place being in jeopardy.

I felt he was over-reacting. I wasn't going that bad. I'd played well in the Munster final win against Cork. You couldn't read anything into the quarter-final.

Then I struggled in the semi-final against Mayo. Kicked a good point under the Hogan into the Hill in the first half when we needed a score, but in general play Ger Cafferkey cleaned me. Still, I wasn't going to let that stop me speaking up if I felt there was something that would help the team. A few weeks before the final against Dublin, Jack called a meeting and opened it up to the floor for suggestions about how to improve our preparation. "Throw everything on the table, lads. Hit me. We're all big boys."

So right away I spoke up about something I'd often thought about. In training we'd pick two teams and just play away without any reference to a score or to what time was left. To me that was a big part of the reason we'd lost to Down the year before – well, that and me missing two sitters. With ten minutes to go, we were six points behind and didn't know what we were supposed to do. I remember being out on the field, *We should have practised for this.* We were trying to get it back all at once and just lumping ball in and then they'd break it away and come out with the ball again. If we'd planned for that scenario, we could maybe have looked to work the ball through the lines, chip over a few points, make them feel edgy, then look to hit them for the goal.

It was something that always bothered me about football. "Oh great session tonight, lads, we're playing great stuff!!"

How do you know it's great football when there's no clock, no score and no consequence for a bad decision? How well are we playing when we're behind? How well are we playing when we're ahead?

In the basketball, we were doing that at sixteen with Joey Boylan and the Irish team. Right, you're eight down with 2:30 to go. What do you do?

Press. To the sidelines. No need to shoot three-pointers straightaway and allow our opponents to stretch the lead to ten, twelve points.

Then we'd run that scenario five times, so you could draw on that experience when the situation arose. *That* was preparation.

So I suggest the same to Jack. "Look, Jack, the football is great and all but we don't know what the score is, what's left on the clock. We should, like, have different scenarios."

Well, once that word came out of my mouth, Jack jumped back as if he'd stepped off a footpath and a car had suddenly flown past.

"Huh! Huh! I'll give you a scenario, Donaghy! There were four balls kicked in between yourself and Cafferkey the last day and you won fuck all of them! *There's* a scenario for you now!"

A part of me now laughs thinking back at his response but at the time it was tense. Marc Ó Sé sensed that and jumped in. "Ah, hold on a minute, Jack, we're just trying to get right for the final…" And then it moved on to the usual. Forwards getting in before training to sharpen up their shooting. That sort of thing.

Jack would still pick me for the final – at wing forward. I hadn't played there since 2005. I'd say he was thinking, "Well, where do we put him? We kind of have to have him on. If we drop him, that's one up for the Dubs."

Of all the All Ireland finals I've played in, that 2011 performance is the one I'm most proud of. Jack probably put me out
on the wing so I could get a few early touches and feel my way
into the game, but I just tore into it from the start. Making sure
I got on as much ball as possible. Catching kickouts. Chasing
James McCarthy back up the pitch. I troubled them then when
I went inside. I kicked my best-ever point for Kerry, the one
under the Cusack to level it entering injury time…

But fuckit, we still lost. It still sickens me. With eight minutes
to go we had a four-point lead. In a low-scoring game, it felt
like a comfortable lead. But two things happened. Joe McQuillan missed a double-hop on their 21 that Bryan Sheehan would
have tapped over, and then showed yellow to Ger Brennan for a
tackle on Declan that was a blatant red card. Dublin were kept
in it when they shouldn't have been. And, fair play to them,
they came along and took it and have hardly let it go since.

MAY, 2012 and I'm in the town square in Munich among thousands of other Chelsea fans for the Champions League final
when the phone buzzes again. Fuckit. It's Jack.

We'd a bit of a row last night. After training I told him I was
going to the game; my friend Gerry Rochford had somehow
got me tickets.

"Jesus, I don't know about that, Kieran," said Jack. "The first
round against Tipp is next week."

"Well, Jack, the flight and hotel is all sorted. I won't be drinking,
I'm back on Sunday and we're not training 'til Monday. I won't
be missing anything."

"No, I'm not happy about this. If you go to that fuckin' match, you won't be starting next weekend!"

Well, that kind of made up my mind for me. Whatever it is, whenever someone says I can't do something, I want to do it.

So here he is, ringing me, to find out what I decided to do, and sure by the foreign dial tone, he already knows. I don't even answer.

Five minutes later, Gooch, our captain that year, calls. "Are you in Germany?"

"I am."

"You're dropped for next Sunday, you know that?"

"Erra, he'll calm down. Sure if I didn't tell him, he wouldn't even know I was gone. Look, I've been following Chelsea since I was a kid. If he wants to drop me over going to see them play in a Champions League final, he can fuckin' drop me."

I hang up the phone in a temper. I hadn't planned on drinking, but fuckit, I'm drinking now. I go into the nearest pub and have a few jugs of beer before meeting the lads. Trying to get my head around that I've just been dropped for the first time since I broke onto the team, yet make sure it doesn't spoil being at one of the biggest sporting events in the world.

A little while later I'm buzzing. I've met up with Gerry Rochford's friend, Denis Diggins, a Mayo man who secured us the tickets. We join in with all the Chelsea fans, chanting to the tune of She'll Be Coming Round The Mountain:

There were eleven German bombers in the air
There were eleven German bombers in the air...
...And the RAF of Chelsea shot one down,
The RAF of Chelsea shot one down!

The Bayern crowd just laughed and returned with some fire of their own. It was like that day in Cork on the doss with Martin Courtney, revelling in the opposing fans slagging each other.

But just like I got suspended for that little escapade, I had to be punished for this one as well. Jack carried through on his threat and dropped me for the Tipp game. As far as he was concerned, he had another good reason to. The night before I flew out to witness Didier Drogba put away the penalty that won the Champions League, I had been late for our trial game. And my excuse was like that of a schoolboy's. Only the dog didn't eat my homework. I went one better. The dog had gone missing and I had to go searching for it.

I didn't think it was an excuse though. Two months earlier the old man had passed away. I was now looking after his dog – or at least meant to be when that evening of the A versus B game, Buddy disappeared.

Hilary and myself were in a panic. I rang Mom to come over and help us with our search. We looked everywhere. I searched down by the town park, making sure to still give myself half an hour to get to Killarney and make training just in time. But when I sprinted back to the house, hadn't my mother blocked my car by parking in front of the driveway. And my phone had gone dead. I couldn't call her and couldn't call a taxi.

Eventually Mom returned and I flew off to training as fast as I could. My brain was fried, between worrying about whether we'd find Buddy and the thought of facing Jack.

By the time I arrived into Fitzgerald Stadium, it was nearly half-time in the A versus B. When I approached Jack he couldn't even look at me, and just flung a bib in disgust. It would be Alan O'Sullivan who'd tell me to go full forward for the Bs.

Afterwards the boys all found it hilarious why I had been late but Jack didn't. It's probably why he snapped over the Champions League final.

When I got home from Killarney we'd find Buddy, two doors down, soaking wet; he'd jumped over some fence, got stuck in a bunch of thorns and couldn't get free, the poor thing.

There'd be another sort of reunion the following Sunday in Thurles. Ten minutes into the second half with the team only two points ahead, Jack swallowed some pride and called for me to get ready. So he put the arm around my shoulder and was giving me instructions when some fella in the crowd shouted out in a big Kerry drawl within earshot of both of us about the best line that could be said to Jack and me at that time.

"G'WAN, DROG-BA!"

THERE would be no fairytale end to Jack's second spell the way there was to his first. We would still have some good days that summer; we finally got to beat Tyrone, in a qualifier in Killarney, a huge one for the team, and obviously with the family connection, a huge one for me – oh, the craic Dad would have knocked out of that one. I palmed in a goal in the second half that put us out of reach but what I'll remember most about that day was the sight of our supporters flocking to Mickey Harte as he made his way to their team bus. It was a measure of the respect and regard there was for the man; that no matter how much heartbreak his teams had put us through over the years, everyone felt for him for the loss of his daughter Michaela and the sham trial that had just finished in Mauritius.

A few weeks later up in Croke Park, a new force in Ulster, Donegal, beat us on their way to an All Ireland, another palmed goal of mine near the end proving to be too little too late. Our year was over, and with it, so was Jack's second coming.

Again, that last game summed up just about where we were in his second stint over the team. He'd me playing corner forward that summer. He didn't want to leave me out but he didn't want to have it all revolve around me. And while I would prefer to have been playing at fourteen, I was always going to keep fighting to the death for him and for Kerry.

Do I regret going to Munich? No. I'd do it again. I'd go looking for my dad's dog and be late for training all over again.

But do I blame Jack for dropping me? No. Maybe he felt, "This guy's all over the shop." I don't think I was. I don't think he was right. A couple of months earlier I had played for Kerry two days after my father had died. That showed how committed I was to Kerry. But a part of me actually likes and respects that Jack didn't bow down to me. Making the big, hard calls was part of what made him a great manager. Bringing in Johnny Crowley for the 2004 final. Bringing in Declan ahead of Brossie for the 2006 final. Going with me in 2006.

To me he was the man who gave me my break, and, one weekend apart, stuck with me to the end. I've always had great time and respect for him. Always will.

Who knows, some day we might even catch a Champions League game together.

CHAPTER 14

A MUNSTER FINAL IN KILLARNEY

'We follow the hordes into town. We take our drinks outside, laughing at the fans' banter. "Gooch." "Yerra." "Boy!" "Cadogan." I spend the evening marvelling at their passion – the joy on Kieran Donaghy's face as he races to the dressing room; the pain on Brian Cuthbert's as he contemplates defeat. This is sport as it was meant to be'

Paul Kimmage, Sunday Independent

I WAS FOUR WHEN MY FATHER BROUGHT ME to my first Munster final. It was the 1987 replay, Kerry and Cork, and we were among 50,000 people who squeezed into Fitzgerald Stadium on a warm summer's day. Dad being Dad and maybe me being me, I got to go one better and squeeze onto the actual field after Dad opened up the wire of the fencing, allowing me to slip in and squat down alongside the photographers.

There's an old black-and-white photo on a wall in The Greyhound taken from that day, with a concerned Jack O'Shea hunched over Pat Spillane who had been sent flying into the low stone wall by the pitch, probably by Niall Cahalane. And there, almost within touching distance of Pat and Jacko is me, ignorant of the sheer greatness right in front of me.

Beside that photo in The Greyhound is another picture of that little boy, only now I'm twenty-three, pulling down a ball above Pearse O'Neill and Nicholas Murphy.

It's from the 2006 drawn Munster final, my first championship start against Cork. That was the day that myself and Anthony Lynch got sent off so I was in a bad enough mood after the game but later a few fellas from the Stacks were raving to me about how high I had got up for that catch. That night they texted me to say the TV had missed it, that at the time they were showing some replay instead, but thankfully the moment was captured by a photographer and now it's framed in my mother's house as well.

It's fitting that photos from the Munster final feature prominently on the wall of my favourite pub and inside the door of my mother's home because it's a fixture that holds a special place in my heart. Outside of an All Ireland final or maybe a semi-final against Dublin, there's not another game that gets the juices going like Cork-Kerry in the championship, especially in Killarney.

That's why I'm struggling a bit getting up for this year's Munster final. Yeah, it's on in Killarney, but fuckit, it's not Kerry and Cork.

With about five or six minutes to go in our semi-final against Clare, I was taken off, job done. I sat down on the yellow steps next to where our subs sit to stretch out my legs. In the row above me in the Ard Chomhairle were our former county chairmen and good friends, Seán Walsh and Seán Kelly alongside Taoiseach Enda Kenny. The two Seáns slapped me on the shoulder, saying well played, and then gave me the news from the other semi-final: Cork were seven points down to Tipperary. And for the next while they gave me constant updates from the game in Thurles.

When the lads told me it was over and that Tipp had won, my immediate response was *Fuck ye anyway, Cork.*

Going by all reports Tipp deserved it and the last few weeks we've been saying all the right things and giving the old party line about not underestimating them. But the reality is that as much as Tipp are improving, they're still a year or two from being a real threat. Cork always test us, especially in Killarney.

For my whole career Cork have been a constant. A constant measure of where we are, a constant enemy. You could never befriend a Cork player the way you would a lad from Galway or Donegal or even Tyrone. I'd have got on well enough with Eoin Cadogan playing International Rules but the following summer then we could both be at some press launch of the Munster championship and we'd just about nod at each other.

In those years when we were always playing them in Croke Park as well as in Munster, you'd keep a wide berth from them at things like the All Stars. At some point in the night alright you were bound to cross paths with one of them, maybe heading to the jacks or beside you up on the stage for the photo, and you'd be civil and shake their hand and say well done to them. But that would be about it. Pearse O'Neill and myself hit it off well in those weeks with the Underdogs but once we both broke onto our respective county teams, there was no point in maintaining a friendship when at least three times a year we'd be going to war against each other.

That's the difference between Cork and Kerry and every other rivalry in the GAA – the other crowd are always there, there's no avoiding them. That time I played for Munster up in Crossmaglen, you had Tyrone and Armagh and Donegal fellas hugging each other at the final whistle when only a few months earlier they'd have been clawing at each other. Even then at the height of their powers the Tyrone and Armagh lads couldn't be sure they'd be playing each other the next year, whereas with Kerry and Cork we always did.

It meant at things like the inter-provincials, we weren't able to bring it together like the Ulster lads could. I'd be coming down in the car with our lads cursing a couple of Cork fellas for the loss, while in their car they were probably going, "That wanker Donaghy cost us today." There was always that odd dynamic which might explain why Munster have only won the competition once since 1999.

So much about playing Cork is about pride. There were a good few years there where they should have beaten us in Killarney and we snatched draws in the last second out of nothing else but sheer stubbornness and to maintain our record of not losing to them in championship in Killarney since 1995. Losing to them down in Cork was always a rough day but we'd high tail it out of there, get across the county bounds, lick our wounds and saddle up then for the qualifiers. If we had lost to Cork in Killarney, I don't know if our confidence would have been able to recover enough to come back and make All Ireland semi-finals and finals. That thought definitely got us through more than one game: *Jesus, we can't lose to Cork in Killarney.*

The 2007 All Ireland final was that then and much, much more. My God, I was never more nervous about a match in my life. Thankfully we beat them in that final and again in 2009. But they were a proud bunch of men too and a part of me was glad for them when they finally got over the line and beat Down in the final in 2010. Fellas like Noel O'Leary, Anthony Lynch, Pearse O'Neill, Nicholas Murphy – they deserved their All Ireland medal.

And Graham Canty. Warrior. Hard as nails yet no dirt in him whatsoever. If he could crunch you, he'd crunch you but he wouldn't go out of his way to pull a nasty stroke on you.

I played with him for Ireland in 2008. At one crucial point in the test in the MCG I saw him at the other end of the field leap over a few Aussies to catch a ball and bring it into his chest. It was a huge play for us, inspirational, and I can only imagine how many times he lifted his Cork teammates the same way. He was their leader and we knew that.

I remember in the 2011 Munster final Canty stripped me of the ball and came out with it along the wing. This huge roar went up from the Cork crowd: *Canty's winning his battle with Donaghy, we'll take them today.* But then Anthony Maher tanked him with a shoulder, Canty spilt the ball, Darran played it into me, I kicked it over the bar and suddenly it was our crowd with the big roar. It was a pivotal moment in that game. By getting that hit in on Canty, Maher had hammered the hammer. It sent out the signal: ye might have won yer All Ireland last year, lads, but ye won't beat Kerry in Killarney.

That's the other bummer about this year's Munster final. The crowd won't be half what it would have been had we been playing Cork.

That first Munster final I was at, the crowd was so big, I got lost: one minute Dad could see me and I could see him and the next moment we couldn't. Luckily, he had told me beforehand that if we got split up, to go straight to a Garda and tell them who I was. So I did: "I'm Kieran Donaghy and I'm lost." That's my one vivid memory from that day: walking out of Fitzgerald Stadium, among the throng of supporters, holding my dad's hand.

It'll be a lot harder to lose a child at this year's Munster final, I'd say. If there's twenty thousand at it, we'll be lucky. Again, it's a balls. With this being my last year, I wanted the atmosphere of Kerry-Cork in Killarney one more time and to savour it.

Even the thought of the drive in to Killarney to play Cork in the championship gives me goosebumps. Normally when you're heading in there to play anyone else, there's hardly anyone about. But half-eleven the morning of a Munster championship game against Cork, the town is already buzzing, you're having to weave your car through streams of people on the streets, all of them with the big smile and the thumbs up, knowing they're at something special. But this Munster final, it won't be like that. That buzz won't be there.

A MUNSTER FINAL IN KILLARNEY

It was the same with our semi-final against Clare. You're on a hiding to nothing with games like them. Every year it's the same, whoever it is we're playing: Clare, Waterford, Tipp or Limerick. Beat them well and people say we got nothing out of it, sure that crowd were useless. Win without playing well and people say we're at nothing this year. When I was working in the bank, you'd have people coming up to you at the counter, genuinely annoyed. "What the fuck's going on with ye? How are ye only beating Tipperary by six points?"

Look, it's like as if you were to bring a champion racehorse to the Dingle Races. He looks around and his ears are down; he doesn't want to be there. He's nearly saying to himself, *This is a pain in the bloody hole. I'll beat all these fellas but I've to go through it anyway.*

But then you bring him over to Cheltenham and there's a hundred thousand in the crowd. The ears are pricked. He's thinking, *Here we go, I'll have a bit of this, I'm ready to go.* The gun goes off and the horse is out of the blocks like a shot.

A Munster championship game against anyone but Cork is the Dingle Races. Even some of the All Ireland quarter-finals we've had – Limerick in 2011, Cavan in 2013 – Dingle Races. But Dublin or Mayo in Croke Park, or seeing that sea of red of Cork flood in to Killarney for a Munster final – that's Cheltenham to us, that pricks our ears. When the ball is thrown in, there's a roar from the crowd like the cheer that goes up for the first race on a Tuesday in Cheltenham, and we're bolting out to win it. You don't get that for any other game in Munster.

We actually went about our business very professionally against Clare. I'd say we were happier with our performance than eighty percent of those games we have in Munster against everybody but Cork. Clare had won the Division Three league final up in Croke Park so we made a big deal of that to make sure we'd the proper focus.

I was happy with my own performance. I was marking Gary Brennan and being up against a racehorse like him, that pricked my ears. I'd to do my homework on him otherwise he was the type of player that could have roasted me; he did it before in a challenge game between Clare and the Stacks two years ago when we were getting ready for our All Ireland club semi-final. I rang Anthony Maher who marked him when Kerry last played Clare in championship. Basically the gist of the message was to thunder into him from the start, beat him to the first few kickouts and see how he responds.

The Saturday morning before the game then, I got out the laptop at home and over breakfast watched some video of him for a couple of hours that our analysis lads, Paudie McCarthy and Pat Duffy, had prepared.

I noticed how for kickouts he likes to break out to the wing, and when he's carrying the ball down the left wing, he'll look for you to tackle so he can ride it and cut back in on his right. But I kept him on the outside, step-sliding along without committing myself to a tackle. I was very physical with him then under the high ball, and just dogged him in general. The fewer touches of the ball Gary Brennan had, the tougher it would be for Clare to win and so it proved. I dominated in the air and on kickouts. Éamonn wasn't slapping me high-fives or anything afterwards but I could tell he was pleased with how I played.

The only thing is my knee has been at me. I jarred it in the trial game last Saturday and had to ice it constantly over the weekend as I was barely able to bend the thing.

Turns out it's a nick in my cartilage that's caused all the fluid to build up around the knee joint.

I go over to Tralee General Hospital where Dr John Rice drains about twenty millilitres of yellow puss out of the knee. I'm generally good with pain but Jesus, this is like an electric shock you'd get touching a farm wire, only more prolonged. But I grit the teeth and get through it, knowing it could have been a lot worse if I had kept training on Tuesday night and done real damage to the knee. I'll be fine for Sunday, thank God.

WE got through that alright. I won't say the team or I set the world alight but we played well enough. I won any kickout that came my way and my man didn't really influence the game. Ten minutes after half-time I won a ball under the crossbar, we were fouled and in that break of play Éamonn took me off. He'd tell me later that he felt I was starting to look leggy, and sure when he had someone like David Moran to bring on, you could hardly blame him for making the change.

We were seven points up at that stage, well in control, and we'd go on to win by ten.

We'd go out again that night. Kieran O'Leary has opened a new bar called the K-Town and he kindly put on a feed of drink for us down there. On the Monday then Marc Ó Sé joined Gooch and myself in Killarney. I was delighted Marc came in. For the first time that I can remember he didn't get any game time in a championship match and it would have hit him hard. He could have sulked and stayed at home but I think it was good for him to be out with teammates afterwards.

I didn't go into his situation with him then with drink in us, but on Tuesday I rang him to say I'd bring him to training later that evening. My nan used to say that if you have some straight talking to do with someone, have the chat in the car because they can't go anywhere. So I reminded Marc that I was in his position after the All Ireland quarter-final against Galway in 2014 but it turned for me.

In fairness to Marc, he totally agreed with me. He'll have his chat with Éamonn and whatever comes out of it, he'll keep with it, work hard and be ready when his chance comes. The other option is to quit and you don't play for fifteen years at the top if you're the kind to just quit.

He's like me. He wants to go out with another Celtic Cross in the pocket. And he can see where the team is at. We could have done with a tougher test in Munster and we're not playing out of our skins but we're coming along nicely with still loads to work on. Nobody is talking about us really. People are saying we can't beat Dublin but within the group there's a sneaky confidence that if our paths cross that we can turn them over.

For a Kerry footballer a game like that is Cheltenham. The ears will be pricked for that one.

CHAPTER 15

YESTERDAY'S MAN

'The hunger that drove this extraordinary young man from nowhere to superstardom disappeared as soon as he became 'Star'. He took his eye off the ball. He is just 31, but his career was over long ago. At the end of 2007 he seemed the natural heir to the legendary Eoin Liston. Sadly two years does not make a Bomber'

Joe Brolly, 'Catch A Fallen Star, Put Him In Your Pocket', June 2014

I'M SITTING IN THE CUSHIEST DUGOUT IN THE country, on one of those nice Recaro seats in the Hogan Stand, but the last thing I am right now is comfortable, warming my arse on it.

It's the August bank holiday weekend, which basically translates as All Ireland quarter-final time if you've spent ten years on the Kerry senior panel. This year, 2014, it's Galway we're playing. The game is in the melting pot. I haven't felt as physically good in a year. And still I'm stuck on this seat.

After five minutes Bryan Sheehan had to come off with a hip injury. Bryan was playing at midfield. In training I've been playing mostly at midfield. But David Moran got the nod, and rightly so. Then after half-time they started to bring in more subs, mostly in the forwards, where I can still play. Galway got a goal there which has brought the game into Oh, Shit territory and that's a place I've always felt I can help the team through. So I'm glancing at the clock, itching in my seat, telling myself to stay focused, positive and be ready for battle.

Eventually, on fifty-eight minutes, I see Éamonn turning away from the pitch and looking up towards us and mouthing the word "Kieran!"

I spring up.

And then I see Kieran O'Leary, our captain that year, flying down the steps.

I sink back into my seat. It dawns on me: I'm not going to play today. And in those remaining minutes, as the team steer safely to a four-point win, I'm there feeling that this is the end. The game isn't over, the season isn't over, but my inter-county career is.

The final whistle goes, a satisfied cheer goes up from our

crowd, and I rise from my seat. On my way down to the tunnel, I become aware of how fresh and dry the jersey still feels on my skin. It's a new sensation for me, the first time since the 2005 All Ireland final that I've been up here, available for selection, and never even broken sweat. No need to shower today, so I don't. The rest of the lads are all giddy and upbeat after the win but I just want to get out of the place.

I walk alone along the underground of the Cusack Stand. There's a gap there as it meets the Canal End, a sort of diagonal tunnel which the likes of the Artane Boys Band come out through. I look out: the second game is on now, Mayo and Cork. And as I stand and watch, I think of all the days I had out there on that patch of grass. All the wins and joy, even the defeats and pain; at least I was out there. The thrill and the comfort of being out there with Darragh Ó Sé, knowing that if there was a ball about to be kicked out, he'd probably catch it. Or if he didn't, Paul Galvin was going to be underneath it. And right there, even though it's Aidan O'Shea and Aidan Walsh that are playing at that moment, it's Paul I see with the ball. He's turning, looking to kick it into Gooch, knowing Gooch is making his run out towards the D. But then Gooch loops around his man and Paul hits him with this little dink pass. That's when I make my run, backdoor. Gooch plays a little one-two with me and it's another score, another win, for Kerry, something I thought would last forever.

But Gooch is injured for the year. Paul finished up at the start of the year. Now it seems I'm finished as well.

Maybe that's how it should be. This is a new team. A new breed of player. All these younger fellas can do twenty chin-ups and bench press huge numbers; they love their gym. I'm from the old school. I started out under the wing of Darragh Ó Sé. Darragh would say to me, "Yerrah, never mind the weights. Sure your man can bench 100kgs but he'd turn his hole to a fifty-fifty ball." Darragh would do the minimum. He'd go in at the start of the year and lift 60kgs, and a month later when we'd be asked to do it, he'd still be at just 60. He wasn't looking for the gym, the gym had to go looking for him, and most of my career I've been the same.

I turn around and make my way to the lifts to get over to the team bus over in Jury's Croke Park. When it reaches level two, the door opens and who do I see to my right only metres away but Darragh. He's talking to someone, probably after doing some media work. But I don't want him to see me. I don't want to talk to him. Because I know it'd be just as awkward for him as it would be for me. I pull back for a moment, take a few breaths and then walk straight towards the main Ard Chomhairle exit.

Just as I walk out the glass doors, a woman with her kids smiles and holds up a camera. "Any chance, Kieran?"

I put on a brave face. "No problem."

"Oh, thanks a million. Well done today. Well played."

When I haven't even played. I don't know if they're even aware of that, but I painfully am.

I head straight over to the bus and dump the bag in my usual seat, second last on the left. For seven years I sat here beside Séamus Scanlon. Tough Guy we called him. When you marked him in training, you were guaranteed an elbow into the face, not because he was awkward as he'd let on but because he was just ruthless.

So now I'm sitting there on our old seats, thinking of the times when I'd slap him on the leg when the upper stands of Croker would come into view – "There it is, Tough Guy!" – and our hearts would quicken.

But now, sitting alone on this bus right across from that same stadium, the heart is low. All I seem to have are memories of past teammates and past games. There was nothing for me today. There seems nothing for me now in the future. At home in the sunroom that I've converted into a gym I've raged against what the likes of Joe Brolly have written about me but now it seems like they're right.

THE groin first started giving trouble up in Omagh at the end of the 2013 league. It was a match we had to win to stay up and we did, playing brilliant stuff in the first half; by half-time we were eleven points ahead. That was the year Gooch won his All Star from centre forward and that day he gave the greatest preview show, spraying in terrific ball, while I was buzzing, kicking three points before Mickey Harte got his team back into the dressing room. But with a few minutes to go and us just about holding off a huge surge from Tyrone, I felt this stabbing pain at the top of my right leg.

I went to Santry for a scan but nothing really showed up. We all just agreed that resting up for a few weeks was best. But my first night back training, about three weeks out from championship, I dropped to my knees taking my first shot at the posts. It was again as if someone had knifed me, only this time the pain had moved up to around my hip-flexor and into my lower stomach. After that I'd to take anti-inflammatory tablets – difene – every morning and every night to get through the season.

I'd still start the first round of the championship, against Tipp, and the next day as well, against Waterford. I felt I was going well and even with the groin I was hopping at the thought of playing Cork in a Munster final in Killarney.

The Thursday morning before the game, Éamonn was on the phone, wanting to meet somewhere quiet in town for a coffee. I was on for that. It would be good to have a chat about my role on Sunday.

So I leave the bank, stroll in to the Abbey Gate Hotel and sit down, when I notice Éamonn is more reserved than usual. Then he lands me with it.

"Kieran, this isn't easy for me, but bad news. You're not starting on Sunday. We're going with Darran inside."

It was such a shock, I started off pleading a case for myself. "What?! It's a Munster final! I won't let you down." But then it hit me: *What I am doing? The man's mind is made up.* We spoke for a few minutes about what my role could be when I came on, but that was about it.

I went back to work in a daze. Every time someone asked me at the counter about the game, I changed the subject. I took the next day off work altogether. With the team in the paper, I just couldn't hack fielding questions on why I had been dropped.

I'd come on after half-time against Cork and, with James O'Donoghue out injured, started the All Ireland quarter-final against Cavan. But when James was back fit for the semi-final against Dublin, I was the one to make way.

So there I was, sitting on one of those Recaro seats, looking at that blue wave on Hill 16, chanting for their boys in blue, and just wanting to quieten them. Midway through the second half, I got the call. The game was right in the balance, just one point in it, ebbing to and fro; epic stuff. But the two or three balls that came in towards me were broken away and then Dublin broke away in the last few minutes for a couple of goals. Kerry once more on the wrong side of a classic.

In general the team came in for a lot of praise but not me or the high ball.

A few days later I got a call from my Uncle Brian, saying one of the local radio programmes was going on about how the long ball game was gone and how Kerry shouldn't be using it anymore. I was yesterday's man.

That following winter I nearly thought as much myself. The club got back to another county final but by then my leg was in bits. The difene had become basically ineffective. The pitches were getting softer and softer which was demanding more of my hip flexor and groin and lower abdominal area, so the pain was getting worse and worse.

The Crokes would hammer us in that county final. Two weeks later we lost the county league final to our town rivals Kerins O'Rahillys. After that game I was frightened; I was moving around the dressing room like an eighty-year-old man. I had to hold my leg and swing it forward. When I got to the house, I had to ring Hilary for her to help pull me out of the car.

Again I hoped rest would be the answer. For the next two months I put the feet up, stayed off the tablets, and enjoyed myself. Hilary and I had just moved in to our new dream house and the pain had settled. I did a couple of weeks in the gym by myself, felt fine. But then my first night back training with the team in Killarney I broke down again.

On the way home in the car I had to pull over at the side of the road. I couldn't concentrate. My playing career looked over.

I'd thought that I could still help the team but now it looked as if the body could no longer help me.

After a couple of deep breaths, I drove on, then took a few more in the driveway before going in to Hilary. We talked. Then the next day I talked to our team physios, Ger Keane and Eddie Hartnett. Within days I was down in Cork to Dr Éanna Falvey, the highly-respected team doctor of the Irish rugby team, in his practice in the Elysian.

Éanna diagnosed it as Osteitis Pubis, something very hard to detect in CT or MRI scans. He then spoke to Ger and Eddie and Enda King up in Santry. It all made sense then. There was hope and a plan then.

So that January I'm up at 6.15 most mornings, to be out in Castleisland with Ger for seven, first doing some gym work inside to strengthen my core and then out to the racetrack. It's dim and it's freezing and the rain is pelting down. I can hear the drops hitting off Ger's umbrella and jacket as he stands there with his phone out, keeping an eye on my times, and more importantly, my technique. I've had to learn a new way to run to ease the pressure on my groin; to get my glutes firing, I've to lift my knee more, almost like I'm marching more than running.

"Okay, Kieran, go at seventy percent."

"Okay, Kieran, technique was very good there for the first two hundred, went away from it then. Keep lifting that knee."

The mornings when I'm not out with Ger, I'm in the Brandon, stretching and doing water resistance work in the pool.

I'm doing this for about six weeks, all the time with a view to getting back for the last couple of league games.

But fuckit, it's still taking too long. It's still not right. I still can't go full pelt. And one morning I unleash on Ger. I arrive at Castleisland at 6.50 and I'm still there, raging and venting, pacing around his physio table at 8.40 before I have to head to work.

"It's not getting better, Ger! I've had this fuckin' thing for a year now!"

That's where Ger comes into his own.

"Okay. So maybe we're not going to be back for the league. We'll move it out now to camp in Portugal. You'll be fine. You'll make it. You're going to be an important player for this team later in the year."

Ger's my saviour. Everywhere else, there are only questions, doubts. You go in when the rest of the group are training and fellas are asking how's the leg and when you'll be back. They don't see any crutches, they can't see any limp, and you can't see any progress. But Ger counters all that doubt with wave after wave of positivity, flooding you with the belief that you'll make it back. If you're on his table all he wants is for you to be off it. So he moves around it, dancing and singing, telling jokes and yarns and laughing at yours as he rubs and laughs away. He radiates good vibes and that rubs off on me.

Ger and Eddie would also give me an exercise that really made a difference. It was basic enough, a sort of pelvic thrust, like a woman would do coming back from giving birth. It really fired the glutes and eased the pressure around the groin and pubic bone area. The only thing was it wasn't the most macho of manoeuvres. I couldn't be doing it in the Brandon so instead I converted the sunroom in the house into a gym, away from any onlooker who'd think Donaghy was away with the fairies.

Portugal was a turning point. I was getting rubs three times a day from Ger and Eddie. Then on the second last day, I brought my boots down to the pitch. The group was down a few bodies from all the knocks and bumps after a testing few days, so I fell in. Felt good. Moved well.

Two weeks later I'd my first game back, with the Stacks. And what happened? I fuckin' dislocated my shoulder. I was in hospital for five hours with two lads trying to put it back in when eventually I just said, "Lads, take me down to surgery and knock me out."

That night after the surgery I just stared at the ceiling. *What am I doing here? What's the point? This just isn't meant to be.* But then it passed. A few days later I was back in with Ger Keane and the lads. I'd be out for another six to eight weeks but Ger kept repeating the message: You'll still be an important player for this team.

So that's what drove me: the likes of Ger's love and then another man's spite. Earlier in the year Joe Brolly had a pop at Kerry when the team had another slow start to the league. How the conveyor belt had stalled, how the production line had run dry. This at a time when James O'Donoghue was coming off winning an All Star and Paul Geaney was now breaking through. I pinned that article to the wall of my sunroom-gym.

Then, the morning before I'd come on towards the end of a hard-fought first-round win in Ennis over Clare, Brolly made it more personal. About how I was a two-year wonder, how soft I'd become and had believed my own hype and no longer had any right to be called 'Star'. Not knowing it was a nickname I was given when I couldn't make my own school team. Not knowing or overlooking the work I did to get back for that All Ireland in 2009 after beating his beloved Derry earlier that year in the league final.

"Distracted?" "Eye off the ball?" For the previous five months

I'd been up at 6.15 in the morning to go to either the pool in the Brandon or the racetrack in Castleisland. At home I was doing these pelvic thrusts. Now he'd given more reason and ammunition to do them. A few days after that Clare game I cut out that article: 'CATCH A FALLEN STAR, PUT HIM IN YOUR POCKET.' And I pinned it beside his earlier one about the Kerry production line. Many is the time that summer that article got me up in the morning and I'd be there, gritting my teeth, thinking, *Joe Brolly, you fuckin' bollix. I'll show you if it's the last thing I do.*

I COULDN'T go out that night after the Galway game. Dealing with strangers asking questions and offering their opinion on what I should do or what I was doing wrong. I went straight home and vented my frustration and fears onto Hilary.

"Fuckit, Hilary, I'm gone."

"You're not gone! You're just back. There's three weeks to the next game. That'll give you more time. They'll need you yet."

That's what people don't see, the support you get from your loved ones. People think the main sacrifice they make is all the time we're apart from each other. But then there's the time when we *are* together and they're hearing you giving out and feeling sorry for yourself. That's what they really have to put up with, and that's what they help you get through.

That night I still couldn't think positively like her. I spent the night turning like a pig on a spit.

I went downstairs, watched some TV, then went back up. At about five o'clock, I finally drifted off.

When I woke up a few hours later, Hilary's attitude was right away up and at them, as always. She made a lovely healthy breakfast and juice for me and then we took the dogs to Banna Strand so the fresh Atlantic air could help clear my head. While the rest of the lads were probably nursing hangovers, I was doing runs and sprints, getting the body and mind right for the battle ahead. I was now up for the fight again. I'd just need to change a few things.

That Tuesday night, I took the old back road to Killarney on the way to training. Just to shake up the routine, change the scenery, and maybe with it, change my luck.

I was one of the first into Fitzgerald Stadium. I still took up my usual spot, the first seat on the right as you come in the door. But this time I tapped more into the mindset of the man who used to sit immediately beside me here: Gally. The way he used to physically prepare himself for training and matches. Foam-rolling, stretching, making sure he was properly warmed up. It wasn't something I'd have religiously done but now it was the road I had to go down.

I was out on the field early, kicking points when I saw Éamonn coming out from the bottom terrace. As he made his way over to me, my heart started to thump. And for a moment I flirted with the idea of fucking him out of it. He'd have known that wouldn't normally be my style and that I must have been really upset about the last day and hopping for the next one. But I didn't. Again, it wouldn't have been my way. Anyway, he knew already by the look I shot him after the game when we went for the cool down in the warm-up room that I wasn't a happy camper.

He explained his reasons for not bringing me on; something

about the mobility of the Galway midfield not being the best match-up for me. I'd like to think I'd have horsed into them and not allowed it to get into a footrace. I said to him I'd been wearing the grass off the sideline the past two summers and that if I couldn't get a game against a team we were expected to beat, how could he have faith in me against the likes of Mayo or Dublin? He assured me that he saw a role for me in the coming weeks. And whatever way he said it, I believed him.

Just before he moved on, I asked him what he wanted me to improve on, anything that would help the team.

"Your tackling," he said.

Right, I nodded. He left. *If it's tackling they want, that's what they'll get.*

All my life I've been a Prove You Wrong person. Dan Nolan telling me I'd fail honours geography. Going to Irish Under-16 trials and being the small fella from the south-west. Jack and the selectors leaving me off the panel for the final in 2004, then the field for the final in 2005. Paul Hearty in 2006. The one-album wonder critics of 2007. Liam 'Frankenstein' Hayes in 2009. Joe Brolly. And now, at least for one night, Éamonn Fitzmaurice and his selectors with their "tackling".

About twenty minutes later, Darran O'Sullivan is coming flying towards me with the ball. I know he's faster than me. But that doesn't mean he'll get by me. I'm able to anticipate things and I've these long arms. Darran comes closer, closer, and then I pounce, knocking the ball cleanly out of his hand.

"Great fuckin' tackle, Kieran!" Éamonn shouts in.

I'm onto the loose ball and drive forward. I see my clubmate Shane O'Callaghan breaking into space and kick the ball down his throat with the outside of my right. And as he pops it over,

I look over towards the management team and nearly feel like giving them the finger. *Well, what did ye think of that?!*

And for the next three weeks, that's how I train. I'm playing mostly with the Bs but we're regularly beating the As. And with every win I'm screaming *Yes!* This is preparing the boys for Mayo and I'm ready for Mayo as well. Just give me the word and I'll be bouncing off that cosy Recaro seat.

THE call comes at a time when Mayo have what Jack O'Connor used to call Big Mo. Ten seconds after half-time James kicked a point that put us five points up. But since then they've been playing like men possessed, even though there's only fourteen of them. They're back on level terms, and as I'm on the side-line, doing my final stretches, waiting for the fourth official to put up his board, Donal Vaughan steams through on goal. Peter Crowley clatters into him and it's a penalty. Cillian O'Connor buries it, and as Brian Kelly is picking the ball out of the net, I slip onto the field completely unnoticed while the stadium is vibrating with this incredible roar from the Mayo crowd.

The game is just helter-skelter. I win the first ball that is kicked out to me at midfield which helps settle me but they're still in control. With six minutes to go Andy Moran kicks a point to put them five clear. The Mayo fans are hopping off the roof. I look over and see Aidan O'Shea sticking it to David Moran, in his face, clenching his fist, jumping up and down.

I'm just about going to hit him a belt of a shoulder when I spot our runner, Padraig 'Paco' Corcoran, frantically racing towards me.

"Full forward, Kieran! Get in there and fuckin' fight for it!"

I'm above at the Hill 16 end when he says this. I have to sprint all the way down towards the Davin, and as I finally get there, I feel wrecked. No second wind yet.

The lippy Mayo runner scurries past me as I catch my breath. "You're finished, Donaghy!"

Another subscriber to the Catch A Fallen Star And Put Him In Your Pocket Club. I feel like catching him and putting his narrow arse on my foot and into the stand. But right now I have other business to attend to.

Last night in our team meeting in the Dunboyne Castle Hotel, each player made three promises to the team. It's a little ritual that started before the Munster final, and after the way we blitzed Cork that day, we've kept with it. It's not quite like running a knife across the palm of our hands like blood brothers but it definitely brings your sense of loyalty and obligation to the group to another level. I guaranteed the boys that if I got on that I'd be aggressive in everything I'd do. I'd be vocal, in fellas' faces, win my individual battle and set up scores. Now that promise has to be honoured.

Paul Geaney runs for a nice pass from David Moran out under the Hogan Stand. He turns and floats one in to me, only it's off, going out more towards my right. Doesn't matter; compared to the ball that was lumped into me this time last year against Dublin, it's perfect. I run out to it and jump, every fibre of me screaming *My ball!* Kevin McLoughlin is under it. I grab it over him. When I land, Donal Vaughan has arrived on the scene but between the two of them, they foul me and Bryan taps over the free. I glance at the scoreboard. Mayo 1-16 Kerry 0-15, sixty-seven minutes gone.

About a minute later, David Moran drops his shoulder to evade Séamus O'Shea. Amazingly, at such a crucial time in a huge match, I'm left one on one with Ger Cafferkey. David spots this and floats in this ball that is just the perfect height at just a perfect pace. I break away from Cafferkey. I spot James breaking to my left, ready to go backdoor on Keith Higgins. I sense a panic among them in the square. I pull it down. I pop it to James. Bang! The assassin fires and hits the target.

I run out, punching the air. I see Declan in front of me pumping his fist as well and that fires me up even more. He has no cartilage in his knee yet he's pounding out to the forty-yard line, ready to die for another breaking ball.

Mayo go back up the field and work the ball into a shooting position. But their corner back, Tom Cunniffe, is the man who shoots and he pulls it wide. I start breathing again.

We come down the field with the ball. Marc keeps the ball in play along the endline, managing to find Fíonn Fitzgerald. Fíonn passes it off to Kieran O'Leary and Kieran nails about the best pressure kick I've ever seen.

A little later Séamus O'Shea catches a long-range free of Sheehan's under the bar. The final whistle sounds. Mayo have survived. We've survived. We'll both go to war again next week.

I hug teammates and shake hands with opponents. One of them is Aidan O'Shea. I haven't forgotten his goading of David Moran. Aidan is more talented and higher-profile than his brother who just made the last catch of the game, but when I clasp his hand, I look him dead in the eye. "Well done, Séamus."

He looks back, confused, as if to say, "I'm Aidan!"

But I've already moved on. I've to get ready for Limerick.

CHAPTER 16

GUESS WHO'S BACK?

'Kieran Donaghy blazed the ball into the crowd at the final whistle. It was as if the big man was releasing three seasons of frustration. You can analyse this all day but in the end Kerry had Donaghy and Mayo didn't. There has never been a player like him to turn a game in the blink of an eye and there may never be another'

Karl O'Kane, The Star

THE MORNING AFTER THE DRAWN GAME, Éamonn rang while I was in work.

"Just so you know, we're going with you from the start the next day."

Mayo hadn't dealt well with me in the drawn game. They tended not to deal well with the high ball in general, at least against Kerry. This was the way he wanted to go. We were going for it. I wouldn't be named in the team and Mayo wouldn't know until the warm-up but he was giving me the heads up right away.

It surprised me. The night before I had said to Hilary that I was sure he'd go with the same starting fifteen and would probably be right to. The lads had been four points up at half-time. Start me and there mightn't be the same impact from the bench. When Éamonn called to say I was in, I nearly said to him, "Are you sure?" It was almost the complete opposite of our brief meeting before the previous year's Munster final.

A part of me was hugely nervous. It was like 2006 all over again, going into the Longford game, the Armagh game. *Jesus Christ, if this doesn't work...* But another – a bigger – part of me was delighted. It was the first time in two years, since the 2012 quarter-final against Donegal, that I was starting a big game for Kerry. I had been through a lot since then. Injury, defeat, dropped, forgotten. This opportunity is why I had stuck with it. To make good on those words Ger Keane would keep saying to me on the racetrack and physio table out in Castleisland. *You'll be an important player for this team yet.*

It was a stressful enough week. There was that element of fear there. But over the years I've found that I play my best when there's a certain degree of fear there. And any excess fear I might have had vanished with the faith Éamonn was showing in his decision and me. He felt very strongly about this call. "This is the way we're going, lads. Get it into him."

It had been a long time since I had heard that. Not since 2009, probably. When I had been at my best, I had been basically our Plan A: I knew the ball was coming all the time. Then when I broke the metatarsal and was out injured, Tommy took over my role – but in a different way. He could do things I couldn't do – run out, take on his man, take a few solos and stick it in the top corner of the net. We'd have won more All Irelands if he hadn't gone to Australia. But he had to go, and when he did, it was like the management, without maybe even knowing it, wanted me to morph into him. I felt at times we forgot what my strengths were – the ability to win ball over the top and overhead. 'Mind the ball' became the mantra. Lads became obsessed with turn-overs – as in not conceding any. They were thinking, "If I put this in and we don't win it, that's a turnover."

This match was like the old days. I knew the ball would be coming. Mayo were a real footballing county and team like ourselves. They didn't play with three sweepers. Win a ball against any of the northern teams or the Dublin team of recent years and there'd be three or four of them around you when you'd land. Although Ger Cafferkey had cleaned me out in 2011, we were happy to have a one-on-one situation on their square.

We weren't overly-pleased that the replay was in Limerick though. Like Mayo, we'd have preferred to be going back to Croke Park. But once we ran out for our last warm-up, there was just this electricity in the Gaelic Grounds. As we moved from the national anthem to take our positions the electricity surged to tripping point.

KER-RY! KER-RY! KER-RY!

MAY-O! MAY-O! MAY-O!

All of a sudden you realised this was different to being up in Croker in front of 50,000 and the place looking half-empty. This was better. This was special. This was unlike anything we'd known before.

> *'Donaghy took himself to the Ennis Road goal, striding brazenly in behind Robert Hennelly and clacking his studs against the butt of both uprights, like a jungle creature marking his territory. For Ger Cafferkey it must have been like watching a lion begin to circle your tent.'*
>
> **Vincent Hogan, Irish Independent**

IN our team meeting in the Clarion Hotel overlooking the passing River Shannon, the three guarantees I gave my team-mates were I'd be aggressive in attacking the high ball, getting out in front, in my body language.

About twenty minutes in, all that was needed more than ever. In the space of two minutes Mayo hit us for two goals to go seven up. We were in serious, serious Oh Shit territory at that point. It was like that moment against Armagh in 2006 when I thought Jack might take me off. Éamonn could have easily brought on some speed merchant for me. The next ball that came up the field, we had to win it. I had to win it.

James got on a ball under the main stand and played a diagonal pass inside the 20m line. It hopped and I managed to hold off Cafferkey with one arm and grab it with the other before being fouled in front of the posts.

When the ref blew for a free in, I gave a massive fist pump. Why?

For everyone – our supporters, Cafferkey, his teammates, my teammates, even me. It was giving the message: *We're still here, fighting. We're still in this. We're not going away.* We just had to take away their momentum. Break it. As a kid watching the Chicago Bulls, I used to notice that when they were struggling, it wasn't always a spectacular play from Michael Jordan that would get them back into it; a lot of the time it was Dennis Rodman diving on a loose ball and into the crowd that galvanised the whole thing. Playing alongside someone like John Teahan with the Tigers, you'd notice how he'd growl that bit louder when he'd win a rebound or make a steal at a time the momentum could have been with our opponent. Small things like that change the whole energy of a match.

A few minutes later, I'd the ball in their net. I'd slag James the following week that he should have passed it over to me straight-away; instead he shot and was blocked by Keith Higgins. But it broke to me to volley in from a few yards out. Now we were the ones with Big Mo.

It would continue to sway one way, then the other. They went four ahead again. Seven minutes after half-time, we levelled it. Michael Geaney took a quick lineball, pumping it into me in the square. I caught it and off-loaded to James who was peeling off me. He was brought down for a penalty which he'd put away.

Ten minutes later he scored another penalty to put us two points up. Over the previous week we'd been on the Fitzgerald

Stadium pitch, just like Gooch and myself eight years earlier, walking through where we should be when the other fella won a ball. Now it was transferring onto the field of play. We could just tell what the other was going to do next and where he was going to go. That day in Limerick, it was just like playing with Gooch.

But Mayo came charging back with two late points to level it. In injury time Rob Hennelly had a free on the '45 to put them ahead – and into a third straight All Ireland final. I sprinted back under our own crossbar in case it dropped short. But when it left his boot, I thought it was sailing over the bar. The more it curled in and soared, the more the Mayo crowd cheered. Then it started flagging, dropping, around the square. Tom Parsons went to punch it over the bar but I was there to block his effort, like a volleyball player at the net. The ref blew his whistle. Full time. Extra time.

I collapsed onto my chest; all cramped up; I could barely get down to the far end where our dressing room was. But I just knew I had to grind it out and play extra time, no matter what. As I hobbled up the field, this huge roar and standing ovation went up for both teams as they made their way to the war hospitals that were their dressing rooms. Because at this stage that's what this was: a war. Aidan O'Shea and Cillian O'Connor on their side had been split open from a first-half collision: they'd come off, then soldier on again. In our dressing room Declan O'Sullivan was violently ripping off his bandages across from me. The man had no cartilage in his knees but at that point he didn't care if he ever kicked a ball again as long as he helped Kerry win that day. It was like Roy Keane that time against Juventus; so what if he missed the final?; lose this and there was no tomorrow for anyone. Fellas who had scored two goals had to come off. Fellas who had been taken off had to come on again. Fellas who hadn't played all summer were coming on. Every body, not just everybody, was going to be needed to get over the line.

Eventually we would. Peter Crowley made a brilliant interception to stop Lee Keegan scoring a goal; the biggest momentum changer of the day. I won a couple of frees for Barry John Keane to put over. Jonathon Lyne came up the field to kick two monstrous long-range points. Mark Griffin turned over Aidan O'Shea with a massive shoulder. David Moran gave the greatest midfield display I've ever seen, with Anthony Maher's not far behind. Paul Geaney kicked a point to put us three up and then we went about killing the game through fair means and foul.

In the closing minutes I was camped inside our own '40. I won a jump ball, fell to my knees, surrounded by a posse of Mayo men, one of them who clipped me in the back of the head. Then the ref blew the final whistle. At that I just ran off and blazed the ball into the crowd.

For me that game summed up everything I am as a footballer. Winning and celebrating that free to try to get the team going. Scoring that scrambled goal. The big catches around the square. Using my arse and my wits to win frees off Cafferkey and then Kevin Keane. Stretching James's groin when he was cramping up. Blocking Tom Parsons. Being in the thick of some of those fights at the end to help kill time. Winning that hop-ball at the end. Just fighting and finding a way to help the team win.

The only thing I was disappointed about afterwards was that I didn't shake hands with any of the Mayo lads. More than any opponent that had been on the losing end of a game I had been involved in, they deserved that courtesy. Limerick had been a war because, like us, they had been warriors.

It was just that when the ref blew that whistle, the blood was up from that clip in the head and I was just so overcome with relief and pride that I took off with the ball, booted it into the stand and roared. Next thing our fans were in on top of me and I was embracing teammates, family and friends. For a few years there I had been the man football had forgotten. Now I was back – and Kerry were back in a final.

That night, on the bus home, we just sensed we were going to win that final. Didn't matter who won the other semi-final the following day: Dublin or Donegal. If Bryan Sheehan's last-minute free had gone over in Croke Park the first day against Mayo and we'd sneaked the win, we very likely could have lost the final. But after prevailing in the battle of Limerick the way we did, we knew we were a team that just couldn't be beaten.

THE Saturday week before the final, I was in bed, resting up for our trial game later on, when I noticed Hilary was all fidgety going about the place. I asked her to sit down on the bed.

"What's up?" I asked.

She started smiling.

"Well, what is it?" I asked again.

And then she said it. The sweetest two words I'd heard since she'd said "I do."

"I'm pregnant!"

We'd been trying for a few months. No joy. But now? Absolute joy. Ever since we'd married, I couldn't wait to be a dad. So there on the bed we hugged and we kissed and we cried. I floated into Fitzgerald Stadium that day. The following weekend, going around Croke Park in the parade, I was feeling on top of the world. I was about to play in an All Ireland final. I'd a baby coming along the following summer. I had gone from absolute despair six weeks earlier, feeling I'd kicked my last ball for Kerry, to now being a father-to-be only seventy minutes away from another Celtic Cross. What more could a man want?

Like myself, the team had been written off earlier in the year. Tomás, Brossie and Paul had all stepped away over the winter. Then Gooch did his cruciate. When Cork hammered us in Tralee in the last round of the league, no-one gave us a prayer. You're talking twenty years since a Kerry team had been so unfancied.

But all the time the group believed in Éamonn and all the time Éamonn believed in the group. We'd a great camp in Portugal. Declan came back in around that time and then ran the Munster final against Cork. Gooch was still about the place, mentoring the younger lads, which was huge; he could have easily gone to America for the summer. So not only were fellas like James stepping up to fill the gap left by Gooch, Gooch himself was helping them as to how they could fill it.

All summer you could see fellas growing right in front of you. Paul Murphy. Paul Geaney. Peter Crowley. Again the older fellas were there to guide them; a lot of lads hadn't been in an All Ireland final before so we'd be telling them to nominate their moms to deal with their tickets so they could just focus on the match.

The first night back after the game in Limerick, I said to Éamonn that we'd have to use me differently in the final.

299

Donegal had won the other semi-final. We couldn't have a repeat of the Tyrone final in 2008 when they had men back and we still kept lumping ball in.

"They're going to put the McGees on me and James. Paddy McGrath is going to be on Geaney. That's a mismatch there – Paul's too strong for him. I'm going to run out and play in the D here to occupy their sweepers and leave space for Paul inside." I didn't care if I touched the ball or not, once Kerry won.

A minute in to the game, Stephen O'Brien is on the ball out on the left wing. I run out towards him, taking two men with me. James has also pulled out the field. Stephen's shot is deflected. Drops on the edge of the small square. Paul Geaney catches it over Paddy McGrath. Sticks it in the net.

Two minutes later, a Johnny Buckley shot comes back off the upright and bounces. James palms it down to me. I turn onto my left foot…

Before 2013 I hardly ever kicked with my left. Two things changed that.

Cian O'Neill joined the set-up and would have us constantly working on our non-dominant side, handpassing and kicking.

And then I did my right groin. Any time I went to kick with it, that stabbing pain would return. But when I kicked off my left, it was fine. I wouldn't wish that injury on anyone but I wished I'd practised off my left a lot earlier. Still, better late than never, and at thirty-one years of age, I kick my first-ever left-footed point in Croke Park, there in an All Ireland final.

Ten minutes later, Johnny plays a diagonal ball into me. I catch it and win the free. 1-2 to 0-2.

But it's still tight. Everything is hard won out here, even having a word with your *maor foirne*. 'Paco' runs in with a message but

Éamonn McGee wants to listen in on our conversation, so there's a bit of pushing and shoving about that.

Just after half-time I knock Neil McGee out over the line with a shoulder. He makes a meal out of it and we have words. Then I chase all the way back to our twenty-metre line only to see Michael Murphy kick a monster point which edges them ahead for the first time, 7-6. On my way back to the Hill end, the two McGees are waiting for me on the 45. So I shove the two of them backwards, saying "This is Kerry's day, boys!" even though they've just taken the lead. I'd hardly be as brave in a bar in Gweedore if they came at me but there can't be any backward step, not here, not now.

Eventually, Neil backs off and jogs back over to mark James. *Good.* A little victory won.

Shortly after that, Paul Murphy slices a beauty over from out on the wing to level it again. It stays at 7-7 for ages. Twelve minutes. Feels even longer. Deadlock.

Then Donncha floats a high ball into their square. I'm in there, but their goalkeeper, Paul Durcan, isn't taking any chances; he fists it away, but only for Killian Young to pick it up and make a great run along the endline and win a free in front of goal. Barry John taps it over. We're one ahead again.

Durcan puts the ball on his tee and steps back to take the kickout…

The last couple of weeks I've studied his kickout closely. I know it's a serious weapon of theirs and that I'm going to be standing right in front of him for the most part of seventy minutes. So I've analysed all the video; of how he runs up when he's kicking short to his left, how he runs up when he goes short to his right, how he runs up when he's going long.

So all day I'm moving when he's about to take a kickout. Gambling.

On this one, I can tell he's going short: he's only standing a few feet back from the ball. With his last two steps he moves to his left and opens up his body. That means he's going to his right. My left. So I shuffle a few steps that way, gambling again.

He scuffs his kick. It bounces just short of the middle of the D.

I'm onto it like a bullet. Without my two-step head start, I might still have got to it first but I'd have been gobbled up by a Karl Lacey or one of the McGees.

But now I'm right through on goal in front of Hill 16, going at what feels like 100 miles per hour when suddenly – ZOOMP! – everything slows down.

It's a sensation I've felt only a handful of times in my career.

Bearing down on Paul Hearty. The point to level it on the stroke of normal time in the 2011 All Ireland. And now.

It's like everything is in slow motion, even though it's probably just the brain running faster than you're actually going.

I take a bounce. He's coming out to me…

I wouldn't be the deftest of finishers, though I've scored a lot of goals for Kerry; normally I just lash it, a real head-down-and-roof-it merchant, trying to take the net off the hinges. But Gooch hasn't been mentoring just the young fellas, he's been talking to me about how to sometimes just pass the ball into the net. So I give Durcan the eyes, as if I'm going to go to my right, hoping he doesn't guess that I'm not going to go that way at all.

I go across my body, and pass it towards my left.

It hits the back of the net.

And then ZOOMP! Everything explodes back into real-time.

James jumps up to chest bump me. Hill 16, between the two

sets of supporters, is a sea of green and gold, but at that moment it might as well be all Kerry. And for a moment, I surf on that wave, the sight of all those people from home going mental.

Donegal don't go away. They rattle off the next three points. But Johnny Buckley swings over a huge point to settle us again. Barry John shows why he's such a brilliant impact sub by winning and pointing a free. And then, for the third different time in the game, a score of mine puts us four points up; Mahony, who has locked down Michael Murphy, sallies up the field, and kicks in a ball around the square. Myself and Éamonn McGee wrestle for it. He has one of my arms pinned, but with my free one I bat it down, turn and punch it over the bar.

A minute into injury time, I'm taken off; Kieran O'Leary comes in. I can't watch. I'm just staring at the ground. We're a goal up but I can tell by the noise from the crowd that they're mounting an attack. One of the lads beside me shouts. "Fuckin' take him down!" But obviously no-one does because the sound from the Donegal crowd grows louder.

I look up. Michael Murphy is inside our D. *Jesus Christ!* He barrels through a wall of our lads to offload to Patrick McBrearty. He gets a shot off which is half-blocked. Brian Kelly palms it away but Colm McFadden hurls himself at the ball and fists it – against the butt of the post. Shane Enright is onto the loose ball and moments later the final whistle goes.

And then?

First, this immediate joy. Then, this huge wave of relief. And then this incredible contentment.

I remember watching the Donegal lads win their All Ireland a couple of years earlier, going around with the cup, the pitch all to themselves. And I said to Hilary: "I'd love for us to have that, to celebrate one on the field." Back when we were winning All Irelands, it was just this haze of madness; the whistle would go, you might get to embrace the nearest teammate and next thing you were just engulfed by this wave of supporters and you were being squashed and bashed in the back.

Now I'm able to bask in the moment with those who've soldiered alongside me. It's why I initially refuse the TV fella who's asking me to do an interview with Joanne Cantwell. But he's hanging off me, breaking me up: No, they want to talk to you.

So on about the fifth time of asking, I say grand, I'll do it.

Joanne says something about us not supposed to be winning All Irelands while in transition. And then it just jumps out. Those couple of articles pinned up on the wall at home. About the production line – and me – being finished.

"WELL, JOE BROLLY, WHAT DO YOU THINK OF THAT?!"

And then I walk off, clenching my fist, leaving it at that, just wanting to get back to my boys, not realising those words will never leave me!

Even if I'd copyrighted that line for that night alone, I'd have made a fortune from all the people repeating it to me at the banquet.

I didn't mind though. Joe had actually been a big fan of mine through the years. That's probably what bothered me about the article and why I pinned it to the wall. But when the chance presented itself, I just couldn't resist throwing that little dig about what he said about me, and more importantly, about Kerry: the 2014 All Ireland champions.

Late that night, at about 4am, we're having a sing-song. Johnny Buckley belting out Luke Kelly.

Beside me, Declan O'Sullivan whispers. "I want to sing a song."

In thirteen years playing with him, I've never heard him sing.

He asks if he can borrow my phone; his own one is dead and he needs to brush up on the lyrics of the song he has in mind.

So we pop out for a moment. Declan holds my phone and silently memorises and rehearses his mysterious party-piece. Then we return to the boys and the last singer selects Declan next.

He closes his eyes, a bottle of beer in his hand. The Parting Glass, sang by everyone from the Clancys to Ed Sheeran, but no-one better than Declan O'Sullivan this particular night. We're there, about fifty of us in the room, just watching and listening, in silent awe. If ever there was a doubt about how much of a legend he is and that he's retiring, it evaporates right there.

Oh all the comrades that e'er I've had
Are sorry for my going away
And all the sweethearts that e'er I've had
Would wish me one more day to stay
But since it falls unto my lot
That I should rise and you should not
I'll gently rise and I'll softly call
'Good night and joy be with you all'

And that's how Declan O'Sullivan bowed out as a Kerry footballer. Out on the Croke Park pitch with his son in one hand and Sam Maguire in the other; then later that night dropping the mic with that parting glass.

If I had known the words, I could nearly have joined in with him. Because back then I was certain I was retiring as well.

305

I'd nearly finished up six weeks earlier after the Galway game; things couldn't get worse than what they were then. Now they couldn't get better. It was the ideal time and way to go out, like Séamo and Darragh had, like Declan was now. Retiring as a champ.

Then the club went on a run.

ROCKIE

'The Austin Stacks supporters are unique. They are loud, they are passionate and they chant and march. They welcome all who join them, no questions asked. Therein lies the beauty of the club, the shared emotions and the sense of belonging it can provide when life is challenging'

Marie Crowe, Sunday Independent

HERE THEY COME, MARCHING UP THE HILL. Like an army. The Black and Amber Army. With their drums, anthems, banners and flags.

We've just begun our warm-up by the dressing room goals in Fitzgerald Stadium for the county final replay, 2014, but we can hear the rumbling in the distance as they make their way up along Lewis Road. And already we feel and feed off the energy. There's nothing like them in the rest of the country.

Twenty years ago, the last time the club won the county, I was there marching with them. I was eleven, around the time Dad had just left home, but he was there with me that day, chanting and clapping away.

> *My old man's a Rockie, he wears a Rockie hat*
> *He went to see the Rockies, and said 'I fancy that!'*

The parade back then maybe wouldn't have been quite the mardis gras it has become now, where megaphones lead out the chants and it's like one big fancy-dress party, with people wearing pirate costumes, Apache-headdresses, Batman black-and-amber emblems and the kids all face-painted.

But the same carnival spirit was there, men and women, from five to eighty-five, dressed up in black and amber, proud to be a Rockie, all proud to be in this tribe.

It was just this great celebration of club, community, life. I don't remember much about the match but I remember the parade.

> *There's only one Black and Amber...!*

The men of '94 would become heroes to me. Eoin Moynihan, a classy forward. Darren Aherne, who captained Kerry the following year on the back of the club's win. Donal McEvoy, a speedy corner forward who'd coach me from Under-14 to minor. Pa Laide, who'd be on the Kerry team that won the '97 All Ireland. Denis Sayers, the Paul Galvin of the team. Cormac Kennedy, who in one game kicked a point from seventy yards.

My favourite was John Galvin. Galla they called him. Left half back. Pure warhorse on the field, pure gentleman off it. The morning after that county final win, I knocked on his door. "Hi, is John there?" His parents told me he was still in bed. I asked could I have his shorts or socks. His dad went rooting through his bag and pulled out these socks, reeking of Deep Heat, the amber hoops at the top, the rest all black.

John died of cancer a few years later, one of too many Rockies that were taken from us far too soon. I wore his socks underneath my socks for ages after that, until the elastic went from one of them. Even after that, I'd put the remaining one on my left foot, because he was left footed.

The next time there was a parade on county final day, I was with the team, but not on it. It was 2001, against An Ghaeltacht; after myself and Daniel Bohane got that late call-up to the Kerry minors, we got another one to the Stacks seniors. My first night training I tried to handpass it over Pa Laide. But I left my chest open and Pa split me in two with a shoulder, welcoming me to senior football. A few weeks later I made my senior debut, getting my substitute slip from club secretary Martin Collins in for the last five minutes of a county league game below in Sneem. Michael 'Nappies' Healy, who worked with me in The Greyhound, was an umpire that day. In the last minute, with us up twelve points, I tried for a point but kicked it a good four yards wide. Nappies ran straight for the white flag.

First point at senior for Star! But I still wasn't ready to feature in a senior county final.

Some of my boys were though. Bohane came on in that final early on. My school pals, TJ Hogan, Brian Dennehy and Mikey Collins all started, even though they were just a year out of minor.

TJ was a savage talent, a real warrior-type player. One year we were playing West Kerry in a minor county quarter-final in Lispole. He couldn't start because of a back injury – even then, the injuries were beginning to give him trouble – but with ten minutes to go, we were behind by three or four points. He came on to win three kickouts, solo downfield and stick it over the bar each time. In the last minute with the sides level, he had a sideline ball about forty-five yards out. He split the posts with the outside of his right boot, just like Maurice Fitzgerald in Thurles. I remember looking at him that day: You legend!

He'd suffer some terrible injuries though. One day in Abbey-dorney they had to break a door down to carry TJ off the pitch after he broke his leg; it still sends chills down my spine, thinking of his roaring pain that day. Yet he was still playing with us right up until last year, 2013, when we reached the county final only to be well beaten by Gooch and the Crokes. TJ's not playing today, but if we win this here, I'd nearly give him my medal.

Brian Dennehy was another inspirational player. He took over the role of Galla, driving the team on from the back while always marking the opposing team's best forward. But by his mid-twenties he had to retire with his hip. Brian had been playing senior football since he was sixteen. Too young, probably, in hindsight; if we'd minded him a bit better he'd probably be out here lining out with us today.

It's a shame he couldn't play for longer because it was around the time he finished up that it started to turn for us. We'd lean times for most of that decade, failing to progress beyond the county quarter-final stage for seven years straight. One year I had to play a relegation playoff against Kilcummin with my ankle swollen like a balloon. Nearly all the '94 lads had retired and then younger fellas left home. Finbarr Smith moved up the country. Billy Sheehan joined Laois. Michael Finn, our captain when we won the Under-21 county final in 2002, went to Australia. Peter Quillinan emigrated to Chicago. There was this huge transition and loss of key players, but then Peter's brother, Wayne, the same man I worked for in Q Sports the summer of 2006, took over the team. Overnight we went from being a club team to almost a county team with the level of professionalism he brought to it.

He brought serious passion too. He was like Al Pacino in the dressing room; he also believed in fighting for that inch. "When there's a ball on the ground," he'd roar, echoing a line of Denis Sayers', "it's not a fifty-fifty ball! It's a fuckin' Rockies' ball!"

In 2009 we'd reach a county semi-final, giving the Black and Amber Army a couple of great days marching through the town. In 2010 we'd reach the final. In 2011 the Crokes beat us by a point in the quarter-final. Wayne stepped aside the following year when they beat us again but he was handing over a good team to our new manager, Stephen Stack.

In 2013 we'd again reach the county final, only for the Crokes to absolutely hammer us, 4-16 to 0-12. It was their fourth year straight beating us and their fourth year straight winning the county. They were a machine at that point; if it wasn't Gooch and Eoin Brosnan killing you, it was Kieran O'Leary or Johnny

Buckley, with brilliant club players like Ambrose O'Donovan and Brian Looney backing them up.

Hail, Hail, the Stacks are here!

The parade has entered the stadium now, marching under the tunnel over by the press box, with their drums and bodhráns, about to take over the whole terrace. People have often compared them to soccer fans in the UK because some of their chants are similar to those the likes of Celtic and Liverpool supporters would sing, but really, they're more like Brazilian fans; there's no hate, just love, like one big party with the samba beats.

In the closing minutes of that county final last year when we were getting beaten up a stick, they kept singing. As Stephen Stack put it afterwards, there was a defiance in their loyalty. When we were at our lowest, they were at their loudest. That helped lift us for 2014.

If any one player sums up that defiance, it's William Kirby. After the Crokes destroyed us in that county final, anybody else would have packed it up. He'd be thirty-nine in a few months. He and Gráinne had five kids at home. It had been eight years since he'd finished up with Kerry because the body had given up on him. And yet eighteen years after his first championship match with the Stacks, he still wasn't going to give up on his county medal dream. Stephen rightly identified that the Killarney boys were far fitter and stronger than us, so he brought in a brilliant strength and conditioning coach, Ciarán McCabe. Two months after the county final there were fellas in the gym at 6am. One freezing January morning they arrived to find Kirby climbing up the ladder he uses from his plumbing job, trying to get in the window. The gym was locked and he'd no key but that wasn't going to stop him from getting in his workout and getting his county medal.

I know well how thick William Kirby can be. He played a bit of basketball, for a team the Stacks have. One night he pulled my arm to play against them, even though I never played for the Tigers in the county league. So I went down for the craic and at the start of the fourth quarter when we were about five or six up, I made a lay-up, drew the foul for the And One, and maybe celebrated it a bit too much. Kirby definitely thought I did. As I was lining up to take my free throw, he said, "If you ever do that again, I'll fuckin' kill you!'

I was looking at him. You're joking, right? The two of us played midfield on the same team! This was only a county league basketball game, a bit of craic. But the look he gave, he made me think he was dead serious. I took myself out of the game; I wasn't going to fall out with anyone from the Stacks over a county league basketball game. Then Kirby took the game over, the Stacks went ahead. The Tigers hauled me back on but it was too late – Kirby and the Stacks had Big Mo. Once the game was over he shook my hand. "Good game, Kieran." Not a hint of gloating, as sincere as anyone could be. I was like: Seven minutes ago you said you'd kill me! He was like it never happened. But it had and that's when I realised it didn't matter if it was football, basketball or marbles he was playing, Kirby had that pride and that toughness about him.

If I had to pick a Kerry team from my time playing for them and we had to win a game, Kirby would be the first guy I'd have on the sheet. Ahead of Gooch, ahead of Darragh. Darragh himself would tell you, Kirby would always do the right thing to get the win. I hated marking him in training when we were both with Kerry in 2004 and 2005. He was the ultimate dog and I must have picked up some of the fleas. He had plenty of football, kicking three points from midfield in the 2004 All Ireland final and, along with Maurice Fitzgerald, was man of the match in the 1997 final. But what made him such a winner was how selfless and intelligent he was. He prided himself on his decision-making, another thing I'd like to think I picked up from him.

It's about time Kirby got his medal. It's about time we brought the Bishop Moynihan back to the Rock. Twenty years without a county is too long for a club of our stature.

> *Sure it's a grand old team to play for!*
> *Sure it's a grand old team to see!*
> *And when, you read, its history,*
> *It's enough to make your heart go OH-OH-OH!*

We're one of the most decorated clubs in the country. The Rock. Rock Street. The Street of Champions. The club named after the Irish revolutionary and hunger striker who captained the county to an All Ireland while he was county secretary. The club of Joe Barrett, Bill Landers and Jackie Ryan and others who came out of the internment camps after the civil war and powered Kerry and the Rock to multiple All Ireland and county titles in the 1920s and 30s. In the '70s there was a time when the club had five reigning All Stars playing for them: John O'Keeffe, Ger O'Keeffe, Mikey Sheehy, Ger Power, and Dennis Long from Cork. Kerry's All Ireland final win over Donegal made it ninety-two senior All Ireland medals for the Rock. Not another football club in the country has won as much.

The Stacks and Tralee in general would be especially known

for producing townie forwards, maybe because there's a good soccer and basketball tradition in the town. Apparently there have been only four players to score four goals or more on the All Ireland senior football final stage. John Joe Landers – Stacks. Mikey Sheehy – Stacks. Yours truly – Stacks. Colm Cooper is the other, a townie who plays for the other black and amber.

Feed the Star and he will score!

The last two county finals we were in, I didn't hold up my end. Injury was maybe a factor in 2013, but I should still have played better. No matter what I've done with Kerry, it'll be a massive failure in my career if I don't win a county for the Stacks. The Tuesday before the drawn final I was over in Stephen Stack's house, going through with him where fellas should be on kickouts, who'd be marking Darran O'Sullivan and Donncha Walsh, when he said to me, "Right, that's great. But from here on now, just you concentrate on your own game and I'll see you on Sunday." I had to go back to just being the full forward again and make sure I got that right.

That first day against Mid-Kerry in Austin Stack Park, I played well; scored a goal just before half-time. But more is needed now.

A minute in, I punch a floating ball over the bar for the first score of the game. Three minutes in, I grab another high ball, this time from Mikey Collins, right on the endline on the edge of the square. A few twists and turns later, I fire a shot across the goal into the net. I just run back over to my spot. I probably over-celebrated my goal in the drawn game. Today, it's all business. Twenty years is too long.

Thirteen minutes in, another high ball to the edge of the

square. I round my man and am about to round the keeper when he pulls me down. Black card. Penalty. Pa McCarthy buries it. 2-5 to 0-1.

There is no let up. Every breaking ball, it's not a fifty-fifty ball; it's a fuckin' Rockie ball.

Daniel Bohane breaks forward. I've been playing with him for as long as I can remember. You could bring him anywhere with you, I've been everywhere with him. One holiday with Kerry, the two of us ended up in a R&B nightclub in downtown Manhattan. We walked outside, looking to catch a cab, when Bohane went over to these black fellas rapping. Next thing he's having a battle rap with them! 'One pop, two pop, three pop, four!' Blending Eminem with his own lyrics. 'You guys don't have shit on me – I'm a white boy from Trá-lee!' Well, it went over and back, about forty people watching on, loving it!

For six or seven years Bohane was on the Kerry panel. Brilliant half back, but he came along at a time when the county also had Moynihan, Tomás, Mahony, Mike McCarthy, Killian Young. His one start in championship for the county, he was man of the match, against Tipperary, but then one of the lads came back in. He'd still get some game time. The man who came up the field to give the last pass to Marc Ó Sé to bring the 2010 replay against Cork into extra time? Bohane. The man who gave me the pass to level it in the 2011 All Ireland? Bohane. Only for injury you'd have seen a lot more of him with Kerry.

Even after he ruptured his Achilles marking me in a Kerry trial match, he'd soldier on for the Rock. He has a very demanding job in the financial services yet he never misses training. He often uses the word 'legacy'. I'd be talking about us having to win a county to leave our footprints. But he'd say, "Yeah, man, but we've to do it the right way. Show the younger fellas how to conduct yourself when you're playing for Austin Stacks."

Now we're on the verge of getting the best of both worlds. Mikey Collins, another friend from school, gets on a ball from thirty-five yards and bangs it over the bar, to put us up ten points again early in the second half. Mikey, you beaut, you!

Other times through the years I've muttered, *Mikey, will you calm down!* Great clubman but he'd fight with himself. One time we were playing a club championship semi-final against our town rivals, Kerins O'Rahillys in Austin Stack Park. It's a black enough rivalry, the Rock and Strand Road. Maybe not Celtic-Rangers black but Liverpool-Everton black, I'd say. It was heated enough anyway for me to be exchanging punches with Micheál Quirke. On the basketball court, Quirke was like a big brother looking out for me, the younger, foolish pup. But with the Stacks I was like a big brother to Mikey, even though he's older than me. This particular day he got into a scrape with Rahillys' John O'Connor, so I backed him up, shouldering Johnno away from him. Next thing, Quirke is over, backing Johnno up, shouldering me. Next thing, we're pucking the heads off each other, the two buddies from the basketball! The photographers are snapping like mad.

The ref finally restores some order and calls Quirkey and myself over. We're certain that's us gone. For two months – Kerry, the All Ireland quarter-final, the lot. The whole of Austin Stack Park is thinking the same. Sure enough, the ref pulls out his card.

Yellow. Yellow.

Then he calls over Mikey and Johnno, the two club fellas who started the whole fracas but didn't throw a single punch.

Red card! Red card!

I don't know who got the other into a jam that day – Mikey or myself – but here in this 2014 county final replay, that point of his from way out has edged us closer to heaven.

We definitely feel heaven's involved today. That there are Rockies up there looking down on us: a couple of saints and one little angel.

This morning I went to the grave of Fr Michael Galvin for a little chat. He died a few years ago, well into his nineties. He was club president for sixty-seven years, through the glory days and the tougher days. *Look after us today, Fr Michael, and hope you're looking after Trevor and little Siún.*

Trevor Barrett was taken from us on Easter Sunday after a short illness. He was twenty-nine. He was one of the best hurlers in the club but he played football as well, one of those lads you need on a panel to push on the other fellas. Today his brother Paul is one of our subs, sitting near Darragh Long.

Darragh is Dinny Long's son, and Siún Long's father. Siún was born to Darragh and Niamh last month, their first child, but there were complications, and a week before the drawn county final, she passed away in Cork University Hospital.

For as long as I've been playing senior football for the Stacks I've been playing alongside Darragh Long. The most solid man you could ever wish to meet. A few years ago we were playing Dingle in a county semi-final. In our last team meeting he had spoken about everyone needing to leave everything out there, not to be holding back, that when you were spent, there were good enough men to come in for you. Darragh kicked our two goals that day, showing why he played minor and under-21 for Kerry, yet in a tight game with a few minutes to go, he put his hand up to let the sideline know his race was run. I remember thinking, *Fair fuckin' play to you, man.* A lot of other fellas would have tried to fake it, living off their two goals and maybe hoping to get a hat-trick, but not Darragh Long.

Now with five minutes to go in this county final, Darragh is coming on, for Mikey Collins, following William Kirby off the bench just before him. When Siún was up in Cork, Darragh had told Wayne Guthrie, our midfielder, to go and win him a county medal; he was going to be away for a while. But a few days after the county final finished in a draw, Darragh was there at training, togged out. Didn't say a word. No-one said a word. There were no words.

It's into injury time now. Mid-Kerry have just got a goal back, but it's academic; we're 2-12 to 1-7 up. There's nothing academic about the next score though. Wayne Guthrie, the man who Darragh Long asked to go get him a county medal, goes and gets him on the ball, fist passing it to him on the 21. Darragh slides across and sweetly strikes it off his left. And as it soars skywards and over the bar, he looks up and points to heaven, to Siún, his Little Rockie Angel.

Once their keeper kicks the ball back out, the final whistle goes. I fall to my knees, a lump in my throat, tears in my eyes.

Next thing Bohane is over me, beaming, shaking me. C'mon, man! Get up! We did it!

Next thing I see Kirby. He squeezes me, I squeeze him. This is for you, buddy. You and Darragh. For twenty years and climbing up ladders at six in the morning.

TJ Hogan comes along, in his civvies, his black-and-amber civvies. The man who was stretchered off on a dressing-room door but came back to give us sixteen years of senior football.

This is his first year not playing but I tell him this is his win too.

A while afterwards, we return to the dressing room. All the lads jumping up and down, singing.

> **There's only one black and amber!**
> **There's only one black and amber!**
> **Walking along, singing a song,**
> **Walking in a Rockie wonderland!**

It settles for a while and we realise the cup isn't here. Next thing, who walks in with the Bishop Moynihan but Darragh Long. He hoists it up over his head, shaking it, furiously, jumping up and down. And sure to see the man there, smiling and grinning after all he's been through, it's the signal for everyone to start again jumping up and down.

We finish the night in the clubhouse. It's brilliant. Stephen Stack has the guitar out. Later, Francie Breen, my old Stacks C teammate who picked up my gloves for me that day down in Lispole, is deejaying. Fellas are dancing on the bar and slipping on the dance floor which is like an ice rink from all the spilt drink. Every time someone falls, a huge cheer goes up.

In a few weeks' time, we'll become Munster champions. We'll beat Ballincollig after extra time here in Tralee. Then the Black and Amber Army will march through Cork and into Páirc Uí Chaoimh, to see us edge The Nire from Waterford in the final.

> **Oh to, oh to be, oh to be a... Rockie!**

But all that is a bonus. All I ever wanted was tonight. Since 2002 I've been coming into this clubhouse at the end of every championship. For twelve years it was always after a defeat. But now, finally, we're champions. Living in a Rockie wonderland.

CHAPTER 18

THE TOUGHEST YEAR

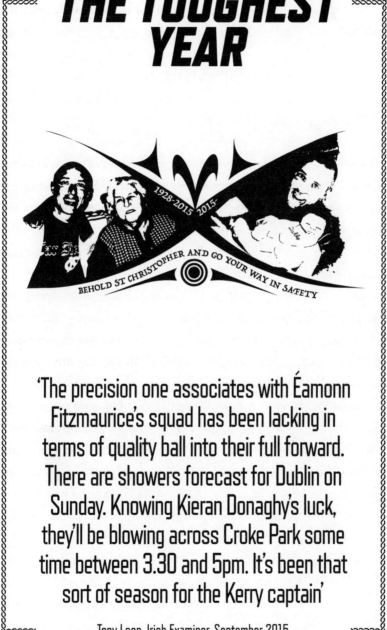

1928-2015 2015-

BEHOLD ST CHRISTOPHER AND GO YOUR WAY IN SAFETY

'The precision one associates with Éamonn Fitzmaurice's squad has been lacking in terms of quality ball into their full forward. There are showers forecast for Dublin on Sunday. Knowing Kieran Donaghy's luck, they'll be blowing across Croke Park some time between 3.30 and 5pm. It's been that sort of season for the Kerry captain'

Tony Leen, Irish Examiner, September 2015

ONLY MINUTES AFTER DARRAGH LONG came bouncing into the Stacks dressing room with the Bishop Moynihan, my uncle-cousin and former C team manager Aidan O'Connor was already talking to me about the Sam Maguire. When I had met him earlier out on the field, he'd said nothing. He couldn't, tears in his eyes, so we just hugged. But back in the dressing room he had to spit it out. He was club chairman at the time, had been for five years. When he took the job he told me we were going to win the county and we were going to bring Sam Maguire back to Tralee. Now the club had won the county. "Next job," he said, "is to get you up the steps of the Hogan Stand to collect Sam!"

That was the first time that it hit me about the Kerry captaincy. In the days leading up to that game I had forgotten all about it.

Another huge fan of mine was less gung-ho about 2015. Nan didn't want any more goals for Nan because she didn't want any more heartache for Keek. I'd call in to her most nights and she knew how much a struggle 2013 and most of 2014 had been for me up until the Mayo replay. It had been stressful enough for her as well; before every game she'd light candles in the house with my Aunt Moira, nervously praying for good luck for me; at eighty-six, did she really need more of that?! Did I need the stress? After we won the All Ireland she said to me, "Kieran, you should go now while you're on top." And I was going to retire. But then the club won the county. And even she had to accept there was no way I could turn down the honour of captaining Kerry.

2015 was only two weeks old when I again met Aidan coming towards me out on a football field. Only this time it was a cold dark evening out in Listowel, and this time he was the bearer of bad news. He didn't even have to open his mouth. Nan had passed away.

She'd been sick for a few days with a swollen stomach and the previous day she had taken a bad turn. I'd been at her bedside in the hospital, along with all her other grandchildren and children and in-laws, knowing these were the final hours. But the club had a challenge game against Clare, as part of our preparation for the upcoming All Ireland semi-final against the Derry and Ulster champions, Slaughtneil. Everyone there at the hospital told me to go on and play the game, that I'd see her when I'd come back, but when I got up to leave, I squeezed her hand, kissed her on the forehead, gave her my usual snug and told her not to be afraid and that I loved her. I just sensed it was the last goodbye.

She was like a second mother to me. After Dad left she took us all into her house. That's why in her later years we'd always call into her, and help my mom lift her into bed and help her get changed; we wanted to be there for her because ever since she broke her hip falling over my size eleven shoes when I was about the same age, she was always there for us. Making our dinners. Getting us out for school and making our breakfast. Trying to get me to do my homework even though I hated it. My primary school principal, Master Michael Hayes, had once said to her that I had "a great brain". And she'd always say it to me, even though I was constantly doing bad in school: "Michael Hayes says you have a great brain!" Like it was gospel!

If something happened in school, we'd nearly go to her before we'd go to Mom. It was like she'd figure out what was the best way to handle it. You could tell her anything. You could have the craic with her. When Sarah was a bit older and would be going to bars and discos, she would turn to Nan for a hop ball. "Would there have been shifting back in your day, Nan?!" And Nan would laugh, a glint in her eye. "No, no! We'd have had none of that!"

She had that bit of devilment, which was maybe why she loved the Ó Sés. When Marc or Darragh would call over to collect me before we'd head for the train to Dublin, she'd come out of the house and bless us all. She thought Darragh was a fierce handsome man altogether.

Herself and Mom used to hop off each other something desperate. Nan was a bit of a nightbird, like me. She'd tell my mom to make her a cup of tea. Mom might say, "God, it's eleven o'clock! It's time for bed, girl, not a cup of tea!" And Nan would pretend to get off her seat, her with her bad hip, making a massive deal of it, knowing full well of course Mom would go "Okay, so!" Then Nan and myself might go into the sitting room and watch any old shit until maybe 1am. "You're like a hatching hen!" she'd say to me. But it wasn't what we were watching. It was who we were with.

Like all of her eight grandsons and two sons, I would get a St Christopher medal on a gold chain from her when I turned eighteen. It was her way of guarding us when we left the nest, St Christopher being the patron saint of children and people who travel. I kept losing mine until on one of my travels, in Miami, when I lost a fourth one in the water, I decided to get it tattooed on my arm. She hated tattoos and didn't find it funny when I'd slag her about getting one, so I hid it from her for three weeks. Then one night when I was putting her to bed, she saw something underneath my t-shirt. I said it was just a bruise and walked on. But she called me back. She wanted to see it up close. I told her what it was, the St Christopher medal, with a Latin term inscribed underneath it. She asked me what it meant. "Two Mothers Bless Me." After that my second mother loved that tattoo.

My head was in a daze playing that challenge game out in Listowel. Gary Brennan destroyed me. Clare beat us well, showing signs that they were developing into a force under Colm Collins. Once the whistle went, I headed straight to the dressing room to get back to Nan, but then just as I came off the pitch, Aidan jogged up behind me. "Kieran…"

Moments later I'd refuse a photograph for the first time in my life. A woman was there with her phone. "Kieran Donaghy! Stand in there for a picture!"

"Sorry, I can't. I have to go."

"Jesus Christ! Can't you just…"

"My nan just died. I'm going straight to the hospital."

I don't think that was quite yet a good enough reason for her; she seemed to be still mumbling, standing there as I headed off.

I cried the whole way driving in to the hospital. But by the time of the funeral, I saw it as much as a celebration than anything. This wasn't like Dad and what could and should have been. She'd had a quick death, surrounded by her loved ones. She'd had a great, long, full life.

A couple of weeks later, we'd play Slaughtneil up in Portlaoise. The first game without Nan lighting the candles, the first game where I couldn't get a goal for Nan. They beat us by a point, compounding the sense of loss and that life was changing.

Nan passed away on the same day as the second anniversary of me and Hilary getting married. We joke now that it's as if she wanted us to be thinking about her every January 18 instead of each other. The timing of her passing is closely connected to another very special woman in our life. 2015 will always be the year Nan left this world and Lola Rose came into ours.

She was born on a Saturday night, May 16, 9.50pm. I couldn't believe she was finally here. Hilary was a star, staying so calm all through, which helped calm me because I'd been a nervous wreck in the lead-up to going to the hospital. So there we were in the early hours of the following morning, the two of us, staring in amazement at what we'd help create, when Hilary pipes up. "I'm starving! We haven't eaten all day! You know what I'd love now? A Big Mac!" This was twelve hours before I had a big championship game for the Stacks against Dingle. Hardly the diet or meal of a champion. But of course I was there in a shot to the local twenty-four-hour McDonald's and back even quicker to my queen and princess. A burger never tasted as good as it did in that maternity ward that night.

THE day before Lola Rose was born, I finished up with Ulster Bank after eight years working for them. It was just time for something new.

I'd joined them at the height of the Celtic Tiger. I was supposed to be a business development officer, with my own car and everything. I was to be out and about, bringing in business. It was a job made for me. Going out to meet a fella, bring him out on the golf course. "Who are you banking with at the moment? We've a good interest rate there; if you have a few bob, you can throw it our way. How many staff do you have? We could maybe get them all to switch over to us if we gave you a good deal."

"Yeah, no problem, Kieran!"

I'd that gift of the gab. People knew me, I knew people and enjoyed getting to know more.

No sooner was I in the job then the arse fell out of the economy. No car. No golf courses. Instead I was behind the counter, like a caged bird, getting my balls broken about football.

I'd still bring in a lot of business for them. I'd work with some great people in the branch, especially my colleagues on the counter: Diane, Breda, Moira, Lorraine. They always had my back: if I had to take a call, or if I messed up, or if I was late back from lunch with fellas stopping me on the street asking about football. Of course I was good to them too! Tickets for games, getting jerseys signed, and things like that. I was something of an agony uncle to them as well; if they had an issue, they'd often come to me with it and then I'd bring it up in the morning meeting with the manager. They'd often say to me that I'd make a great branch manager. And I would have. But I didn't have the papers. That's where the dyslexia caught me.

AT the start of the summer of 2006, I faced a test that daunted me far more than facing Francie Bellew in Croke Park a few months later. For the third time I was sitting my maths Leaving Cert exam. I felt extremely embarrassed and self-conscious in there, at twenty-three years of age, in the classroom in Tralee Community Centre, surrounded by these teenagers probably wondering what that big dope Donaghy was doing in there.

But the reason I was there was I wanted my Leaving Cert. I'd failed it twice before because I'd failed maths. I knew I was never meant for college and college was never meant for me, but I had seen how my other friends were moving on in their careers and lives. If I was to work somewhere else other than Supermac's as I was at the time, I needed to get my Leaving.

Every Friday for a year a great Stacks man, Timmy McMahon, gave me grinds. And one big fuckin' grind it was too. But Timmy was brilliant. Patient. And pragmatic. He'd tell me, "I'm going to get you to pass it, man. Forty percent is all we're looking for. We're not going to worry about the hard ones."

I remember being terrified opening up the results. Twice before, I'd seen that big E beside mathematics. If I didn't get it this time, I didn't know what I was going to do with myself. But it was a D. I'd passed my maths. I'd my Leaving. I could get a job like one with the bank.

The only thing was in the bank there were more exams. QFAs: Qualified Financial Advisor exams. I studied like mad for them, Hilary as my Timmy McMahon. But still I failed three times.

You'd have these multiple choice questions, four options.

With each of the options, there were only a few words different from the others, and by the time I'd get to the third one, I'd forgotten the first two. So I'd have to go back and read the first two, but then I'd not know what the third and fourth were.

The frustration. The confusion. The panic. ARRRGGGHHH!

At the start going out with Hilary, I'd try not to let on that I had any trouble reading; here was a girl who could have anyone she wanted, not some thicko who couldn't read or pass maths. But once we got comfortable and I knew we were going to be a long-term thing, I'd say, "Hilary, can you help me spell…"

Like most people, she'd tell me to sound it out. My mom used to say that. My teachers in school used to say that. "Sound it out, Kieran!" But it was no good. I'd snap back to them, especially Mom, "Will you stop asking me to sound it out! If I could sound it out, I'd sound it out! I can't sound out a word!"

It was when Hilary saw how I was struggling with the QFAs that she said there was something not quite right here.

She organised for me to have an assessment with an educational psychologist. I was diagnosed as having dyslexia when it came to numbers and spellings.

It had taken until I was twenty-five for it to be identified.

I'm the better for the diagnosis. That I'm okay, that I'm not alone; there are other good people who face the same challenge.

I do still struggle with some words. 'HEAVEN' is a killer for me. I'll often spell it 'H-E-V-A-N.' 'TOMORROW' is another. The second 'R', I always leave out.

And I couldn't get enough QFAs to advance like I would have wanted to in the bank.

So now you know. That's why I left the bank.

As opposed to another reason that you may or may not have heard.

A COUPLE of weeks after Lola Rose was born, Micheál Quirke rang as he often does. This time it wasn't to talk about some match or going for a game of golf.

"Listen, just so you know, there's a rumour going around that you're having an affair and have some girl pregnant."

When I think of it now, my reaction said it all. If the story had been anyway true I'd have gone in to panic mode. Tiger Woods job. Instead I sat down in the living room and went, "What?! Man, that's bullshit. Forget about it."

When I hung up the phone, that's what I did. I thought no more of it. I didn't even think to tell and worry Hilary about it. There'd always been groundless rumours about me flying about the place. That I was taking over a bar. That I was going working in Sherry Fitzgerald auctioneers where Hilary works. And they're just the ones since I'd left the bank.

About an hour later I got a text from Daniel Bohane.

Can you take a call?

I texted back. **Yeah. I think I know why you're ringing.**

And sure enough, he'd heard the same thing as Micheàl.

I told Hilary then. I was standing by the fireplace. She was holding Lola Rose. "There's a rumour going around about me."

"Go on, what is it?"

"That I'm having an affair. That I have a blonde girl pregnant."

It would have been funny if it wasn't so serious. My wife was blonde. And earlier in the year, she was pregnant, with Lola Rose. So yeah, I had got a blonde girl pregnant – my wife! Is that okay?! But somewhere someone intentionally or innocuously made the wrong calculation and the story spread like wildfire about the pace.

That night Micheál and Bohane rang, I put out a message on all the WhatsApp groups I'm in – Stacks, my family, Hilary's, two or three different ones with Kerry alone. 'Just so you know, there's a rumour going around about me that's bullshit.'

Hilary put out a similar message to her groups – her family, work, the Kerry team's girlfriends and wives. 'Hey, you may or may not have heard but there's a rumour going around about

Kieran. Just to let you know, it's not true. If anyone says it to you, you can set them straight. Thanks.'

So, just like that, we got the message out and we moved on.

But the only problem with social media is that it works the other way. Just as you can quash a rumour much quicker than you would by word of mouth, you can spread one quicker as well. I'm in about fifteen WhatsApp groups. If someone came to me and said, "It looks like Ronaldo's going to Chelsea," that goes up. And boys will be bouncing it over and back until it becomes clear it's not true. We don't see him playing for Chelsea so we know it's not true. But that's how easy it is for something that's not true to go up on social media. And when it comes to things like it being said you've had an affair, how do they realise then that it's not true?

After Hilary put the message up on the Kerry girls' WhatsApp, a lot of them came back to her. Some said they hadn't heard it. A lot of them said they had. And they wouldn't be human if some of them didn't think it might be true. Talking to her after Lola Rose was born and thinking, "Bloody Kieran's having an affair on her." Or some of the nurses that helped her give birth to Lola Rose. Seeing the two of us in the ward that night. "The poor girl." "That Donaghy…" We'd only be fooling ourselves to think none of them had heard the rumour and that none of them thought it could well be true.

Hilary has been brilliant with it all. She's a strong woman. If anything, the whole thing brought us closer together, the way we handled it and rose above it, our three-person home team. But of course it hurt. At times it still hurts. When it was announced this book was being published, Hilary saw one of the comments on a website: 'I wonder will he talk about his affair?!'

So, actually, that's why I am. To say it was complete and utter bullshit. And that the next time you hear a Chinese whisper on the wind, take a moment and really think should you be quick to believe or spread it. Or to even say, "Did you hear that…?" "I heard…" That's a great one. "I heard…" What you heard might not be a fact, but that you heard it is a fact. So you can't lose. You're not saying it's true, but in case it is, it can't be said that you hadn't "heard"; you're in the know.

I once read a great line that said all it takes for an injustice to prevail is for good people to say nothing. But what this has shown me is that sometimes all it takes is for someone malicious to make something up and then good, decent but easily-influenced and weak-minded people to believe and spread it.

I'm not the first Irish sportsperson to have an untruth fly around about them. And I probably won't be the last. But I hope for the next man's or woman's sake, people think a bit more about what they're saying and spreading about someone or something they don't even know.

Did you hear that?

THAT summer I decided not to look for a new job until the championship was over. It would give me a chance to spend time at home with our new arrival and Hilary, start writing my autobiography which a few publishers had approached me to do, and more than anything, to help make a huge push to lift Sam Maguire on behalf of Kerry.

Unfortunately, the only cup I lifted that year was after the Munster final replay. The first day we were very fortunate to get away with a draw; although I'd score an early goal, it took a last-minute Fíonn Fitzgerald kick to sail over my head and over the bar to deny Cork their first win in Killarney since '95. We'd win the replay in a monsoon on a Saturday evening, Gooch turning the game when he came on for me by setting in motion a goal for Paul Geaney. After I lifted the cup in near darkness, I made a balls of the speech. You must have heard the line a thousand times: "*Tá an athás orm an corn seo a ghlacadh ar foireann...*" I got *corn* and *foireann* mixed up. I looked down and could see Marc Ó Sé, a *gaelgoir*, breaking his hole laughing. It sort of summed up my captaincy really, even in its finest hour: although I had the best intentions, it just didn't happen.

I was in good form in training going into the All Ireland quarter-final against Kildare, but then did my groin on the Thursday. That rattled me. That Sunday was one of the few dry days we'd have that year, and the lads would hit Kildare for seven goals. If I had stuck in a few goals, I'd have been brimming with confidence going into the Tyrone game. Instead I went into the semi-final on the back of a groin injury on a day when it was pissing down as bad as it did the second night against Cork. It was never going to be easy against a defence like Tyrone's anyway, and although I kicked a point on the stroke of half-time, management had made the decision to replace me with Paul Geaney.

It worked too; Paul turned the game for us. Then in the other semi-final Dublin coped well with Mayo's Aidan O'Shea on the edge of the square. It all added up to them giving Paul the nod over me for the final. He earned it but it was a very tough one for me to take. Telling family that instead of leading Kerry around in the parade, I'd be on the bench, to not let it spoil their day. "It's not about me starting. It's about who wins and who'll lift the cup. In ten years' time no-one will remember whether I started; they'll just know Kerry won and Donaghy lifted the cup."

But, of course, I didn't. We'd a poor run in by our standards. Injuries had quite a bit to do with it. David Moran couldn't train after the Tyrone game with his back. Anthony Maher was also struggling from a knock he took in that match. A week out, Marc Ó Sé did his hammer and James dislocated his shoulder.

For the 2014 final fellas had been hopping off the ground. Our A versus B games were ferocious, because fellas on the Bs felt they could still get onto the As. In 2015 we went back into training after the Tyrone game and on the wall you'd see the teams posted up: A versus B. I was on the B team, which was fair enough. But that night, I was on fire. In the car back I counted that eleven balls had come in to me and I'd won nine. I was playing like I had in the Mayo replay twelve months earlier, just dominant. But then the next night I went in and saw the teams and there I was on the B team again.

We were hammered that night. Something like 2-25 to 0-6. We were short of too many bodies to make the Bs competitive. We had our trainer, Paco, playing at half back. It was just a false game. With the injuries and everything, we were just off.

But that was 2015.

We'd be in a lot better shape to have a go at them in 2016.

CHAPTER 19

THE GO HOME GAME

"Donaghy has been doing jobs in midfield that people aren't giving him credit for. Gary Brennan was coming into the quarter-final with an All Star in his pocket, and well, there's no All Star there now. But Kerry have to ask questions of Dublin and to ask questions, that means Donaghy at full forward. No doubt about it"

Pat Spillane, August 2016

TUESDAY IN THE WARM-UP AREA OF FITZGERALD Stadium and it's giddy and edgy, a real buzz about the place. We're only days out now from August 28, a date that we circled with red pens in our heads over ten months ago, so fellas are bouncing off one another.

Aidan O'Mahony is at the centre of it. The two of us have been hopping off one another for twelve years now. A lot of the time, just ball hopping, having a laugh; other times then, thumping the head off each other, having all-out war.

Last year we were marking each other in a trial game over in the Crokes' main pitch. One of the lads kicked a wayward ball and as it was bouncing over the sideline, I slowed down, saving my energy, knowing it was a lost cause. But Mahony kept going, ploughing straight into my back, giving me whiplash. I turned round and went for him. I didn't care who he was or how tough he was, he was fuckin' getting it.

Éamonn took no notice of the two old billy goats, gruff, locking horns; the game continued. But so did our wrestling match until the two of us went crashing over the metal sponsorship sideline signs.

I still have a scar on my shoulder from it. Mahony got cut as well. A few minutes after we'd dusted ourselves off and jogged back to the edge of the square, he'd to run off to hospital. I still slag him about it, that he was the one who needed six stitches.

This evening, our exchanges are more verbal and light-hearted, even if we're still throwing a few digs at each other. Mahony's a Guard, so I give him a touch about how his colleagues were stopping people on the way into Tralee on the Monday of the Rose of Tralee festival. Fuck's sake! Of all the days?! The traffic!

He shoots back, saying that the mad fella dressed as a priest who stormed the stage must have been a Rockie!

But before the rest of the boys even get to go WOOOW!, I go, "Hold on now, boy! There were about fifty of your Garda buddies playing flutes and fiddles in front of the stage and I didn't see any of them coming to the rescue!"

WOOW! And all the boys laugh as Mahony mumbles out of the side of his mouth before finally giving me a little smirk.

There's nowhere else in the country we'd rather be right now than here, together, in Killarney, the sun still high in a clear sky outside. Or actually there is. Croker. We can't wait for Sunday. We can't wait for this week to be over. We just want to get on with it.

A week like this is about killing time. You can't go flat out in training. All you're doing is constantly thinking of the game. Every time you do something – eat the right food, stretch, drink your water, try and get a good night's sleep – you think of the game because you're doing it for the game.

From Wednesday on I have to do a bit more to be ready for it. Later on in training on Tuesday while making this sharp turn to shoot, I tweaked my groin. Colin Teahan, my boss at PST Sports, has given me the rest of the week off work to get it right. So I'm down in Poll Gorm twice a day, doing high knees in the cold ocean water up to my waist. I go to the Brandon for another water-resistance session in the pool. By the weekend I feel it's fine to play, though on Saturday morning, when I visit Nan's grave before getting the train, I ask her for a blessing and that the groin will be fine.

I'm starting full forward against Dublin. A few days after we beat Clare in the quarter-final, Éamonn told me that's where he was looking to play me in the semi-final and that we'd be doing more drills kicking the ball in. The last couple of weeks, it's been like the last couple of games of 2014: lads, this is the way we're using Kieran. And don't just be thinking of him long. I've been winning ball in over the top and out in front, kicking points, scoring goals, linking up well with the lads around me.

Only the group know who is lining out and where. Mahony isn't named to start but he will. Darran O'Sullivan isn't named to start, but he will. Anthony Maher the same, in midfield. Which means I won't be in midfield. But that's all in house. Loose lips sink ships so only our crew know the line-up for Sunday. Family can't.

On Friday Hilary's dad, Frank, comes over and throws himself down on the couch beside me. Frank is very excitable when it comes to Kerry, especially since I came on the scene. Two years ago he left the Gaelic Grounds when Mayo drew level towards the end of normal time. He couldn't take it. When he asked a guy in a chip van outside the stadium what was the latest, he was told that Mayo had a free to win it. He headed off depressed, sure a Cillian O'Connor close-in free had ended Kerry's season, only to realise when he reached his car that the epic game he'd left was still going on. I don't know what he'll be like on Sunday.

"God, I'm very disappointed with that team!"

"What do you mean?"

"Sure you have to be in at full forward!"

"No. I'll be out in the middle of the field with David Moran."

I get on great with Frank. But you have to be a good liar to be a county player these days. Not even my mom knows where I'm playing on Sunday. That's the discipline.

We get the train up, then the bus out to Dunboyne Castle Hotel. For the quarter-final I was rooming with Barry Dan O'Sullivan, the youngest fella on the panel. It was his first weekend away with us. He's a gas man. It's scary how it feels like it's come full circle and how much he's like me when I was a rookie away with the seniors for the first time, rooming with Dara Ó Cinnéide. He's all go, all questions. What time do we go to mass? Do we all go to mass? What time do we have to be at this meeting? What time do we have to be down for breakfast? He doesn't want to be late for anything.

On the Saturday evening he asks what time do I go to bed.

"Nine o'clock, lights out," I tell him. "Be back early; I don't want my sleep disturbed."

"Oh! Oh, okay, so, I'll be back soon!" he says, heading out the door, when I call him back.

"I'm only messing, man. Whenever you want!"

So there he is all weekend, all polite, always punctual. But the most important time to be early is on Sunday. Our game against Clare is on at 2pm. The pre-match meal is at 11am. Our pre-match meeting is at 11.45. So you have your bag ready before that. Ten minutes before the meeting, I'm in the room, and still no sign of Barry Dan, even though the place is like a bomb site with his gear scattered all over. *Where is this young fella?* I stride down the corridor, and find him in Tom O'Sullivan's room, door open and Barry Dan laughing on the phone.

Hey, c'mon, you! All weekend you've been "What time's this? What time's that?"

So he heads back to the room with me and I'm helping him pick up his stuff and firing it into his bag, until we both just about make it down in time for the meeting.

For the Dublin game, I'm rooming with a veteran: Gooch. Fifteen years on this very weekend from when we first shared a field playing for Kerry, also against Dublin, as minors.

On Saturday evening, at about eight, he heads to the shop with a few of the other boys. I pop over to Seán Boylan who lives five minutes from the hotel here. I just find talking to him and listening to him over some tea and brown bread helps put my mind at ease.

I sleep well that night. In the morning, I open the curtains. It's sunny. "That's the first win today, anyway, Gooch."

We don't talk much about the game. We watch some YouTube clip of Tommy Tiernan that Peter Crowley sent on to me, until Gooch says, "That's enough of Tommy, big fella." So I switch it off and he rolls back over and goes for another bit of a snooze.

A few hours later we're on the bus in, sitting across from each other. I've the earphones on. Mr Brightside gets another blast as Croker comes into view. We pull in under the stadium. Again we let everyone else get off first, then I let him off before me.

We all go out and look at some of the minor game to size up the conditions. Kerry are well up on Kildare and on their way to a third straight All Ireland title in the grade. The production line in Kerry is looking pretty good, Joe.

Back into the dressing room. The usual. Foam rolling. A last visit to the jacks. Clasp hands. Deep breaths. C'MON!!!!

We dash out for the warm-up. Then this bullshit handshake protocol with the Dubs. We line up for the parade. I catch my uncle Brian and Mom in the lower Hogan and wink. *You are your people.* We break from the anthem and our huddle, I make my way straight up to full forward, leaving the jump ball to Maher and Moran.

Philly McMahon, is waiting for me. He doesn't put out his hand. Fine. That suits me absolutely fine. I won't shake your hand so. Then, at the last second, he sticks it out. But I'm already committed to not shaking hands. Jesus Christ, we just shook hands a few minutes ago! This isn't a cheese and wine party! Enough shaking hands.

The Hill notices our little exchange. Again, the boos rain down. Again, that's fine. They were going to boo anyway. Someone has to wear the black hat around here. Let it get a rise from them. I'm just being bould. If I was wearing fourteen in blue they'd love me, but right now let them hate me.

Throw it in, ref. Time for war.

FUCKIT, anyway. We lost. Unlike last year, we performed, we brought it, we left everything out there. But here we still are in this dressing room and it's like a morgue.

The last time we were in here, at half-time, it was a different place. We'd run in, the sound of our supporters ringing in our ears, roaring "KER-RY! KER-RY! KER-RY!" rising to their feet to cheer us off the field. We'd just hit Dublin for two quick goals to go five points up.

Then I made an awful fuckin' mistake by sitting down for twelve minutes, getting my breath break. I should have been walking around, keeping it loose, been maybe on a bike, to stop the groin seizing up. For an experienced player to allow that, it just wasn't good enough.

Instead, I went out for the second half and going for the first ball, I felt it tighten. Jogging back into the square, I was thinking, *You're in trouble here, Kieran.* I went for another ball and it tightened worse. And then after about fifteen minutes, I turned to go after John Small and felt it go properly then. That's why I swung off him; to stop him, take a black card and get someone else to come on for me.

As it turned out, I only got a yellow, but it didn't matter: I was gone anyway. So I'd to watch the rest of it from the front row of those Recaro seats, sitting beside Darran. All year we'd prepared for this game, this moment, and then the two of us hobble off injured and there's not a thing we can do now to influence the outcome. At times I couldn't even watch; then when I did, I'd kick the metal barrier in front of me out of frustration. They got a soft free or two and then a '45 they shouldn't have. Then we didn't get a free and a '45 we should have had. But all the time you still thought and trusted the boys would pull through. And they nearly did. But fuckit, fair play to Dublin, they made even more great plays than our lads in the end, and they edged it.

I only played okay. Barely touched a ball in the first fifteen minutes; we were all over the shop at the start. Then I got on a good bit of ball. I was involved in a lot of our scores; getting out in front, laying it off. But I didn't get a shot off. I wasn't enough of a scoring threat. I'd say if you were to mark my performance out of ten, I was a six and a half; a seven maybe, tops. For us to beat that Dublin team, I needed to be at least an eight.

When the final whistle went, I made my way to the bottom of the steps. And for a moment I thought of shooting straight down the tunnel. But then I said: No.

First of all, I wanted to shake hands with Gooch, Marc and Aidan out there. It's likely that's the last time we'll ever be on a pitch together. Ever since I first walked into the Kerry dressing room back in 2004 under Jack, they've been there. They've always been there, for me, for Kerry. So this time I wanted to be there for them.

And I wanted to shake hands with the Dublin players. To look them in the eye and say, "Fair play to ye, we put ye to the pin of your collar, ye might have folded, but ye came again, ye were better than us."

I got to shake hands with nearly all of them. Philly McMahon included. "Well done, man. Great battle." Because at the end of the day, I respect him. I respect what he's done with his life, what he does for his community, and a lot of what he does to help his team win. I respect Johnny Cooper. I respect James McCarthy. I respect all of them. You have to give it to them – they're a great team.

But, that hardly makes this easier to take. It's purgatory, a losing dressing room in Croke Park. A part of you is too deflated to even move, another part of you just wants to get the hell out of there. But you can't. Instead there's this awful hanging around, between lads having to be drug tested and waiting for your manager to come back from talking to the media before he and the captain say a few words.

So I'm still here in my gear, staring at the ground, when out of nowhere comes something to ease my pain: Lola Rose. Hilary had come down from the premium level and been outside the dressing room door. The guy in the luminous jacket wouldn't let her in, but our kitman, Niall 'Bottie' O'Callaghan, spotted Lola Rose with her, and knew I could do with seeing her.

So Bottie comes over across the dressing room and puts her on my lap. And she looks up into my eyes, while I look into her eyes, and we cushion each other's heads. She knows there's something wrong with me; she knows there's something after happening here. Normally she'd be climbing down and moving around but instead she stays still and quiet, probably because the room is so quiet.

Eventually, she gives a little whine and starts to clamber down. So instead of having her bother lads and roaming all over the dressing room which is like a wake anyway, I take her by the hand and into the green warm-up room. And then when we're in there I decide sure I might as well take her out onto the pitch altogether.

So we go back out through the tunnel, and out into the biggest playground in Ireland.

The stands are empty now but they still tower above us. Lola Rose is looking around, taking in the place. I can only think of what she makes of it; even now I'm struck by just how massive it is. It must be like the World Trade Center all the way around for her.

I lie down on my side as she runs around. She does this little thing with her feet, almost like a dance, that I haven't seen before, and I laugh. And for those few minutes, nothing else matters, just her and this moment.

I'm not thinking of what just happened here earlier today and the year that we've had, or of what will happen in the weeks and months ahead.

When I will, I'll look back on this year with pride as well as some regret. The body for the most part was good to me all year. From Newry to today, I got to start in eleven straight competitive games, a run I haven't had in years, if ever. I felt in good shape. I felt I contributed to the team. Whatever job Éamonn gave me, I just went out and did it. If stopping Gary Brennan touching the ball meant I hardly touched the ball, I didn't care, once it helped the team win. And then the last three weeks was hugely enjoyable, back being a focal point at full forward. If only for the groin and letting it seize up...

A few days from now I'll be on the road with the job, finalising another pitch that we're installing. And I'll come across Radio Kerry's commentary of the five minutes before half-time and have a lump in my throat. Hearing how passionate they were about us getting the few goals, and the crowd chanting 'KER-RY! KER-RY!' It'll just bring it home to me, what it all means. You can become so obsessed about winning the All Ireland, you nearly forget how lucky you are to be out there playing; the privilege it is to be wearing the green and gold jersey, that you're one of only thirty men chosen to make up the best army the county can put out to win battles. You can get so consumed about trying to get to the destination, you don't get to take in and enjoy enough of the journey.

And if you do that, you're missing out on a lot. It's like driving through Kerry itself; if you actually take a look around, it's just beautiful. The camaraderie. The friendships. The craic. Even the suffering, like busting a gut on the dunes of Banna with all the boys.

A couple of weeks after being out on the pitch here with Lola Rose, Éamonn will meet me. And he'll tell me he wants me back for 2017, that I brought so much to the team in 2016. And it'll be great to hear that. But there'll be a lot to consider. Family. Work. The body and how it'll be in the new year.

The week after this Dublin game, the Stacks will beat the Crokes in the club championship final and I'll play as well as

I have all year. A few weeks later the Irish TV Tralee Warriors will bring Superleague basketball and Showtime back to Tralee. We'll be coached by Mark Bernsen, the American who coached the Tigers to that epic league final win down in Limerick in 2008. The Complex will be packed to the rafters like when the Tigers were winning leagues and Cups. Before tip-off in our opening game, the lights will go off and the spotlight will shine onto the court for the team introductions, exciting and hopefully inspiring another generation to fall in love with the game like I did over twenty years ago.

Lola Rose waddles towards me. I take her by the hand. Come on, we've to go see Mommy.

We start making our way off the pitch. A few Kerry supporters are still lingering about, over by the tunnel. As we make our way across, they clap and ask us if they can take a picture. So we stand in with them, Lola Rose in my arms, before we turn to go back down the tunnel.

I was sure this year, this game, against Dublin was the Go Home game. Like Flamingo Park. Like the time I'd be over in the Smiths' as a teenager, playing Pro Evolution Soccer on their PlayStation. Didn't matter if I lost the Cup. Didn't matter if I lost to them in the league. I wanted another crack. "Look, lose this and I'll go home!" But the thing about it was, even if I lost that last game over in their house and was spitting fire cycling home in the dark, I'd always be back the next day or the day after. There'd be another Go Home game.

I don't know if there'll be another Go Home game with Kerry. All I know right now, little lady, it's time to go home.

Acknowledgements

IN thanking people who have been there for me in life and in putting this book together I'll start with family as they mean the world to me.

To Mom, for what you have done for us as a family through all the tough times, I will always be indebted to you. You showed us to be kind, caring and mannerly at all times, especially to elders. To this day you are still looking after me and you're always there to help look after Lola Rose too. Thanks for helping me become the man I am today; all I did was follow your lead on how to be a good person.

To Nan, you might be reading this on a cloud version in heaven but thanks for taking us into your home as a family and helping to rear us just like a second mother. My tattoo was for you – Two Mothers Bless Me. Even though you hated tattoos in general I think you loved mine. I miss you every day.

To Hilary, what a little legend you are. I love every minute in your presence. I love what a great job you did bringing Lola Rose into our lives. You're the best wife a man could ask for, always there for me in good times and in bad. You are creating a beautiful home environment for us as a family. I love you and can't wait to grow old with you.

To Sarah and Conor, I'm proud of what you have become

and the people you are; loyal to the core. The fights when we were young were epic; I think they paid off.

To my two uncles in Kerry, Ciarán and Brian. You are two polar opposites but I learned so much from both of you. Thanks for always being there for us when we were young, helping to raise us. You went above and beyond the call of duty expected in the role of an uncle and still are to this day, especially in the DIY and grass-cutting departments!

To the rest of the Kerry family, I love you. I love how close we are and I love knowing that if or when a crisis hits we are always there for each other and rally like no other family I know. We needed all that when Ronan, my youngest cousin in Kerry, nearly died from a head injury suffered while playing for Tralee rugby club. It's thanks to the medical staff in Tralee General Hospital and the brain surgeons in Cork University Hospital that he is alive today. It's great to see you getting stronger every day. I'm so proud of how you are handling it all.

To Ciara who lives out in San Francisco, I know you miss home and you miss all the occasions but we miss you just as much. We can't wait to see you again some day soon.

To my family in Tyrone and beyond, thanks for all the good wishes before games, even when we played against the Red Hand. To those who went the extra mile looking after and helping Dad after he left Tralee, I thank you.

To Frank, Angela and all the Stephensons. Thanks for welcoming me to family with open arms. Frank, thanks for all your help and sound advice – even when it was on the greens in Waterville in many a battle with the Cork boys, Barry Golden and Roy Horgan. Angela, thanks for being a great grannie to Lola Rose.

To all my teachers who persisted and went the extra mile with me, thank you.

To everyone who offered their advice to me on a basketball court, I am forever grateful. The basketballer everyone helped out in a way produced the footballer I am today.

To Austin Stacks and all the coaches that helped me reach my potential as a player, I thank you. To all my Rockie teammates, thank you for the ups and downs, the wins and losses, the drinks and banter. Some of you are now acquaintances, some friends and some are as close as brothers; but I respect you all.

To everyone involved with Kerry GAA who helped me to be a part of the greatest sporting tradition of all. Our great chairmen in my time, Seàn Walsh, Jerome Conway and Patrick O'Sullivan, thanks for always ensuring we wanted for nothing when chasing our dreams.

To my managers Jack, Pat and Éamonn and their respective management teams and physical trainers, thanks for giving me the opportunity to represent you and this great county and entrusting me to deliver on the biggest of occasions. I would like to thank you too for the endless hours of preparation, the tough decisions, and the passion and honesty you showed me during our time together.

To all the physios, doctors and trainers in the Kerry setup, thanks for keeping me out on the pitch as much as possible and extending my career when I thought 2013 was the end.

To Seàn Boylan, Anthony Tohill and all the backroom staff, thanks for giving me the opportunity to represent our great country and go up against top professionals from the AFL in three different International Rules series from 2006 to 2011.

To my new employers, Ger and Colin Teahon and all the PST

Sports team, thanks for all your support during a very busy year of my life.

To Eddie O'Donnell, thanks for what you do, as always.

To Paul Dove and all the Trinity Mirror Sport Media team for putting so much into this book and producing something that I will be proud of for ever more. Also to Roy Gilfoyle, Rick Cooke and the creative art team at Trinity Mirror for helping a dyslexic reader like myself by making this book so easy to read. The bigger letters, all the artworks and quotes at the start of each chapter, the extra picture section I begged for, all with the view to making this an easy, enjoyable read. Thanks also to publishers' agents Gill Hess for their help making this all happen.

To Kieran Shannon, thanks for all your efforts and hours of dedication. I rang you as a dyslexic person who was trying to write his own book, probably because someone told me I couldn't, but I must admit I was struggling. You took over and added, moulded and shaped this book into something special, while making sure my words and voice come through.

Kieran and I would also like to thank the love and support of his wife Ann Marie and children, Aimee and Andrew. The time and support Tony Leen and Colm O'Connor – two proud Kerrymen – in the Irish Examiner gave Kieran in this project is also appreciated.

To you, the reader, I hope you understand now why I play the way I play. Thanks for taking the time to read this book and I hope you enjoyed it.

Any comments post to @starryboy14 on Twitter and Instagram or on Facebook at KieranDonaghybasketball.